Canada's Balance
of International
Indebtedness, 1900-1913

Canada's Balance of International Indebtedness, 1900 - 1913

AN INDUCTIVE STUDY IN THE THEORY OF INTERNATIONAL TRADE

Jacob Viner

With an Introduction by H. C. Eastman

The Carleton Library No. 86
McClelland and Stewart Limited

© *McClelland and Stewart Limited,* 1975

ALL RIGHTS RESERVED

ISBN 0-7710-9786-7

This volume was first published in 1924 by Harvard University Press
from the income of the David A. Wells fund.

The Canadian Publishers
McClelland and Stewart Limited
25 Hollinger Road, Toronto 374

Printed and bound in Canada

CONTENTS

INTRODUCTION

CHAPTER I

Method and Scope of the Present Study 3

The *a priori* character of the classical theory of international trade, 3.
The place of induction in the theory of international trade, 5. The
scope of the present study, 9. Canada, 1900 to 1913, the field of the
present study, 11.

PART I

THE CANADIAN BALANCE OF INTERNATIONAL INDEBTEDNESS

Introductory 21

CHAPTER II

The Commodity Balance of Trade 24

The Canadian commerce statistics, 25: Methods of compilation, 25;
Methods of computing values, 26; Accuracy of the statistics, 27; Omissions and inclusions, 28; Fiscal years *vs.* calendar years, 30; Imports
and exports of gold coin, 32. The commodity balance of trade, 35.
Comparison with earlier period, 36.

CHAPTER III

Non-Commercial Items in the International Balance
of Indebtedness 39

Introductory, 39. Immigrants' capital, 41: Capital per capita of immigrants from the United States, 41; Capital per capita of immigrants
from other countries, 44; Capital brought into Canada by immigrants,
45. Capital taken out of Canada by emigrants, 45: Emigration from
Canada to the United States of natives of the United States, 45; Emigration of persons of British nativity, 50; Emigration of Canadians to

CONTENTS

CONTENTS

PART II

THE MECHANISM OF ADJUSTMENT OF THE CANADIAN BALANCE OF INTERNATIONAL INDEBTEDNESS

CHAPTER XI

CHAPTER XII

CHAPTER XIII

Introduction to the Carleton Library Edition

The name of Jacob Viner was one of the most illustrious in economics during his long life-time. It lives on in his scholarly works many of which were seminal contributions or constituted major advances in economic theory and the history of economic thought. Some of his works are definitive in their field.

Viner was born in Montreal in 1892. He received a B.A. from McGill University where Professor J. C. Hemmeon, among others, taught him economics. He then studied at Harvard under the influence and guidance of Professor F. W. Taussig who was then nearing the conclusion of his career in which he had developed the most complete statement of classical economics. As so many intellectuals who left Canada at the time, Viner did not return. In 1916, he went on to teach at the University of Chicago where he also edited the *Journal of Political Economy*, from 1929 to 1946. He joined the faculty of Princeton University in 1946, from which he retired in 1960, but he continued his scholarly activities in Princeton until his death in 1970. Viner's contributions to economics were recognized by the American Economics Association which elected him President in 1939 and awarded him the Francis A. Walker Medal in 1962. Thirteen universities gave him honorary degrees, among them Queen's, McGill and Toronto. He received many other honours.

Viner's writings reflect an interest in Canadian economic matters that declined with the years of his absence from Canada. *Canada's Balance of International Indebtedness, 1900-1913*, his major work on Canada, published in 1924, began as his Ph.D. thesis. Thereafter specifically Canadian questions were peripheral to his interests though he participated in some conferences relating to Canadian subjects under various auspices. He wrote a brief on the tariff for the Province of Manitoba and another on the debt problem of Alberta during the 1930's. His concern for objectivity led him to preface the first Alan B. Plaunt Memorial Lecture (1958) at Carleton University, for which he had chosen Canadian-American relations as a topic, with the declaration that, while he had an abiding affection for his native land, he had affection also for the United States to which, in addition, he felt obligation.

While the foundations of Viner's greatness were his analytical power, his erudition and his exactness of judgement, his personality extended his influence. In his years at Chicago, he had the reputation of a formidable character, because of the standards imposed on his students by his exemplary command of economic theory and literature, his concern for intellectual rigour, his dialectic and expository powers and the severity with which he treated inadequate performance. His graduate course in economic theory was reputed to be the best such course given in the United States, perhaps the world, in the nineteen thirties. The direct stimulus that Viner gave tirelessly to learning and research was directed at colleagues as well as students. Stories abound of the vigour of Viner's discussions, of how the halls of the Social Science Research Building at Chicago would resound on occasion as Viner debated with others, often with Frank H. Knight, some major point of economic theory, perhaps whether economies that are external to a firm must be internal to another firm in the same or another industry, and the implications of the result. Legend has it too that Ph.D. candidates had difficulty both in avoiding this subject and in dealing with it.

At Princeton, where he spent another very productive period, Viner was especially celebrated for his graduate course in the history of economic doctrine in which his scholarship, his sense of the continuity of thought and his love of knowledge for its own sake were apparent and contagious. At this time too, his interests extended further beyond his principal discipline into the history of social and religious thought; into general intellectual history.

Viner's help to the scholarship of others came from far more than classroom teaching and debate. Despite the immense burden of his own work, throughout his life he was unstinting in the time he would devote to giving others the benefit of his unique erudition, analytical powers and experience.

Research and teaching were not Viner's only professional activities. He was also interested and involved in questions of economic policy. He wrote and gave public testimony on a host of practical matters. He wrote on the tariff, on the organization of world trade, taxes, public debt, reparations and the transfer problem, banking legislation, credit control, anti-trust, international monetary organization, international lending, economic development, defence and yet more.

Viner's views were not only offered, they were sought: he was an influential economic advisor in Washington. He wrote that he had a "faithful adherence to the modes of thought and the values of 19th century free-trade liberalism" and it is certain that his views and advice were invariably based on these principles. Viner was a vigorous exponent of liberal views, but he was not doctrinaire. His prescriptions for specific problems were influenced by concern that theory, the intellectual basis for making decisions, should take into account the complexity of reality. His practical advice was guided by a sense of balance and realism as to the use that policy makers could extract from economic theory. This is discussed in his Presidential Address to the American Economic Association, "The Short View and the Long in Economic Policy" (1939). He also had an awareness of the limitations of theory. In 1951, shortly after his periods of most active involvement in advising on policy, despite the future progress in economic theory that he foresaw, he put this point in an extreme form: "It seems that the old [classical] theory was sufficiently elastic, especially through its monetary phases, to absorb without friction the Keynesian contributions, and that it is now on the verge of systematic rehabilitation. Despite my belief in its merit and its relevance during the period of its dominance, I am convinced, however, that it would be a mistake to carry its rehabilitation so far as to claim for it, even in its improved and modernized form, adequacy as a theory to guide policy in the modern-day world". Viner's command of theory and sense of its limitations gave his advice on pressing problems such great practical value that he was sought out at the highest level by the United States Treasury during the hey-day of the New Deal and during the Second World War though Viner's basic philosophy was not then in fashion.

Viner was a renowned teacher, a reputed adviser, but his greatness lay in his scholarship. The breadth of his knowledge and interests and his versatility were remarkable. His 1931 article on "Cost Curves and Supply Curves" was a definitive contribution to the pure theory of the firm. Its famous error, identified by his draughtsman, in drawing the long run envelope curve did not lessen its impact, but added at the time an element of fun at the expense of the otherwise infallible Viner and later entered the folk-lore of economists some of whom have at times been comforted by its rememberance. Another article, "The Utility Concept in Value Theory and Its Critics" (1925) would today be considered in the category of history of economic thought of a very technical sort. He wrote articles on major writers, authoritative owing to his scholarship and uniquely structured in the balance of considerations of theory, historical antecedents and implications for policy. "Adam Smith and Laissez Faire" (1927), "Bentham and Mill: The Utilitarian Background" (1948), "Marshall's Economics, in Relation to the Man and His Times" (1940), among others, are on most university reading lists.

The theory of international economics was the field of Viner's principal contributions. He wrote many articles and several books in the pure theory of trade and international monetary theory. He developed theory to apply to policy problems. His first book, *Dump-*

ing: A Problem in International Trade (1923), is the classical theoretical and institutional study of the subject. The analysis developed there sets out the cases and obtains all the important results. It differs from present method of analysis only in greater use of average rather than marginal conditions. His most celebrated book in the field of policy oriented international trade theory is The Customs Union Issue (1950) in which he made the crucial contribution to the understanding of discriminatory tariff reduction by distinguishing between its trade creating and its trade diverting effect. This work, which thus analyzed the effect of tariff discrimination on production, inspired a great deal of very fruitful research by others. The principal contribution of this later work has been to indicate that gains may also arise from such tariff reductions because these increase efficiency in consumption. These gains are a more conjectural matter than the production effects. Viner also wrote on International Trade and Economic Development (1953).

There are few fields in international economics to which Viner did not contribute significantly. But one work stands out: his monumental Studies in the Theory of International Trade (1937), a history of chiefly English thought in international economics from medieval to modern times with emphasis on the period from the classical economists onward. It is not an antiquarian piece, but an evaluation of the views of earlier writers in terms of modern economic knowledge that reveals an astonishing mastery of the literature. Its pages are studded with insights into the thoughts of others and with independent theoretical contributions, some of which are derived, of course, from Viner's earlier works. An instance of the latter is the well-known analysis of the relation of types of imperfections in the labour market to presumptions of gains from free trade. This early, incisive application of the theory of the second best comes from Viner's review (1932) of Manoilesco's book. This superb Studies, a model for studies of the evolution of economic theory, remains the definitive work in its field.

Canada's Balance of International Indebtedness, 1900-1913 is also one of Viner's major works. Though based on his doctoral thesis under Taussig, it was published only in 1924 and was by no means his first publication. Taussig had developed the classical theory of adjustment in the balance of payments in the tradition of J. S. Mill and Henry Thornton, but he believed that a theory without inductive verification did not constitute real knowledge. He and his students engaged in case studies of the adjustment process in various countries. The best known of these studies in addition to Taussig's own for the United States, are J. H. William's study of Argentine experience under a paper standard from 1880 to 1900,

W. H. White for France 1880-1913, but especially Viner's *Canada's Balance*. Little empirical work on the transfer process has been done since.

The purpose of Viner's study was to test the classical theory of the mechanism of adjustment in the balance of international payments under a gold standard. Canada in the period from 1900 to 1913 was an appropriate case for study because its balance of payments showed a huge change during that period. It shifted from no net capital movement at its inception to a capital inflow that was very large whether measured as a proportion of Canadian trade or of national income. What mechanism had brought about this change?

As was to become characteristic of so much of his work, Viner included in his book a careful analysis of economic doctrine on the subject of his research. He established that Mill's theory descended from Thornton, but that Ricardo believed an adjustment in the balance of payments to a capital flow could occur owing to "shifts in relative demand" without a gold flow and a change in the terms of trade. Viner himself adhered to the classical theory against Ricardo, though he recognized that part of the adjustment might take place directly by an increase in expenditures on imports and exportables, because the loan increased the income of the borrowing country. Thus part of the loan would be transferred directly without a change in the terms of trade. Viner assumed that the marginal propensity to spend on imports and on exportables would be equal to their average propensity and he left out the changes in expenditures caused by the income change owing to financing the loan in the lending country. Thus Viner stated only part of the correct formulation of the classical transfer mechanism which is that the transfer will be exactly effected without gold flows and price changes if the sum of the proportions of expenditure change falling on the two countries' export goods is equal to unity. In any event, he would not have considered this outcome to be likely and would have adhered to the necessity for a change in relative prices.

Viner's first task was to establish the facts and he laboriously composed estimates of the balance of payments for Canada for that period. The reader should remember that Viner's terminology does not correspond to that used today. The present meaning of the balance of international indebtedness is the outstanding claims on foreigners and liabilities to them; whereas Viner's use corresponds to the modern term "the balance of international payments" or to changes in the claims and liabilities. The modern reader will be struck by how the world has changed. In those relatively non-inflationary days, it was possible to borrow at long term at about four per cent. The exchange rate was truly fixed and "movements in the exchange normally show a strong aversion to reaching the gold points".

In accordance with the Mill-Taussig formulation of classical theory, Viner assumed that the flow of capital into Canada was the disturbing autonomous phenomenon. The funds borrowed abroad would initially be transferred in bullion, thus permitting an increase in Canadian money supply and an increase in expenditures including imports and exportable goods. Increased prices for Canadian output would raise the balance of payments deficit so that it would be financed by continued new borrowing abroad.

Viner adapted the traditional theory to take into account the peculiarities of Canadian banking practice and traced the effect of changes in bank liquidity on the quantity of money, on relative prices in Canada and abroad, and on the balance of payments. He reached the conclusion that the mechanism of adjustment in Canada's balance of payments operated much as explained by the classical theory. The flow of gold, modified to correspond to the practice of holding outside reserves by Canadian banks, was consistent with that expected by classical theory as were the movements in the relative price levels of the borrowing country Canada, the United Kingdom in which the borrowing took place, and the United States from which most imports came. Viner conceded that Canadians may have borrowed abroad to finance settlement and industrialization, but he contended that the investment expenditures would not have had a direct role in the adjustment of the balance of payments and the capital flow that was observed. He believed that the relative inflation in Canada and the change in the terms of trade could only be explained if the foreign borrowing was the disturbing factor.

Later Viner wrote in his *Studies in the Theory of International Trade* "that in the case of Canada before the war the fluctuations in the trade balance were much more the effect than the cause of fluctuations in the long term borrowings abroad", thus adhering to his earlier view in *Canada's Balance*. For his part R. H. Coats, the Dominion Statistician, in his *Report of the Board of Enquiry into the Cost of Living* (1915) of which Viner had himself made much use, had emphasized the role of dynamic factors in the Canadian transfer mechanism without, however, developing a specific economic model. Since 1945 a number of writers have returned to Coats' view and claimed that Viner over-emphasized the role of monetary factors as against that of autonomous expenditure changes in his explanation of the adjustment in Canada's international position. Indeed, the sequence of events identified by Viner as being consistent with the classical process of adjustment is also consistent with other mechanisms in which the capital movement is endogenous to a process of growth rather than the exogenous cause of the disturbance.

A surge in economic development, led by Prairie expansion, occurred from 1895 to 1913. It resulted in increased exports and was accompanied by rising imports and domestic prices. Only after 1904 was it accompanied by the sizeable capital imports from the United Kingdom that Viner was analyzing. They permitted an excess of imports over exports and the process of development to continue unimpeded. Thus the theoretical basis of *Canada's Balance* is incomplete and undoubtedly leaves out of account changes of income and expenditure that elicited at least part of the flows of capital and that also played a larger role than Viner envisaged in the adjustment in the balance of payments to autonomous capital flows.

The theory of adjustment in the balance of payments has progressed during the 50 years since *Canada's Balance* was published, yet this book remains a landmark in empirical economic research and a major contribution to Canadian economic history. The contribution resides not only in its analysis of the payments mechanism, but also in the observations and the analysis of other economic phenomena characteristic of Canada then and in part now. Viner explained that the basis of direct foreign investment was the technological and management abilities of the foreign firms that established themselves here, a view that has only very recently been elaborated and widely accepted. He noted the contrasting behaviour of British and United States' businessmen, the former concerned with portfolio investment, the latter with control and management of enterprises in Canada, often using the funds of others. He understood that the Canadian tariff was a factor encouraging the establishment of foreign firms in Canada as were also the suitability of American methods to Canadian markets and the need of foreign industry for Canadian resource-based products as United States sources became depleted. These are questions of interest still. He also wrote of unwise investments, mostly undertaken with governmental encouragement, in overbuilt railways and municipal facilities, especially in the West. His pessimistic estimate of the prospective yield on much investment made in the boom turned out to be correct and this added painfully to the financial burden borne by Canadians in the depression years.

This book is a classic, a work of lasting significance for its interpretation of the functioning of the balance of payments mechanism under the gold standard and for its description and analysis of a remarkable period in Canada's economic development. It bears the marks of its author's genius in its sophisticated theory, its respect for the views of earlier writers and its painstaking concern for the facts.

H. C. Eastman
Department of Political Economy
University of Toronto

PREFACE

THIS study is intended primarily as an inductive verification of the general theory of the mechanism of international trade, and its treatment of Canadian matters is incidental to its main purpose. It should nevertheless prove of some utility to students of Canadian economic affairs. The changes in Canadian financial, monetary, commercial, and industrial conditions consequent upon Canada's participation in the war make 1913 the terminal year of a distinct period in Canadian economic history. It is mainly for this reason that I have made no attempt to carry this inquiry beyond the year 1913. The study of Canada's balance of international indebtedness during the war and post-war period would encounter problems which in many respects would be essentially different from those analyzed in the present inquiry; most important of all would be the effect on the mechanism of international trade of Canada's departure from the gold standard. Statements of fact in this study should be understood to be intended to apply to the period 1900 to 1913, and not necessarily to later years, even though no warning is given in the text of later changes.

I am indebted for assistance in gathering the statistical details upon which the present study is based to my former teacher, Professor J. C. Hemmeon of McGill University, to the Canadian Pacific Railway, to the Dominion Securities Corporation, Toronto, and to many kind government officials at Ottawa. To Professor F. W. Taussig, at whose suggestion this study was begun many years ago, and to whose kind and unflagging interest therein its final completion is due, I owe special thanks for inspiration, advice, and criticism.

JACOB VINER.

UNIVERSITY OF CHICAGO
October 10, 1923

CHAPTER I

METHOD AND SCOPE OF THE PRESENT STUDY

The *a priori* Character of the Classical Theory of International Trade

The modern theory of the mechanism of international trade is almost wholly the contribution of the English classical school of economists and its later followers. Its first principles, stated rather clearly by Hume and more haltingly and inaccurately by Adam Smith, received systematic and comprehensive development at the hands of a group of English economists writing in the first two decades of the nineteenth century, most notable of whom was Ricardo. The subsequent contributions of Cairnes and Mill to the theory of international trade, although not unimportant, were in the nature of amplification, explanation, clarification, rather than of vital addition or emendation to the logical system expounded by Ricardo. These later writers followed closely not only Ricardo's statement of principles, but his methods of expounding and illustrating them. Those contemporary economists, such as Taussig, Edgeworth, and Bastable, who have been interested in the explanation of the mechanism of international trade have carried the reasoning of the older writers a few steps further in some detailed aspects of the problem, and have improved the method of statement, but they also have adhered closely and faithfully, except for minor details, to the classical tradition. Alike with the remainder of the economic system of the classical school, the theory of international **trade** has in recent years been submitted to severe criticism from **several** points of view. Something will be said later of the sources, the methods, and the validity of these various attacks, but it is unquestionably true that the classical explanation of the mechanism of international trade has, of all the classical economics, been subjected to least criticism, both in quantity and in effectiveness, and remains to-day in every important particular the authoritative doctrine accepted even by most of those economists who in other respects have largely abandoned — or believe that they have abandoned — the classical economics.

The classical economists, in keeping with their general methodology, developed the theory of international trade on lines almost wholly abstract and *a priori*. Even the arithmetical and other illustrations utilized to facilitate the exposition of reasoning necessarily difficult because of the complexity of the problem, often had little resemblance to actual conditions. In only a few instances did they make any attempt to derive or even to verify their theories by an inductive analysis of factual data.[1]

The classical theory of international trade is *a priori* in the sense that it begins with a few fundamental generalizations, largely psychological in character, assumed to be of universal validity, and that from these few principles it derives all of its important conclusions, no significant use being made of any additional data other than a few facts characteristic of our industrial and commercial structure — facts of common experience and observation, not requiring systematic observational study and analysis for their understanding and interpretation. With a background of rationalistic prudential psychology to start from, the classical school stressed the individual character of each transaction in international trade, in which each of the parties, being ruled by egoistic motives, demanded a value equivalent in return for everything he exported or imported. From this they derived the further principle that all exports must tally in value with all imports, and that relative price differences are the proximate cause of all international transactions. Adjustments of the necessary balance of international transactions to a commodity and service basis with a minimum of gold movements are effected, they explained, through preliminary gold movements, initiated by individuals in the pursuit of economic gain. The influence of gold movements on price levels,

---

[1] Ricardo made extensive and effective use of factual data for the purpose of inductive verification in his *Reply to Mr. Bosanquet's Practical Observations on the Report of the Bullion Committee* (1811). Other instances would be hard to find.

explained by the quantity theory of the value of money, and of price levels on the profitability of export and import of commodities and services, always tended to bring about an even balance between commodity and service imports and exports. The absence of such equivalence, temporary or continued, was to be explained only as due to temporary ill-adjustments, to credit transactions, that is, loans and repayment of loans, and to noncommercial unilateral transactions not requiring an exchange of considerations, such as tributes, subsidies, and gifts.

Criticism on *a priori* grounds of this *a priori* reasoning has been directed mainly against three particulars: first, the apparent dependence of the theory on the questionable validity of the quantity theory of money; secondly, the precise part played by gold movements in the mechanism of international trade; and thirdly, the details of the reasoning regarding the order of events in the adjustment of trade balances when the currency of one or both countries engaged in trade is depreciated in terms of the standard metal. Attempts to apply the inductive method to the problem of the mechanism of international trade have been relatively few, and also, with one or two exceptions, relatively unimportant. Most of them rested on the explicit acceptance of the classical doctrine, and confined themselves to the attempt to establish statistically (1) the equivalence at some definite date, or during some closely defined period, between debits and credits in the international balance of payments of a selected country, and (2) the amounts as measured in money of the constituent items in the debit and credit sides of the balance. Two recent studies have gone somewhat further. C. K. Hobson, in *The Export of Capital*,[1] has added to the quantitative establishment of the items in the balance of international transactions some analysis of the quantitative changes in the individual items which result from a disturbance in an original *status quo*, and of the mechanism whereby such changes are brought about. J. H. Williams, in his *Argentine International Trade under Inconvertible Paper Money, 1880–1900*,[2] tested the validity of the classical doctrine in so far as it dealt with those phases of the mechanism

[1] London, 1914.   [2] *Harvard Economic Studies*, 1920.

of international trade which were different, or might be supposed to be different, in trade under depreciated paper as compared with trade under the gold standard. Various writers on the theory of the foreign exchanges have also examined inductively, although generally only for purposes of illustration of accepted *a priori* principles, the part played by variations in exchange rates in the adjustment of international balances of payments. The classical explanation of the mechanism of international trade between gold-standard countries, in its larger and fundamental aspects, has not yet been submitted to a comprehensive and thorough inductive test.

This study is primarily an attempt at such a test. It rests its case on the belief that, given a systematic and comprehensive quantitative record of economic phenomena directly or indirectly related to international transactions, and given circumstances favorable to the application of the more highly developed methods of inductive inference, a number of valuable results may be obtained by the inductive method in addition to those reached by the *a priori* method: (1) the validity of the conclusions of the *a priori* theory can be tested by comparison with actual situations; (2) a more accurate and more detailed description of the mechanics of trade-balance adjustments can be obtained; (3) inspection of the factual data may suggest possible hypotheses amending or extending the accepted *a priori* theory, these in turn to be tested by the logical methods of deduction and of induction.

THE PLACE OF INDUCTION IN THE THEORY OF INTERNATIONAL TRADE

What has just been said should not be interpreted as intended to question the value of the deductive method as a method of adding to human knowledge, or as a claim that the inductive method can replace and render superfluous the deductive method. A generalized description of a social process from observed data can completely take the place of deduction only if it is induction from "complete enumeration," that is, only if all the relevant facts in every situation have been completely and accurately measured, recorded, classified, and analyzed. Induction from partial evidence, or from incompletely classified data, itself waits upon hypotheses, upon the mental anticipation of possible causal correlations, before it can yield logically convincing inferences. The limitation of specific knowledge of facts is perhaps the chief obstacle to the use of the inductive method. This limitation of knowledge is due to the inadequacy of recorded factual data; to the difficulty of attribution of effect to cause where a combination of causes produces a joint effect; to the human element in the collection and arrangement of facts which leads to their distortion and their loss, in the process of manipulation, of their purely objective character; and, probably most of all, to the inaccessibility to the student, under conditions usually governing his research, of the facts of mental experience necessary to a complete explanation, subjective as well as objective, motivating as well as external and physical, of a process in which man plays a part.

The deductive method in economics, when its general psychological assumptions have not been too much divorced from the true psychology of the market-place, and when the generalizations concerning the environmental data which are used as premises have also been reasonably accurate, has brought valuable results. Deductive conclusions would differ, perhaps, from the results obtained by an inductive investigation of the same problem with a complete record of facts to work from; but they would differ only because they were incomplete. The differences would tend to disappear as the deductive results were supplemented by the results of inductive analysis resting on inference from the facts omitted in the fundamental abstractions of the deductive study. This assumes, of course, that the abstractions of a valid deductive theory are not inconsistent with the facts. They should be abstractions, not in the sense that they are untrue, but in the sense that they do not tell the whole truth.

In the field of the theory of international trade, as in all other fields in the social sciences, there are aspects which in practice can be investigated by only one of the methods; and there are other aspects in which both methods can be more or less completely applied, and the results of the one corroborated or dis-

credited by the results of the other. In developing a complete
theory both methods must be used; and the utilization of the
one method as a means of verifying the other is made possible,
not only in that portion of the field to which both can be applied
but practically throughout the field, by a study of the success
with which one part of the theory obtained by means of one
method can be made to fit in with the other portions obtained
by the other method or by both together, so as to form a complete and consistent system satisfactory to the reasoning intelligence.

As has been indicated, the special field of deduction in the investigation of the problems of international trade is the explanation of the subjective phases of the problem, and particularly the
motivation of individuals in their international activities. To
the explanation of the objective mechanism of the process, the
devices used and the manner of their operation, and the objective
manifestations of human behavior as it reacts to the environment
under the stimulus of the main incentives operating, the inductive method can make important contributions, partly because
these phases are objective, and partly because they rest on a com-
plicated and detailed industrial and commercial organization, of
which even the most satisfactory abstract theory could take into
consideration only the main framework. The two methods can
be used as tests on each other chiefly in that common portion of
the field where what the deductive theory would lead us to expect to find men doing can be compared with what the inductive
theory actually finds them doing, and can be made to suggest a
rational explanation of these doings.

In the theory of international trade there must be left to the
deductive theory, as its exclusive field, the exposition of why men
act as they do in their international transactions, and of the
subjective results of such action. The remainder of the theory
is available to the inductive method, provided the facts have been
collected and recorded. Induction can be utilized generally in
cooperation with deduction, to describe and explain the changes
in the volume and character of trade, the movements of price
levels, the part played by exchange rates and gold movements in

the adjustment of trade balances, and the reaction upon internal economic conditions of changes in international trade. The quantitative determination of the division of gains from international trade appears to be a problem beyond solution by either method. But quantities which are incapable of direct measurement are sometimes subject to measurement of their relative changes. The inductive method can be utilized here, both to test deductive conclusions as to the direction of the change in the division of the gains following upon a specific change in the conditions of international trade, and, given the direction of the change, to supplement this by an objective measurement of the degree of change in the ratio in which the gains are divided. The present study will pay most attention to those phases on which an inductive investigation can throw most light, although a considerable amount of deductive reasoning will inevitably make its appearance, mingled with the principles obtained inductively from a systematic factual study of a specific situation.

THE SCOPE OF THE PRESENT STUDY

No logically precise division can be made between the problems which are problems of international trade, and those which are not. In a country whose commercial relations with other countries are important, no significant element of its internal economic structure is free from important influence by factors wholly external in their origin, and the degree of importance of this influence is directly dependent upon the extent to which international trade has been developed by that country. In countries highly developed economically there is a remarkable degree of interdependence between the various economic factors at work. Furthermore, the character, direction, and extent of a country's foreign trade are always closely related to its material and human resources, its physical situation, its political and legal institutions, its sentimental affiliations, its internal industrial, financial, and commercial structure. It would be absurd to attempt an analytical study of a country's foreign trade without correlating it with its domestic industry, or, on the other hand, to make a general survey of its internal industry without paying considerable attention to the influence upon it of its foreign trade.

In the present stage of development of statistical data, some phases of great importance must often be ignored in an inductive study, while other phases of less significance receive detailed analysis, because of differences in the relative completeness of the recorded data bearing on different problems. Partly because of the survival of mercantilist beliefs concerning external trade and partly because of fiscal necessity, many phases of commerce are subjected to official accounting only at political boundaries, and are thus available for inductive inference only in their international aspects. It is obvious, therefore, that the particular situation studied and the data there available must play a considerable part in the determination of the scope of a study such as this. The particular situation examined may further affect the character and scope of the study inasmuch as special factors may be prominent in that situation, or may have been subject to particularly marked variations, and may thus more readily lend themselves to inductive investigation.

It is on these grounds rather than on the basis of any claims to logical consistency that the writer defends his acts of omission and commission in his choice of phases for investigation. As a result of the emphasis laid on the inductive method, this study should offer as its special contribution a more detailed, more concrete description of the mechanism and the objective results of external trade than is to be found in the primarily deductive treatments of this subject. But even in the problems of the distribution of gains and of the ratios of international exchange, detailed study of a general situation and analysis of the mechanism may suggest new solutions for old problems and may reveal new problems affording valid justification for occasional excursions into deductive analysis. Above all, the description and analysis of the objective data, in addition to providing material for independent inductive inferences, should make possible a critical examination of the accredited deductive theory, with a view to verification where such is justified, and to correction where the evidence demands it.

Canada, from 1900 to 1913, the Field of the Present Study

The particular field in which the data for a thoroughgoing inductive analysis of the mechanism and effects of external trade have been sought is Canada during the fourteen-year period from 1900 to 1913, inclusive. There are a number of weighty considerations pointing to Canadian trade history during this period as a particularly fruitful field for research. To begin with, an inductive investigation of social phenomena, in order that it may bring results of any definiteness and reliability, must confine itself to factors which in the situation studied are of sufficient importance to influence appreciably the phenomena causally related to it. If minor factors in a complex situation are investigated with the intention of measuring the extent of their influence, it is often found that their effects are so mingled with the effects of other causes as to be lost in the complexity of the situation. Under such circumstances no inductive attempt to learn their effects, no matter how detailed and painstaking, will succeed in obtaining results not open to question. How ascertain that a small variation in an effect of a combination of causes is due to the particular cause studied, and not to some undetected variation in some other causal factor, or to some error or inaccuracy in the recorded data? And so, if the effects on each other and on the commercial and industrial structure of a country, of the factors at work within the mechanism of its external trade, are to be analyzed and measured with any reasonable degree of accuracy of results, the external trade of that country must be of great importance relative to its internal trade and to its industry and commerce in general. Otherwise their effects will be indistinguishably merged in the effects of the internal factors at work.

To Canada its foreign trade is of supreme importance. With its inhabited territory situated wholly within the cool temperate zone, Canada can produce within her own boundaries, even with the highest degree of artificial stimulation, only a small percentage of the range of commodities demanded by her people. Limited by the character of her climate, soil, and natural resources, and by the sparseness of population, to comparatively few exporting industries, she must with the products of these industries pay for the commodities of other countries which she cannot, or cannot profitably, produce for herself, but which she insists on having. The Canadian manufacturing industries are much more dependent on imports for their raw and semi-manufactured materials than the American, and even than the British. Cotton, hemp, silk, wool, jute, rubber, hides, coal, tin, copper, iron ore, raw tobacco, raw sugar, all have to be obtained from abroad. Tropical fruits, corn, vegetable oils, tea, coffee, cocoa, spices, must be imported from warmer countries. Even where the natural and technological conditions are not unfavorable for the development of domestic production of commodities of a sort demanded by Canada, there are often social forces at work which prevent their domestic manufacture, at least in all its stages, from developing, and which force Canada to obtain these commodities by importation in return for the inchoate products of her great primary industries.

Chief of these forces is the influence exerted upon the Canadian consumer by the standards of consumption of Great Britain and the United States. Canada has only imperfectly developed a national consciousness, and not to any appreciable extent national standards of taste and consumption. With the exception of daily newspapers, her periodicals of general circulation are mainly American or English. Thus not only do New York and London, through prestige and sentimental, racial, and lingual kinship, mould and direct the demands of the Canadian consumer, but through their periodicals, which circulate in huge numbers, with their advertising contents often more bulky than their literary features, they train him to demand the special brands and styles of the United States and England. As a result, the native production of similar articles is checked. The great distances between the centres of population within Canada, combined with, on the one hand, the proximity of American producing regions to Canadian markets and of Canadian producing regions to American markets, and on the other hand, the cheapness of water-transportation to and from Europe, further promote foreign trade.

Table I presents a comparison of the per capita foreign trade, in 1911, of the great trading nations populated by Europeans. Of the countries listed, four had a per capita trade in 1911 greater than that of Canada. All these four countries use the value on arrival (c. i. f.) for their import statistics, whereas Canada uses the lower value in port of lading (f. o. b.). For New Zealand and Australia, distant as they are from the important markets, this has a substantial influence on the statistics of trade. Transit, *entrepôt*, and reexport trade make a large fraction of the total trade of Belgium and the United Kingdom, but are unimportant in Canada. It is probable that, if proper allowance were made for these factors, the basic per capita foreign trade of Canada would be exceeded only by that of Australia and New Zealand, and only by narrow margins even in these instances.

TABLE I

Per Capita Trade of Various Countries in 1911 [1]

Country	Aggregate trade *thousands of dollars*	Population *thousands*	Per capita trade *dollars*
Canada	$874,638	7,207	$121.36
Belgium	1,494,578	7,424	201.32
New Zealand	187,850	1,008	186.36
Australia	713,207	4,455	160.09
Great Britain	6,024,365	45,369	132.78
Argentina	670,107	7,172	93.43
France	3,471,745	39,602	87.67
Germany	4,439,331	64,926	68.38
Chile	224,511	3,415	65.74
United States	3,267,031	91,972	35.52
Italy	1,039,063	34,671	29.97
Brazil	583,343	23,071	25.28
Russia	1,299,429	167,003	7.78

[1] Computed from data for 1911 or nearest year in *Statesman's Year Book*, 1913.

The data presented in the table suggest the generalization that per capita foreign trade varies inversely with the number of inhabitants. For the smaller European countries the explanation probably lies in the importance of their transit trade, in their limited range of natural resources, in their peculiar adaptation to certain industries, and in their proximity to foreign producing and consuming markets. For Canada, in addition to these reasons there should be noted the fact that since Canadian manufacturing technique is closely modelled on the American, with its large-scale mass production of standardized commodities, the limited extent of the domestic market, in so far as population is concerned, and the limited supply of labor, restrict the range of industries to which, under Canadian conditions, this technique can be intensively applied. If comparison between the relative importance of production for domestic and for foreign consumption were feasible, the importance to Canada of its foreign trade would probably appear to be even greater than is indicated by this table.

Another factor of great importance in making Canadian trade experience a favorable field of investigation is the high degree of compactness and unity of the Canadian industrial and commercial structure. At first glance one should not expect much economic interdependence between the various parts of the Dominion. The population is practically all to be found within a narrow strip of land extending across the continent, and even this narrow strip of land is broken up into a number of distinct sections by the projection of Maine into Canadian territory, by the barren lands north of Lake Superior, and by the Rockies. But whatever may be the situation geographically, the social factors have all contributed to the development of what is, under the circumstances, a remarkably unified economic organization. The effect of a high protective tariff in forcing traffic into east and west channels, and the deliberate policy of the Canadian federal and provincial governments of stimulating transportation service of this character by money and land subsidies of the most generous character, have been most effective in building up a transportation system both by land and by water, which serves to tie together province and province rather than province and American state.[1]

Furthermore, centralization of economic control, with the

[1] While tending to unify the economic organization of Canada, these factors tend, of course, to restrict somewhat the volume of foreign trade and thus operate counter to the natural tendencies enumerated above.

whole Dominion as the economic unit, has also been carried to great lengths. Practically all long-distance transportation was, during the period under study, in the hands of the government and three or four giant corporations; and in a country of specialization in industry, sparse population, and great distances, transportation is bound to be one of the most important industries, if not the most important. The reserve system for Canadian currency, government and bank, is highly centralized, while banking is in the hands of less than twenty-five banks. In manufacturing, and even in primary industries such as mining, the fisheries, and lumbering, similar centralization of control obtains. It has often been said, and with greater truth as applied to Canada than to any other important country, that every consumer's product and many of the raw materials are monopoly or quasi-monopoly products.[1] The imports of the west either originate in the east or are bought through eastern merchants and transported through the east, while the products of the west are largely sold to the east, whether for eastern consumption or for eventual export, and are shipped to the eastern provinces in either case. Add to these the important financial interrelations between the industrial and the banking, financial, and transportation magnates, and the further centralization which is procured through the powerful influence wielded by the Canadian Manufacturers' and the Canadian Bankers' Associations, and it becomes clear why all these factors must operate to establish an unusual degree of economic interdependence between the various parts of the Dominion, with the result that there is little likelihood that an important financial or industrial phenomenon arising in one part of the country will be neutralized by counteracting phenomena in another part and will thus not have a visible effect in the national statistics. Canada, because of these circumstances, presents opportunities for statistical analysis and research not available in countries which are economically more loosely organized and in which there is less likelihood of all important factors operating on a national scale.

[1] Cf. James J. Harpell, *Canadian National Economy*, Ch. iii: "Canada's Combines."

The smallness of Canada's population of itself has been suggested as a factor in making Canada a fertile field for economic research:

We are often reminded that Canada's population is small and her trade a modest affair. But the smallness of the scale has its advantages, not only when we watch the workings of a political experiment in federal government, but when we watch the movements of trade. The daylight of first principles may shine more easily through the figures of a comparatively small commercial nation than through those of countries which have seven or eight times the population, and have been doing business for centuries. Along with the larger numbers and the older business come the complexity and perplexity due to the increasing plurality of causes; and the interpretation of figures becomes less simple even though the guiding clues are the same for all cases, great or small. It is well for those that have "a passion for statistics" to seize their opportunity; it will not last long.[1]

Perhaps the most weighty justification for seeking in Canadian experience a field for the inductive investigation of the theory of international trade is to be found in the fact that during the years 1900 to 1913, chosen for special study, there occurred in Canada a great importation of foreign capital, rising from a few million dollars in 1900 to almost half a billion dollars in 1913, and amounting for the entire period to over two billion dollars. This tremendous import of capital created a situation peculiarly favorable for the application of the inductive method, especially in its special form of the method of concomitant variations. The inward movement of capital dominated all other factors in Canada's foreign trade during the period of heavy borrowings, and the variations in the inward flow of foreign capital were marked enough to effect sharp correlated variations in other elements in the situation. As a consequence, an inductive study of Canada's international trade during this period becomes largely a study of the adjustment of Canada's trade balance, currency and banking system, price levels, and industry in general, to a heavy import of foreign capital.

Finally, an important prerequisite to the use of the inductive method, the availability of adequate and comprehensive statistics, is for the particular subject of investigation more nearly ful-

[1] James Bonar, "Canada's Balance of Trade," *Proceedings of the Canadian Political Science Association*, 1913, p. 82.

filled in Canada than in most countries. Many statistical series, which in other countries are not obtainable or are available only for districts or states, are available for Canada as a whole. Complete currency and banking statistics are published monthly under official auspices. The problem of measuring gold movements is simplified by the fact that no gold coin circulates in Canada and all gold coin in the country is centralized in government or bank reserves. Detailed and excellently classified commerce and price statistics are regularly compiled. Original statistical investigations under government and under private auspices have made available for our present purposes important data which ordinarily are not similarly obtainable for other countries.[1]

The study is divided into two parts. In the first part statistical estimates are made of the important items entering into the Canadian balance of international indebtedness. The second part comprises a detailed analysis of the mechanism of adjustment of the balance of indebtedness.

[1] Special acknowledgment must be made to *The Cost of Living Report*, vol. ii, 1915, prepared under the direction of R. H. Coats, Dominion Statistician. This is a mine of statistical and other information, much of it bearing directly upon international trade problems. The indebtedness of this study to the *Cost of Living Report* is abundantly evidenced by the frequent citations and references thereto.

PART I

THE CANADIAN BALANCE OF INTERNATIONAL INDEBTEDNESS

INTRODUCTORY

THE terminology used in the theory of international trade is rather formidable, is sometimes confusing, and is often involved in ambiguities. It will be well, therefore, before proceeding to the body of the investigation, to forestall misunderstanding by carefully defining the more important terms used.

A transaction which creates a pecuniary obligation on the part of a person in Canada toward someone outside Canada is called a debit transaction; and one which creates an obligation toward a Canadian by a person outside Canada is called a credit transaction. For example, a commodity import is a debit transaction; a commodity export is a credit transaction. By the Canadian balance of international indebtedness is meant the difference between the totals of Canadian debit and credit international transactions. If the debits exceed the credits, there is a debit balance; if the credits exceed the debits, there is a credit balance. In accordance with customary usage the term balance is used also, sometimes to signify an even balance or equilibrium between debits and credits, at other times to designate the balance-sheet itself, that is, the tabulation of all the debit and credit items, without special reference to the quantitative relations of total debits to total credits. In such cases the context will show what meaning must be given to the term balance. The balance of payments, or, if it be assumed that all immediate obligations are immediately liquidated, the "balance of immediate obligations," refers to the difference between *immediate* debit and credit obligations, and not to the difference between *all* debit and credit transactions. If some of the transactions are on a deferred-payment basis, as is generally the case, there may be a debit balance of indebtedness at the same time that there is a credit balance of payments, and *vice versa*. The commodity balance of trade, the balance of service transactions, and the balance of non-commercial transactions indicate, respectively, the differences between the amounts of commodity imports and exports, of debit and credit international service transactions, and of debit and credit international non-commercial transactions, irrespective in each case of whether or not the obligations created thereby are immediate or deferred. The total of these three balances equals the total balance of international indebtedness.[1] This total balance of international indebtedness for any period is, of course, the same thing as the difference between total foreign loans and total foreign borrowings for that period.

In Part I the commodity balance of trade, the balance of non-commercial transactions, and the balance of service transactions are first estimated for each year in the period, and the total balance of international indebtedness is then computed from these partial balances. The addition, to the debit balance of international indebtedness so obtained, of the volume of investments of Canadian capital abroad gives as a result an indirect estimate of the foreign investments of capital in Canada. The accuracy of this estimate of foreign investments in Canada, and, indirectly, of the entire calculation of the balance of international indebtedness, is then tested by a direct estimate of the volume of foreign capital invested in Canada, based upon the available information relating to such investments.

The only other comprehensive attempt to estimate the Canadian balance of international indebtedness is that made by R. H. Coats, Dominion Statistician, in connection with his cost-of-living inquiry, published in 1915.[2] Coats' analysis of the balance

---

[1] The Harvard *Review of Economic Statistics*, in its calculations of American trade balances, appears to use the term "balance of payments" interchangeably with the term "balance of indebtedness," and so tabulates and describes its material as to make it impossible to determine with certainty whether in particular instances balance of payments or balance of indebtedness, as the terms are here defined, is meant. Usage is not uniform, but the weight of authority and considerations of economy and clarity in terminology are in my opinion both opposed to the attribution of identity of meaning to the two terms. In any case, there is an important difference in meaning between what is here called the balance of payments, i.e., the balance of immediate (and honored) obligations, and what is here called the balance of indebtedness, i.e., the balance of all obligations, immediate and deferred.

[2] *Report of the Board of Inquiry into the Cost of Living.* Summary and vol. ii, Ottawa, 1915.

of indebtedness covers approximately the same period as that investigated in this study and, in general, follows the same lines. While it proved of great aid to the writer, its results, for reasons later to be explained, are not in close agreement with those obtained in the present study.

CHAPTER II

THE COMMODITY BALANCE OF TRADE

By the commodity balance of trade is meant, of course, the difference between the value of the exports and that of the imports of physical goods. The trade in coin and bullion is sometimes excluded and sometimes included in the striking of the commodity balance. Where the purpose is to ascertain the balance of immediate obligations which is not liquidated by shipment of commodities (or services) and must therefore be settled in money, it is proper to exclude coin at least, and perhaps also bullion.[1] For our present purpose, the ascertaining of the debit balance of international indebtedness, or the amount of obligations of Canada to other countries which were *not* met during the period, whether by shipment of goods or money or in any other way, the trade in coin and bullion must be included alike with the trade in other commodities.

Information as to the amounts of commodity exports and imports is to be obtained from the official commerce statistics of practically all civilized countries, and it would appear at first glance to be a simple matter to strike off the balance by setting exports against imports. Commerce statistics, however, like all other statistical data, have their peculiarities. It is generally advisable to examine carefully the basis of their compilation, what is included and what excluded, and the time-units for which the data are collected, before proceeding to use such data as the foundation for important conclusions.

[1] It is true, of course, that a balance of immediate obligations cannot be struck without allowance for imports and exports of capital, i.e., deferred obligations, and for obligations contracted through other than commodity transactions. Where the commodity balances of trade are alone being considered, there is no obvious justification for excluding coin imports and exports. In Canada, bullion moves in foreign trade purely as a commodity, as it does not enter into the currency in its unminted state, and little of it is minted in Canada.

THE CANADIAN COMMERCE STATISTICS

Method of Compilation. — The Canadian statistics for exports and imports are primarily collected and tabulated by the Department of Customs, by months and by years, on the basis of declarations of value by importers and exporters, checked, especially for imports, by the valuations of the customs inspectors. The tabulated statistics, during the period under study, were published by the Department of Customs, but the Department of Trade and Commerce reworked the statistics of the Customs Department into other forms, elaborated the classification thereof, added to the amount of comparative statistics, and published monthly and annual reports based on the data originally collected and issued by the Customs Department. Most of the commerce data used in this report are obtainable in both sets of reports. Statistics of imports are published both for "total imports" and for "imports entered for consumption." "Total imports" are all imports which reach the customs warehouses. "Imports entered for consumption" are all imports which pass *through* the customs warehouses and enter into the Canadian channels of trade. "Imports entered for consumption" is a technical term, used in both Canada and the United States for imports to which it does not always accurately apply, since it includes goods not consumed in Canada, if they are reëxported after passing through the customhouse.

Statistics of exports are published for "total exports," for "exports of Canadian produce," and for "exports of foreign produce." These terms are self-explanatory. Included in exports of "foreign produce" are foreign goods exported from customs warehouses without having passed into the channels of Canadian trade, and foreign goods exported after having been "entered for consumption in Canada." The amount of exports of foreign produce is generally greater, therefore, than the difference between "total imports" and "imports entered for consumption." [1] To obtain the commodity balance of trade, the statistics of "total imports" and "total exports" must be used.

[1] Since 1916 a comprehensive reorganization of Canadian commerce statistics has been effected, and what is said here should be understood to be applicable to

Methods of computing Values. — There are important divergencies in the methods used by various countries in computing the values of their imports and exports.[1] Most countries use c. i. f. values for imports, or the values on arrival at the port of import, including freight, insurance, and other transport charges. Many countries use official valuations, which in some cases are arbitrary or obsolete and have little relation to actual values. Canada follows the American usage of basing its import statistics on the values of imports in the countries whence the goods were consigned to Canada. The values used for imports are the " fair market values of such goods when sold for home consumption in the principal markets of the countries whence, and at the time when, the same were exported directly to Canada." The term "direct" does not exclude shipments passing in continuous voyage through the ports or other territory of a third country. Unless either "dumping values" or undervaluation are discovered in the values declared and sworn to in the invoices, the invoice values are taken. Except for the relatively insignificant amount of goods which are undervalued to evade customs taxation *without* discovery by the customs officials, or which are discovered by the customs inspector to have been sold at dumping prices, the recorded statistics of imports represent, therefore, the actual, f. o. b. charges made for the goods by the foreign exporters.[2]

The importer pays not only the f. o. b. invoice price, but also the freight and insurance and other charges incurred in transporting the goods to the point of destination. Nevertheless, import statistics based on f. o. b. values have the advantage that they

the period under study, but not necessarily to subsequent years. Statistics of " total imports" are, since the fiscal year 1920, no longer published, and statistics of goods exported from warehouses are collected and published separately as "transit trade." The Customs Department has informed the writer that the difference between "total imports" and "imports entered for consumption" was due almost wholly to imports of wheat in bond from the United States, for reëxport overseas, when it appeared in the statistics of exports of foreign produce. Such wheat would now appear only in the statistics of transit trade.

[1] Cf. United States Department of Commerce, *Misc. Series*, No. 59, "Methods of Computing Values in Foreign Trade Statistics."

[2] For a qualification of some importance with regard to trade discounts, see *infra*, p. 71.

are accurate as far as they go. Those countries which base their import statistics on values at the port of entry usually obtain these values either by adding an arbitrary percentage, kept uniform throughout long periods, to the invoice values, or by valuing the goods more or less arbitrarily and independently of the invoice value, on the basis of their supposed values at the port of entry. Even with the inadequate data available as to freights, a careful estimate of the amount of the import freights added to the invoice values should give more acceptable results than the arbitrary usage of customs officials.[1]

The values used in compiling the export statistics are: for goods "the produce of Canada," their value at the time of exportation at the "port"[2] whence shipped; for exports of foreign produce, the "actual value" of such goods, which means in practice the value declared by the exporter, and probably includes as a rule the accretion in value to the goods between arrival in Canada and reshipment from Canada abroad.

Accuracy of the Statistics. — For the items which they cover, with the exception of gold coin, the Canadian statistics of exports and imports are probably as close to accuracy as is reasonably to be expected of any comprehensive statistics. An exceptionally efficient Customs Department collects with great care the data for both the import and export statistics, and no allowance need be made, with the exception noted, for inaccuracy in the published statistics. Until June 30, 1900, the statistics of exports were regarded by the Customs Department as inaccurate for shipments overland to the United States, and an addition of five per cent was made annually to the collected statistics of exports to the United States, to cover unrecorded exports. In 1900, however, the Customs installed a new system of collection of export statistics for overland shipments, and abandoned as un-

---

[1] In the *Final Report of the Dominions Royal Commission* this question is enlighteningly discussed, with special reference to Canada, and the conclusion reached that the c.i.f. method of computing import values would result in great inaccuracy if used in Canada, because of the great range in the ad valorem proportions of the freight charges of imports overland from the U. S. (Gt. Br. Parl. Papers, Cd. 7971 [1917], p. 166).

[2] Includes inland towns, and indicates merely the point of shipment.

necessary the allowance for unrecorded items. The defects in the statistics of imports and exports of gold coin are discussed later.

Omissions and Inclusions. — A careful study of the commerce statistics of any country generally reveals some unusual omission or inclusion in the items of commodity trade for which data are collected, the result of conditions peculiar to the trade of such country or due to some tradition or practice of long standing in the department which gathers or publishes the statistics.[1]

The most important aspect of the Canadian statistics requiring attention in this connection is the inclusion, in the recorded statistics, of imports and exports of settlers' effects. As these move in or out of the country with the owner, they create no international obligations, and, in this sense of the term at least, are non-commercial in character. While the movement of settlers' effects in or out of the country is a movement of capital, it differs from the ordinary import or export of capital in that it involves no payment of interest or repayment of principal to or from Canada as the case may be. The statistics of imports and exports of settlers' effects are therefore to be deducted from the statistics of total imports and exports in the present study, whose purpose it is to ascertain the balance of Canadian indebtedness to other countries.

Ships purchased by Canadian companies for use in the foreign trade and ships of British registry and construction imported for use in the coastwise or internal trade are not subject to duty in Canada, and no statistics of imports of such ships are collected. All, or practically all, the Canadian-owned ships engaged in the foreign trade and not constructed in Canada are of British origin. It may be assumed, therefore, that all the imports of ships for which no data are collected are of British ships. The annual statements of the trade of Great Britain record exports by destination of *new* ships, but exports of old ships are not recorded. These are not unimportant. In one year, 1903, the Canadian Pacific Railway purchased for approximately $7,000,000 a fleet of

---

[1] In the British statistics, for instance, there are not included imports and exports of precious stones, exports of old ships, and exports of bunker coal.

fifteen old vessels belonging to an English company.[1] For new ships, the statistics of British exports to Canada during the period under study are added to the statistics of total imports into Canada. For old ships, correction has been made for the purchases abroad of the most important company, the data having been obtained by private correspondence.

The statistics of imports include a few items which would demand some further investigation as to their significance for this study, if their amounts were not so small as to render them unimportant, however disposed of. It may be well, however, at least to make mention of them. Prizes won in competition (import in the fiscal year 1914, $10,861) should be excluded as non-commercial, but their amount is insignificant. "Articles ex-warehoused for ships' stores" (imports entered for consumption, 1914, $1,041,782) apparently represent goods generally dutiable but not subjected to duty because taken out of customs warehouses for use in vessels engaged in the foreign trade. These goods, however, should properly be included in the statistics of exports as well as of imports, but no evidence can be found that such is the procedure. Several items consisting wholly or in part of advertising material are valued for purposes of duty and included in the import statistics. Much of this material is distributed in Canada free of charge for advertising purposes, and no offsetting payment is made. To the extent that this is the case, not only should the amount of the recorded imports be deducted from the total imports, but the amount of the duty collected should be reckoned as a payment to Canada from abroad. (The chief item of this character, consisting of advertising pamphlets, showcards, circulars, etc., amounted in the fiscal year 1914 to $830,841; duty thereon, $399,320.) Allowance for the goods ex-warehoused for use as ships' stores will be made when freight charges are considered.[2] The remaining items are disregarded as unimportant. All the items here enumerated were in much greater amount in the fiscal year 1914 than in most preceding years.

[1] *Canadian Annual Review*, 1911, Appendix, p. 68. [2] P. 72, *infra*.

Fiscal Years vs. *Calendar Years.* — The Canadian commerce statistics are collected and issued primarily for a fiscal year differing from the calendar year. This makes the commerce data inconvenient for purposes of comparison with other statistical data collected for calendar years. Moreover, during the period under investigation there was a change in fiscal years: the fiscal year ended on June 30 until 1906, and on March 31 after 1907, with an intercalary period of 9 months from July, 1906 to March, 1907. The series of fiscal years from 1901 to 1914 inclusive therefore covers only 13 years and 9 months, instead of 14 years.

TABLE II

UNRECORDED IMPORTS AND EXPORTS OF GOLD COIN, 1900 TO 1913

In thousands of dollars

Year	I	II	III	IV	V	VI
	Gold coin held by Canadian banks			Gold held by receiver-general[3]	Total gold coin in Canada	
	Total[1]	Outside Canada[2]	In Canada (I — II)		Amount (III + IV)	Increase over preceding year[3]
1899	9,584	2,797	6,787	12,444	19,231	....
1900	11,773	3,475	8,298	14,931	23,229	3,998
1901	11,571	5,330	6,241	16,224	22,465	764
1902	12,892	6,324	6,568	21,266	27,834	5,369
1903	16,101	5,861	10,240	28,679	38,919	11,085
1904	17,617	6,598	11,019	35,742	46,761	7,842
1905	19,649	7,491	12,158	34,289	46,447	314
1906	23,752	10,912	12,840	38,685	51,525	5,078
1907	25,119	9,079	16,040	39,685	55,725	4,200
1908	27,099	11,374	15,725	61,674	77,399	21,674
1909	27,456	12,765	14,691	69,525	84,216	6,817
1910	33,411	11,998	21,413	74,566	95,979	11,763
1911	37,464	13,703	23,761	100,408	124,169	28,190
1912	33,780	14,798	18,982	103,854	122,836	1,333
1913	46,620	19,478	27,142	115,153	142,295	19,459
Total....	....	....	....	....	....	123,064

[1] *Canada Gazette*, data as of December 31. $1,197,000 in Central Gold Reserves included in 1913 figures.

[2] Not separately reported until 1913. For previous years, estimated to be 17 per cent of deposits outside of Canada, which was the average for the period July, 1913 to January, 1914, when these holdings were separately reported. Deposits outside Canada, from *Canada Gazette*, as of December 31.

[3] *Canada Gazette*, as of December 31.

To avoid these difficulties statistics of commerce for calendar years were sought. The Customs Department issues calendar year statistics of "imports entered for consumption" and of total exports, but neither monthly nor calendar year statistics are collected for "total imports" or for trade by countries. The difference in amount between "total imports" and "imports for consumption" for the period under study never exceeds $25,000,-000 in any one year, and can be computed for fiscal years from the fiscal year statistics of total imports and of imports for consumption. The method followed in this study has been to use

TABLE II

UNRECORDED IMPORTS AND EXPORTS OF GOLD COIN, 1900 TO 1913

In thousands of dollars

Year	VII Recorded imports of gold coin [4]	VIII Gold coin minted in Canada [5]	IX Total recorded accretions of gold coin (VII + VIII)	X Recorded exports of gold coin [4]	XI Recorded net accretions or losses of gold coin [6] (IX − X)	XII Unrecorded imports or exports of gold coin [7] (VI − XI)
1900	4,524	....	4,524	3,697	827	3,171
1901	4,882	....	4,882	2,367	2,515	3,279
1902	5,968	...:	5,968	290	5,678	*309*
1903	6,741	....	6,741	310	6,431	4,654
1904	10,369	....	10,369	2,330	8,039	*197*
1905	7,128	....	7,128	1,366	5,762	6,076
1906	7,860	....	7,860	15,360	7,500	12,578
1907	4,606	...:	4,606	18,718	*14,112*	18,312
1908	8,943	3	8,946	4,140	4,806	16,868
1909	4,467	79	4,546	1,420	3,126	3,691
1910	7,260	136	7,396	1,984	5,412	6,351
1911	20,438	1,248	21,686	5,733	15,953	12,237
1912	7,496	1,478	8,974	13,805	*4,831*	3,498
1913	12,495	1,909	14,404	12,561	1,843	17,616
Total	113,177	4,853	118,030	84,081	33,949	89,115

[4] 1904–1913, calendar year statistics, compiled from Dept. of Customs *Unrevised Monthly Statements of Imports and Exports*; 1900–1903, fiscal year statistics from Dept. of Trade and Commerce, *Annual Reports*, adjusted to calendar years partly on basis of hypothesis of equal monthly distribution, partly on basis of incomplete monthly reports.

[5] Canada: *Public Accounts*, 1913, p. xiv, for 1908–1912. By correspondence from Dept. of Mines for 1913. None minted before 1908.

[6] Decreases in italics.   [7] Net export in italics.

calendar year statistics wherever available, supplementing them whenever necessary with the fiscal statistics adjusted to a calendar year basis, generally on the assumption of equal monthly distribution throughout the fiscal year. In most cases more detailed monthly statistics were available at the beginning and the end of the period under study, which made it possible to obtain accurate totals for the period as a whole, even though there was some error in the distribution among the individual years.

Imports and Exports of Gold Coin. — The Canadian statistics

TABLE III

THE COMMODITY BALANCE OF TRADE, 1900 TO 1913

In thousands of dollars

Year	Debits					
	I Imports for consumption [1]	II Imports for reexport [2]	III Unrecorded imports of gold coin [3]	IV Unrecorded imports of British ships [4]	V Settlers' effects to be deducted [5]	VI Total imports (I + II + III + IV −V)
1900	180,665	8,998	3,171	....	3,558	189,276
1901	187,477	9,329	....	....	4,160	192,646
1902	209,169	8,452	....	720	5,511	212,830
1903	252,421	7,586	4,654	7,221	6,600	265,282
1904	256,639	6,328	....	781	6,921	256,827
1905	270,386	4,417	....	2,603	8,169	269,237
1906	320,477	3,650	12,578	1,332	8,477	329,560
1907	372,825	10,112	18,312	1,225	9,935	392,539
1908	292,289	11,753	16,868	128	8,463	312,575
1909	351,962	14,902	3,691	941	9,634	361,862
1910	443,805	11,727	6,351	1,610	13,122	450,371
1911	524,851	11,453	12,237	503	14,876	534,168
1912	645,547	15,346	3,498	2,576	15,735	651,232
1913	673,241	17,016	17,617	2,264	15,932	694,205
Total....	4,981,754	141,069	98,976	21,904	131,093	5,112,610

[1] Dept. of Customs, *Unrevised Monthly Statements of Imports and Exports.* December issues give revised returns for calendar years ending in December of previous year.

[2] Dept. of Customs, *Annual Trade and Navigation Returns.* Obtained for fiscal years by subtraction of imports for consumption from total imports. Adjusted to calendar year basis on hypothesis of equal monthly distribution in each fiscal year.   [3] From Table II.

[4] United Kingdom: *Annual Statements of Foreign and Colonial Trade,* exports to Canada of new ships, British produce. Converted from sterling to dollars at £1 = $4.87. To these figures were added

of imports and exports of gold coin are admittedly imperfect,[1] and it is easy to demonstrate their shortcomings. Gold coin is used in Canada only as banking and currency reserves, and there is no, or practically no, gold in circulation as money. The total recorded excess of imports of gold coin over exports from January 1, 1900, to December 31, 1913, amounted to only $29,096,000. During the same period the gold reserves of the government and the banks increased by $123,064,000, of which only $4,853,000

[1] Cf. *Cost of Living Report*, vol. ii, pp. 848, 849.

TABLE III

THE COMMODITY BALANCE OF TRADE, 1900 TO 1913

In thousands of dollars

Year	Credits				Balances	
	VII "Total exports"[1]	VIII Unrecorded exports of gold coin[3]	IX Settlers' effects to be deducted[5]	X Total exports (VII + VIII − IX)	XI Debit (VI − X)	XII Credit (X − VI)
1900	186,129	....	1,189	184,940	4,336	....
1901	203,292	3,279	1,402	205,169	....	12,523
1902	217,083	309	1,492	215,900	....	3,070
1903	228,153	....	1,354	226,799	38,483	....
1904	199,241	197	1,379	198,059	58,768	....
1905	224,624	6,076	1,602	229,098	40,139	....
1906	269,478	....	1,741	267,737	61,823	....
1907	273,325	....	1,999	271,326	121,213	....
1908	270,005	....	1,948	268,057	44,518	....
1909	290,962	....	2,293	288,669	73,193	....
1910	298,850	....	2,202	296,648	153,723	....
1911	303,763	....	2,152	301,611	232,557	....
1912	378,094	....	2,370	375,724	275,508	....
1913	474,414	....	3,013	471,401	222,804	....
Total....	3,817,413	9,861	26,136	3,801,138	1,327,065	15,593

the difference between (1) the purchases of British ships, new and old, by a Canadian company which supplied the information to the writer, and (2) the British exports of new ships to Canada, in every year for which the former were in excess of the latter.

[5] Dept. of Customs, *Annual Trade and Navigation Returns*, for fiscal years. Adjusted to calendar year basis on hypothesis of equal monthly distribution in each fiscal year. Monthly returns of Dept. of Customs also used in obtaining figures for imports for calendar years 1900 and 1913.

was minted in Canada. The remainder, $118,211,000, must therefore have been obtained by importation from abroad. The excess of this amount over the recorded net import of gold — $89,115,000 — should measure, therefore, the unrecorded gold imports.

There are, however, two possible sources of error in this calculation. (1) It has been stated above that there is no gold in circulation in Canada. This is essentially true, but some of the gold coin minted in Canada passed into the hands of private persons in Canada and elsewhere as parts of coin collections, and did not enter into the monetary gold reserves of Canada. The amount of gold coin remaining in Canada out of monetary use should be added to the amount of unrecorded imports of gold, since the calculation made above assumed that all gold coin minted in Canada was added to the monetary gold stocks. Available data indicate that less than $2,000,000 of Canadian gold coin remained outside of Canadian gold reserves. (2) "Specie held by the banks," assumed in the above calculation to consist wholly of gold coin, includes all coin held by the banks, including subsidiary silver and bronze coins. The banks do not report the proportions in which this specie consists of gold and other coins. It is known that the bulk of the specie held by the banks consists of gold, and in May, 1913, the Canadian Minister of Finance stated in the House of Commons that it was "probable" that of the $39,000,000 specie reported as held by the banks, only two to three millions were in Canadian silver currency.[1] This appears to be a reasonable estimate. The total issue of Canadian silver and bronze coin from 1858 to 1914 amounted only to approximately $20,000,000,[2] of which some must have disappeared, and the bulk of the remainder must have been in general circulation. It will be assumed that the amount of increase in specie holdings by the banks from 1900 to 1913 which is to be accounted for by increased holdings of subsidiary coin is offset by the amount of Canadian gold coin which did not enter into the reserves.

[1] *Toronto Monetary Times*, May 24, 1913.
[2] Canada: *Public Accounts*, 1914, p. xviii.

The Commodity Balance of Trade. — Tables II and III present the estimates reached for unrecorded imports of gold coin and for the commodity balance of trade, respectively.

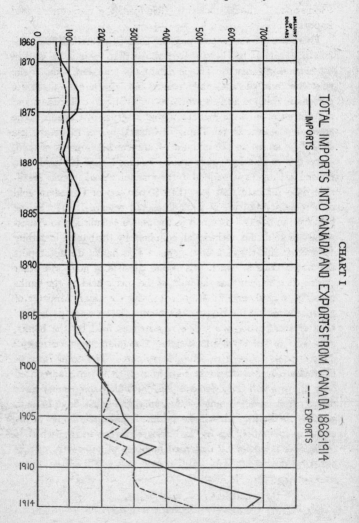

DATA OF CHART I

Total Imports into Canada and Total Exports from Canada, 1868–1914 [1]

In millions of dollars

Fiscal Year	Total Imports	Total Exports	Fiscal Year	Total Imports	Total Exports
1868	73	58	1891	120	98
1869	70	60	1892	127	114
1870	75	74	1893	129	119
1871	96	74	1894	123	118
1872	111	83	1895	111	114
1873	128	90	1896	118	121
1874	128	89	1897	119	138
1875	123	78	1898	140	164
1876	93	81	1899	163	159
1877	99	76	1900	190	192
1878	93	79	1901	190	196
1879	82	71	1902	212	212
1880	86	88	1903	241	226
1881	105	98	1904	259	214
1882	119	102	1905	267	203
1883	132	98	1906	294	257
1884	116	91	1907 [2]	260	205
1885	109	89	1908	371	280
1886	104	85	1909	310	262
1887	113	90	1910	392	301
1888	111	90	1911	472	297
1889	115	89	1912	559	315
1890	122	97	1913	692	393
			1914	651	479

[1] *Canada Year Book*, 1913, pp. 227, 228.   [2] Nine months only.

The results tabulated above show that, in so far as the commodity balance of trade was concerned, there was approximate equilibrium between debit and credit obligations from 1900 to 1903, and that only with the year 1904 did there appear a marked debit balance against Canada. The debit balance persisted throughout the remainder of the period under study, and showed an almost constant tendency to increase from year to year.

Comparison with Earlier Period. — A study of only the commodity items in the international transactions of Canada provides an inadequate basis for definite conclusions, but it is of interest to compare the situation from 1900 to 1913 with the situation existing during the three preceding decades. Chart I presents the imports and exports as given in the official returns, for the fiscal years from 1868, the first fiscal year of Confederation, to 1914, the last fiscal year before the outbreak of the Great War. The data presented in this chart, it should be noted, are the statistics as they appear in the official returns, without correction for unwarranted omissions or inclusions.

With the exception of the single year 1880, there was throughout the period from 1868 to 1894 an excess of imports over exports, substantial and, if averages for five-year periods are taken, fairly constant in amount. As there is no reason to suppose that the excess of imports during this period is to be explained by a balance of indebtedness in favor of Canada arising out of the transactions in international commerce which escape measurement at the frontier, the so-called invisible items, the chart indicates that the period from 1868 to 1894 was marked by a steady flow of foreign capital into Canada, and this is borne out by what is generally known of the economic history of the period. The greatest excess of imports over exports occurred during the years 1871 to 1875. These were years of industrial growth and of extensive undertakings in capital investment in Canada. In these years the building of the Intercolonial Railway was in active progress, the Canadian Pacific Railway was begun, and there was considerable expansion in manufacturing and in large-scale lumbering operations. Most of the capital necessary for these enterprises was borrowed from abroad, especially Great Britain. During these five years the excess of imports over exports totaled $171,000,000.[1]

The period from 1876 to 1890 was marked by a less spectacular but steady growth of business enterprise in Canada, and the excess of imports over exports shown in the chart for these years is probably roughly representative of the inward flow of capital.

The years from 1892 to 1895 were years of acute financial and industrial depression in Canada, brought on mainly by the collapse of a real-estate boom, a succession of crop failures, and a decline in business activity in sympathy with the disturbed

[1] For an outline of the economic history of Canada during this period, see R. M. Breckinridge, *The History of the Canadian Banking System*, pp. 264-272.

economic conditions then prevalent in the United States. The annual excess of imports over exports declined steadily from 1889 on, and in 1895, for the first time, with one exception, since Confederation, the trade statistics showed an excess of exports over imports, an indication that a check had occurred to the inward flow of capital from abroad.

The years from 1896 to 1901 were years of slow but gradual recovery from the antecedent period of depression, and the excess of exports over imports during this period indicates that the flow of new capital into Canada from abroad was overbalanced by the liquidation of old indebtedness to other countries and by interest payments on old investments.

The period after 1901 was marked once more by industrial expansion, speculation, and a great increase in public works and improvements, railroad building, and other investment enterprises, a movement which continued in ever-growing volume, except for a temporary set-back resulting from the disturbance in the world's money markets in 1907, until shortly before the outbreak of the World War. A comparison of the movement of the balance of indebtedness with the conditions governing capital investment in Canada during this later period is postponed until the figures for the commodity balance of trade are supplemented by an analysis of the other items in the international balance of indebtedness. It is to be noted, however, that, while the excess of imports over exports during the decade preceding the war had its counterpart in the earlier period from 1870 to 1894, the excess of imports during the later period marked a reversal of conditions from the excess of exports in the eight years immediately preceding. Moreover, in the period after 1903, as compared with the period from 1870 to 1894, the excess of imports was much greater in amount and was an excess over a much greater volume of exports.

CHAPTER III

NON–COMMERCIAL ITEMS IN THE INTERNATIONAL BALANCE OF INDEBTEDNESS

INTRODUCTORY

UNDER the heading of non-commercial items are grouped those transactions which consist, in their international aspect, of the movement of goods into or out of Canada, which does not involve an offsetting movement in the opposite direction because no payments have to be made for such shipments. Remittances by aliens in Canada to their relatives in the home country and by Canadians abroad to their relatives at home, and settlers' effects and monetary capital brought in by immigrants and taken out by emigrants, are the important transactions in this class.

Non-commercial remittances by aliens in Canada to friends abroad are made immediately by sending money orders or other financial documents. Funds must be provided in the foreign country for the cashing of these documents, and the two main methods whereby this is accomplished are the export of goods for sale in that country or a reduction in the amount of the goods which would otherwise have been imported from that country. Non-commercial transactions involving payments by Canadians to persons abroad affect the commodity balance of trade, therefore, in either or both of two ways: they increase the exports, or they decrease the imports. In either case they tend to bring about an excess of exports over imports. Per contra, non-commercial transactions involving payments to Canada from abroad increase the imports or decrease the exports, and in either case tend to bring about an excess of imports over exports.

Settlers' effects, that is, the personal property other than money of migrants and moving with them, differ in some important respects from the other non-commercial items. They are separately and immediately recorded in the official statistics of exports and imports as settlers' effects; because money is not used in any stage of the transaction, they do not require the use of financial documents to mediate their transfer from one country to another; and they invariably represent *additions* to the recorded imports and exports. They have already been considered in connection with the discussion of the commodity balance of trade, and the existence of official statistics, not necessarily of their true volume but of the extent to which they have been permitted to affect the recorded statistics of imports and exports, made it a simple matter to account for them.[1] Imports of advertising material not sold for a price resemble settlers' effects in these respects, but are too small in amount to demand special consideration.[2]

There is, unfortunately, but little statistical information bearing directly on the other items here to be considered, and resort must be had in these cases to estimates of a very rough sort. But for the main purpose of this study the variations in the balance of indebtedness from year to year are of much greater importance than the absolute amount of balance for any year or series of years. The method mainly followed here, in reaching estimates for "invisible" items in the balance, consists of the resort to official annual statistics for data as closely related as possible to the actual transactions whose value measurement is sought, and the building up from these data of estimates of the volume of such transactions for the corresponding years. This procedure perhaps has little advantage over the method usually followed in like circumstances, of estimating the volume of transactions in round numbers for the entire period, in so far as reaching totals for the period are concerned. It has the distinct advantage for the purpose of this study, however, that it gives a reasonable degree of assurance that the trend from year to year in the volume of the transactions has been indicated with approximate accuracy. Use is made also of all available means of checking up on the estimates reached, including comparison with similar estimates made by other writers for Canada and for other countries. But the main defense against possible criticism of the statistical

---

[1] See *supra*, p. 28, and Table III.   [2] See *supra*, p. 29.

methods used must rest on the impossibility of obtaining more certain results and on modesty of claims for such results as are obtained.

IMMIGRANTS' CAPITAL

An estimate for the amount of capital brought in by immigrants, not including settlers' effects, will be reached by estimating the per capita amount of capital brought in by each class of immigrant and multiplying by the number of immigrants in such class.

Capital per Capita of Immigrants from the United States. — Immigrants into Canada from the United States bring with them considerable amounts of capital. Many of these immigrants are farmers who sell their farms in the United States and bring the proceeds of such sales, together with some of their live-stock and implements, to Canada, where they take up free homesteads or buy cheaper land than was available at home. For the calendar years 1906 to 1912, official figures of the total value of effects and cash brought in by immigrants from the United States were issued as follows:

TABLE IV

IMMIGRATION BUREAU ESTIMATES OF CAPITAL BROUGHT IN BY AMERICAN IMMIGRANTS, 1906 TO 1912 [1]

Calendar year	Number of immigrants from the United States	Effects and cash per capita value *dollars*	Total value *thousands of dollars*
1906	63,782	809	51,600
1907	56,687	885	50,168
1908	57,124	1,152	65,807
1909	90,996	811	73,798
1910	124,602	1,061	132,203
1911	131,114	1,539	201,784
1912	140,143	1,444	202,366

[1] *Canada Year Books*, 1911, p. 398, and 1912, p. 44.

The figures given above were issued by the Superintendent of Immigration, and are presumably to be regarded as estimates based upon actual data collected by Canadian immigration officials from immigrants. They include, it will be noted, both effects and cash. To the extent that the effects were recorded as imports, they have already been dealt with. But the import statistics of "settlers' effects" are collected by the Department of Customs, and not by the Immigration Department. Settlers' effects are free of duty; they are mainly old articles, not accompanied by invoices to aid the customs officials in their valuation; and their accurate valuation, owing to their non-commercial character, is of slight importance. The recorded statistics of imports of settlers' effects are, therefore, probably underestimates.[1] The value of settlers' effects which escapes official record does not concern us here, since it does not affect the recorded balance of trade. But because of the possible discrepancy between the valuations of settlers' effects by the Department of Customs and the Immigration officials, it is not permissible to take the Immigration Branch's figures given above, less the amount of settlers' effects recorded by the Department of Customs, as measuring the amount of cash brought in by immigrants from the United States.

But even if very generous allowance be made for the value of effects, the Immigration Branch's figures for cash brought in are unquestionably great overestimates. As Dr. Bonar points out, the total imports from the United States do not greatly exceed the estimates of the Immigration Branch for cash and effects brought in by immigrants from the United States.[2] The litera-

[1] Cf. James Bonar, "Canada's Balance of Trade," *Proceedings of Canadian Political Science Association*, 1913, p. 88: "This [the value of imports of settlers' effects from the United States as recorded in the official import statistics] is a modest figure. . . . Through the courtesy of the Superintendent of Immigration I learn that it is furnished by the Department of Customs, and, as a great part of settlers' effects is not subject to duty, the full value would not be shown." There is an unwarranted implication here that statistics of imports of non-dutiable goods are necessarily unreliable.

[2] *Ibid.*, p. 89, in reference to the statistics for 1911: "With every allowance for the difference between a calendar and a fiscal year, the figure seems very high. The value of all the imports from the United States in the ordinary way of trade would be about 277 millions; and we are asked to believe that the said 130,000 settlers brought wealth to nearly three-quarters of that amount, about 202 out of about 285 *minus* [the recorded imports of settlers' effects] about 8 millions. . . . In absence of the data on which this estimate is founded, we can place much less confidence in it than in the recorded value of the effects; and the authorities have done well to exclude it from the records of imports." Cf. also Professor Stephen Leacock,

ture issued by the Immigration Branch gives evidence of the
influence of a "boom" psychology, and little confidence can be
placed in statistical data presented by it which are not collected
according to routine methods prescribed by statute.

F. W. Field estimates on the basis of the kind of evidence submitted by immigration officials that the value of effects brought
in by settler immigrants from the United States is $350 per capita,
and of cash is $500.[1] Coats accepts Field's estimate and applies
it to all immigrants from the United States.[2] There is ground for
belief that even this estimate is not conservative enough. Not all
the immigrants from the United States to Canada are prosperous
farmers. Farm laborers and their families and the families of
farmers are all included in the Canadian official statistics of immigrants, according to occupation, under the heading "farmers
and farm laborers," and less than one half of the total immigration from the United States is in this class. Many of the American immigrants who take out homesteads or buy farms in Canada
are sons of American farmers, whose capital is borrowed from

"The Canadian Balance of Trade," *Journal of Canadian Bankers' Association,*
vol. xxii (April, 1915), p. 173: "The average figure of $1000 per person seems ex-
tremely high."

[1] *Capital Investments in Canada* (1913 ed.), p. 181.

[2] *Cost of Living Report,* vol. ii, p. 902. The Canadian Minister of Finance, the
Honorable W. I. White, in his Budget Speech of May 12, 1913, made the following
reference to capital brought in by immigrants from the United States: "From
compilations carefully made by the Department of the Interior [the Immigration
Branch is a division of this Department] it has been conservatively estimated that
the class of immigration we receive from the United States, that is to say of farmers
who have sold out their holdings in the States, and have taken up land in western
Canada, brings with it capital (including settlers' effects) to the amount of over
$1,000 per head or say $5,000 per family of five persons. The total number of
such immigrants for the calendar year 1912 was 140,143. Applying the rate above
mentioned per head the amount of capital and effects accompanying this immigration would reach a total exceeding $140,000,000, in value. When considering the
excess of imports from the United States over our exports to the United States this
large influx of capital to be productively employed in our agriculture must, as I
have pointed out previously, not be overlooked." It should be noted that the Department of the Interior thus stands sponsor for two markedly different estimates
of the per capita wealth brought in by immigrants from the United States, namely,
$1441, as given in Table IV, and $1000, as reported here by Mr. White. Mr. White,
like Mr. Coats, assumes also that all of the immigrants from the United States
are well-to-do farmers.

their fathers in the United States, and is repaid after a few successful crops. The remaining immigrants from the United States
consist almost wholly of general laborers, mechanics, miners, and
domestic servants, persons with but small capital who come to
Canada in search of employment. Estimates of $500 per capita
for farmers and farm laborers and $100 per capita for other
immigrants from the United States are probably generous enough,
and will be used here.

   Capital per Capita of Immigrants from Other Countries. — The
Canadian immigration statistics for arrivals by ocean ports cover
only those who travel steerage, and immigrants who travel on
first-class tickets are not included. The Immigration Branch publishes statistics for saloon passengers arriving at ocean ports,
which give data of total saloon passengers, returned Canadians,
and tourists. Statistics of saloon immigrants can be obtained by
subtracting the figures for the two last-named classes from the
total figures. Coats[1] estimates that Continental European immigrants bring on the average $25 each, and, following F. W.
Field, that British immigrants bring on the average $100 each.
He bases the higher estimate for British immigrants on the ground
that many of the British immigrants are agricultural, and bring
sufficient capital to settle in the west. Paish[2] estimated at $50
the average sum brought into the United States by immigrants.
As in the United States a much greater percentage of the immigration comes from eastern and south-eastern Europe, a class
of immigrants who bring little money, his estimate may be regarded as in reasonable agreement with the ones here made for
Canada. The estimate of $25 per capita for steerage immigrants
from Continental Europe will be used here. For saloon immigrants, who come almost wholly from Great Britain, $500 per
capita is estimated, and for steerage immigrants from Great
Britain, $50.

   Canada levies a head tax on Chinese immigrants, other than
merchants and students, upon their entrance into Canada. The

---

[1] *Cost of Living Report*, vol. ii, p. 902.
[2] Sir George Paish, *The Trade Balance of the United States* (U. S. National
Monetary Commission), 1910, p. 182.

receipts from this tax during the period under study amounted
to $13,000,000,[1] and Coats includes this sum in his estimate of
the capital brought in by immigrants.[2] After 1904 the tax
amounted to $500 per capita. As Chinese immigrants of the class
subject to the tax are not financially in a position to meet so
severe a demand, there can be no doubt that the tax is paid for
immigrants wholly or almost wholly by Chinese already in
Canada. The proceeds from this tax are therefore not included in
the present calculation of the amount brought in by immigrants.

Capital brought into Canada by Immigrants. — Table V, on
pages 46 and 47, presents the estimated amounts of capital
brought into Canada by immigrants.

Capital taken out of Canada by Emigrants

No statistics of emigration are published by Canada. As some
knowledge of the amount of emigration is necessary for an estimate of the amount of capital taken out by emigrants, resort
must be had to rough estimates based on the statistics of immigration from Canada published by other countries, on census
statistics, and on other relevant data.

*Emigration from Canada to the United States, of Natives of the
United States.* — From June 1, 1901, to June 1, 1911, there was,
according to the Canadian census returns, an increase amounting to 175,781 in the number of persons in Canada who were
born in the United States.[3] The Canadian immigration statistics
are collected on the basis of the countries from which immigrants
come, and not on the basis of nativity. For the period from June
30, 1909, to June 30, 1914, there are available, however, statistics
for the number of immigrants into Canada from the United States
who were citizens of the United States. Included among citizens
of the United States would be naturalized aliens, including persons of Canadian birth, but the last-named are not included as
immigrants in the Canadian returns. The census reports of the
United States give the foreign-born population of the United

[1] *Canada Year Book*, 1913, p. 111.
[2] *Cost of Living Report*, vol. ii, p. 903.
[3] *Canada Year Book*, 1913, p. 73: 127,899 in 1901, 303,680 in 1911.

States as 13.6 per cent of the total population in 1900, and 14.7 per cent of the total population in 1910.[1] Allowance being made for returned Canadians who had been naturalized in the United States and for the smaller proportion of foreign-born to total citizens than of foreign-born to total population,—due to the fact that practically all natives, but only a fraction of the foreign-born, are citizens,— it is estimated that 10 per cent of the immigration into Canada of citizens of the United States other than returning Canadians consisted of United States naturalized aliens.

Of the total number of immigrants into Canada from the United States during the period from July 1, 1909, to June 30, 1914, amounting to 510,799, 78.2 per cent, or 399,533, were citizens of

[1] *U. S. Statistical Abstract*, 1914, p. 45.

TABLE V

CAPITAL BROUGHT INTO CANADA BY IMMIGRANTS, 1900 TO 1913

| Year | From the United States | | | | Saloon immigrants | |
| | Farmers and farm laborers | | Others | | | |
	Number[1]	Capital ($500 each) *thousands of dollars*	Number[1]	Capital ($100 each) *thousands of dollars*	Number[2]	Capital ($500 each) *thousands of dollars*
1900	8,176	4,088	12,257	1,226	2,537	1,268
1901	9,705	4,852	12,482	1,248	3,338	1,669
1902	22,455	11,227	15,475	1,547	3,660	1,830
1903	24,105	12,052	23,216	2,322	4,397	2,198
1904	20,175	10,087	24,181	2,418	4,414	2,207
1905	32,735	16,367	17,933	1,793	4,882	2,441
1906	40,802	20,401	11,199	1,120	5,977	2,988
1907	42,385	21,192	12,976	1,298	7,436	3,718
1908	42,976	21,488	16,501	1,650	5,164	2,582
1909	58,085	29,042	34,720	3,472	4,174	2,087
1910	63,544	31,772	53,494	5,349	3,311	1,655
1911	60,588	30,294	70,477	7,048	3,715	1,857
1912	48,724	24,362	89,099	8,910	3,526	1,763
1913	42,855	21,427	82,438	8,244	3,614	1,807
Total....		258,651		47,645		30,070

[1] *Immigration Facts and Figures*, 1911 and 1920 editions. Adjusted to calendar year basis from fiscal year statistics on hypothesis of equal monthly distribution.

[2] *Immigration Facts and Figures*, 1911, and *Annual Reports* of Immigration Branch, Department of

the United States.[1] Deduction of 10 per cent from this amount leaves 70.4 per cent. This will be used as an estimate of the percentage of the total immigration from the United States into Canada for the period under study which consisted of native-born Americans. From June 1, 1901 to June 1, 1911, the total

[1] Data obtained from Canadian official sources by United States Commissioner of Immigration for Canada, given in *Annual Reports* of United States Commissioner of Immigration, 1911, p. 158; 1913, p. 170; and 1914, p. 212. W. W. Husband, Secretary of the United States Immigration Commission, stated that about two thirds of the emigrants to Canada from the United States were American citizens, the remainder being almost entirely Canadian citizens and aliens of European birth who had resided for a time in the United States (*American Economic Review*, Supplement, March, 1912, p. 79). The apparent discrepancy is explained by the fact that returned Canadians are not classed as immigrants in the Canadian returns.

TABLE V

CAPITAL BROUGHT INTO CANADA BY IMMIGRANTS, 1900 TO 1913

| Year | Steerage Immigrants | | | | Total capital brought by immigrants; *thousands of dollars* |
| | From Great Britain | | From Other Countries | | |
	Number [1]	Capital ($50 each) *thousands of dollars*	Number [1]	Capital ($25 each) *thousands of dollars*	
1900	11,046	552	19,887	497	7,631
1901	14,534	727	21,542	538	9,034
1902	29,525	1,476	30,415	760	16,840
1903	46,083	2,304	35,942	898	19,774
1904	57,866	2,893	36,075	902	18,507
1905	76,077	3,804	40,918	1,023	25,428
1906	80,592	4,030	45,048	1,126	29,665
1907	108,732	5,437	74.388	1,860	33,505
1908	69,720	3,486	46,626	1,166	30,372
1909	58,066	2,903	42,447	1,061	38,565
1910	107,206	5,360	61,266	1,532	45,668
1911	134,343	6,717	78,458	1,961	47,877
1912	147,435	7,372	105,261	2,631	45,038
1913	171,310	8,565	154,494	3,862	43,905
Total.....		53,626		19,817	411,809

the Interior: Total Saloon Passengers minus Returned Canadians minus Tourists. Figures for 1909 and 1910 estimated from incomplete data. Adjusted to calendar year basis from fiscal year statistics on hypothesis of equal monthly distribution.

immigration from the United States into Canada amounted to 633,190. Of this total, 445,765, or 70.4 per cent, is estimated as the immigration of native-born Americans. Subtraction from this amount of the amount of the increase in the same period in the number of natives of the United States in Canada, 175,781, leaves 269,984 as the number of natives of the United States who during this period returned to the United States or died in Canada.

No vital statistics are published for Canada as a whole, and the statistics published by the provinces are not free from criticism. By taking the death-rates of 1911 for eight provinces [1] and weighting them in proportion to their population in the same year, 13.9 per thousand is obtained as an estimated death-rate for Canada.[2] In calculating the number of deaths of Americans in Canada during the period, allowance is made for the following factors: the probability that the death-rate is higher for persons in Canada born in other countries than for natives of Canada; [3] for those who migrated to Canada during the period under consideration, the length of time which elapsed between their admission into Canada and the final date of the period, June 1, 1911; departures from Canada of natives of the United States between June 1, 1901 and June 1, 1911.

It is estimated on the basis of the available data covering these factors that the deaths in Canada amounted to 16 per thousand for 10 years for the natives of the United States already in Canada on June 1, 1901, before allowance for departures, and 13.9 per thousand, the Canadian rate, after allowance is made for those who returned to the United States.[4] For natives of the United

[1] New Brunswick is excluded, because of inadequate statistics. The recorded death-rate of Saskatchewan in 1911 was only 5.54 per thousand as compared with death-rates in the same year in the neighboring provinces of 12.03 for Manitoba and 9.69 for Alberta. The mean between these two rates, 10.86, is taken as the death-rate for Saskatchewan instead of the recorded death-rate.

[2] The calculation is made from data given in *Canada Year Book*, 1913, pp. 51, 100, 101.

[3] The death-rate advances, of course, with the average age, once the infancy period is passed. Adults preponderate among immigrants; moreover, the children of natives of the United States born in Canada would be classed as natives of Canada.

[4] The bulk of the departures probably consist of recent arrivals who do not

States who entered Canada between 1901 and 1911 it is estimated, after allowance for those who returned to the United States, that the average stay in Canada up to June 1, 1911, was 2½ years.[1] It is assumed that the Canadian death-rate applies to the last-named group. This gives an estimate of 33,470 for the total deaths in Canada of natives of the United States between June 1, 1901, and June 1, 1911.[2] Subtraction of the number of deaths from 269,984, the number of natives of the United States who either left Canada or died in Canada, leaves 236,514 as the emigration from Canada of natives of the United States between June 1, 1901, and June 1, 1911.

From the period beginning with July 1, 1909, there are available official United States statistics of United States citizens returned to the United States from Canada after having settled in Canada.[3]

These are as follows:

Year ending June 30	Number
1910	22,832
1911	31,432
1912	38,317
1913	54,497
1914	44,013

If, as was probable, the departures from Canada of natives of the United States were preponderantly in the later years of the period 1901 to 1911, these statistics, including, as they do, naturalized aliens, are lower for 1910 than those indicated by the estimates made here.[4] Some natives of the United States, however, may leave Canada for countries other than the United States. Moreover, 1910 was the first year in which such statistics were collected, and it takes some time before the organization

find conditions to their liking, and not of those who have been resident in Canada for a long period.

[1] The Canadian statistics of immigration would show an average stay up to June, 1911, of approximately 3 years if none died or returned to the United States before June 1, 1911.

[2] $(127,899 \times 0.0139 \times 10) + (451,564 \times 0.0139 \times 2\frac{1}{2}) = 33,470.$

[3] Reports of U. S. Commissioner of Immigration for Canada in United States. Commissioner of Immigration, *Annual Reports*, 1910, 1912, 1914.

[4] See Table VIII, p. 57, *infra*.

for the collection of a new set of statistics can be developed to function efficiently, especially where, among the difficulties to overcome, are a 3000 mile border and the reluctance of United States citizens to submit to cross-examination where it can be avoided without adverse effects.[1] The figures given for the years subsequent to 1910 in general are confirmatory of the present estimate.

Emigration of Persons of British Nativity. To Great Britain. — Great Britain published statistics for the period under study giving the numbers of persons of British, including colonial, nationality who entered the United Kingdom from Canada and who departed from the United Kingdom for Canada. The aggregate arrivals and departures of British tourists visiting Canada and of Canadian tourists visiting Great Britain should approximately balance each other in a series of years, and the recorded immigration into Canada from Great Britain minus the excess of British departures for Canada over the arrivals in Great Britain from Canada should closely represent the emigration from Canada to Great Britain. Since April 1, 1912, Great Britain has collected immigration statistics, and for the period of this study covered by these statistics a check of the present calculation is possible.

The total immigration into Canada from the United Kingdom from January 1, 1900, to December 31, 1913, of persons traveling steerage was 1,113,188. In the four years for which statistics of arrivals of saloon passengers by country of origin are available, passengers from Great Britain averaged 80 per cent of the total. Assuming that this percentage held true throughout the period

---

[1] Cf. U. S. Commissioner of Immigration for Canada, quoted in *Report* of U. S. Commissioner-General of Immigration, 1910, p. 140: "The year also witnessed considerable growth in the number of U. S. citizens who were returning to their former homes after previous residence in Canada, reports already submitted to the Bureau showing the total number to be, 22,832. It is my judgment, however, that said number does not show even approximately the actual number of citizens returning to the U. S. from Canada. As such passengers are immune from the operations of our immigration laws and regulations, they are especially resentful of any attempt at examination on the part of our officers, and the number of returning citizens reported represents only those who have manifested willingness to answer such questions as would establish the place of immediate previous residence."

for the proportion of saloon immigrants who came from Great Britain, the total saloon immigration from Great Britain for the period amounted to 48,167. This makes the total immigration from Great Britain for the period 1,161,310. The total excess of departures for Canada from Great Britain of persons of British nationality, over similar arrivals in Great Britain from Canada, amounted for the period to 1,003,591. Subtraction of this amount from the total given above for immigration into Canada from Great Britain leaves 157,719 as the total emigration from Canada to Great Britain during the years from 1900 to 1913. This total is distributed among the different years on the assumption that the emigrants from Canada were in each year the same percentage of the total arrivals in Great Britain from Canada, giving the results presented in the table which follows below:

TABLE VI

EMIGRATION FROM CANADA TO GREAT BRITAIN, 1900 TO 1913

Year	Arrivals in the United Kingdom from Canada of persons of British nationality [1]	Emigrants from Canada to the United Kingdom [2]
1900	10,640	3,937
1901	8,636	3,196
1902	11,563	4,279
1903	13,786	5,101
1904	18,397	6,807
1905	19,934	7,376
1906	23,596	8,731
1907	33,691	12,467
1908	39,866	14,752
1909	33,509	12,400
1910	41,309	15,286
1911	50,095	18,537
1912	52,586	19,458
1913	68,622	25,392
Total		157,719

[1] *Statistical Abstracts for the United Kingdom.*

[2] The figures in this column are 37 per cent of the figures for corresponding years in the preceding column, which is the percentage of emigrants from Canada of the total arrivals in the United Kingdom from Canada for the entire period.

The present calculation shows an emigration from Canada to Great Britain in the two years 1912 and 1913 amounting to 44,850. The British statistics for immigration, collected since April, 1912, show a total immigration into Great Britain from Canada, including persons not of British nationality, of 42,831 from April 1, 1912, to December 31, 1913, the months of January to March, 1912, thus not being included.[1] Migration of aliens between Great Britain and Canada, except en route to or from a third country, is negligible in amount; from April 1 to December 31, 1912, of a total recorded immigration into the United Kingdom from Canada of 11,941, only 52 were aliens. The months of January to March of each year are months of little travel; in the fiscal year ended March 31, 1914, of the total immigration from Canada into the United Kingdom amounting to 27,969, only 3,998 arrived in these months. The results obtained by the present calculation coincide almost exactly, therefore, for the only part of the period for which a check is possible, with the British statistics.

To Other Countries. — The estimate made above, of the emigration to Great Britain from Canada of persons of British nationality, including Canadians, leaves unaccounted for the substantial movement from Canada to the United States of persons who originally came from Great Britain to Canada. The Canadian census returns showed an increase amounting to 394,507 from June, 1901, to June 1, 1911, in the population in Canada born in the British Isles.[2] During the same period the total immigration into Canada from Great Britain, including saloon immigrants, amounted to 765,343. Subtraction, from this total, of 394,507, the amount of increase in Canadian population of British birth from 1901 to 1911, leaves 370,836 as the number of persons born in the British Isles who left Canada or died in Canada between 1901 and 1911. To account for the deaths in Canada, the death-rate estimated for Canada as a whole is applied for 10 years to the number of persons of British birth

---

[1] These statistics and the other data in the remainder of this paragraph are from Great Britain: *House of Commons Returns, Annual Statements of Emigration and Immigration,* 1912–1914.

[2] *Canada Year Book,* 1913, p. 73: 390,019 in 1901; 784,526 in 1911.

already in Canada in 1901, and for three years to the total immigration from Great Britain from 1901 to 1911.[1] This gives 86,541 as the number of deaths in Canada,[2] leaving 294,208 as the number who departed from Canada.[3]

From 1901 to 1911 it was estimated that approximately 75,000 persons born in the British Isles returned from Canada to the British Isles.[4] This leaves 219,000 as the approximate estimate for persons of British nativity who left Canada for countries other than their mother country.

Emigration of Canadians to the United States. — The United States census returns showed an increase in the population of Canadian birth in the United States between 1900 and 1910 amounting to 23,382.[5] The annual average death-rate per thousand for the period 1901–1910 for the registration districts of the United States was approximately 15.[6] Application of this rate for ten years to the population of Canadian birth in the United States in 1900 gives 177,188 as the total number of deaths for the period. Adding this to the increase in population of Canadian birth gives 210,570 as the total net [7] emigration of Canadians to the United States from 1900 to 1910. The following statistics are available from American official sources bearing on the immigration into the United States from Canada:

---

[1] The statistics of immigration indicate that the average stay in Canada before June 1, 1911, was four years without allowance for departures from Canada or deaths in Canada before 1911. It is estimated that the average stay was three years after allowance for these factors.

[2] $(390,019 \times 0.0139 \times 10) + (775,255 \times 0.0139 \times 3) = 86,541$.

[3] $380,748 - 86,541 = 294,208$. Since some of the immigrants into Canada credited to the United States are of British nationality, this calculation underestimates the total immigration into Canada, and consequently the emigration from Canada, of persons of British nationality. As all of the immigrants from the United States who are not natives of the United States are classed in a subsequent section as of nativity other than British or American, this underestimate should be offset by an equivalent overestimate of emigration of persons born in countries other than the United States, Great Britain, or Canada.

[4] See Table VI, p. 51, *supra*.

[5] U. S. Immigration Commission, *The Immigration Situation in Canada*, p. 36 (61 Cong. 2d Sess., *Sen. Doc.* 469), and *U.S. Statistical Abstract*, 1914, p. 49 (1,181,255 in 1900; 1,204,637, in 1910).

[6] *Ibid.*, p. 75.

[7] *I. e.*, over and above Canadians returned to Canada.

TABLE VII

IMMIGRATION INTO THE UNITED STATES FROM CANADA, 1900 TO 1913

Year ending June 30	Total[1] (admissions)	Canadian citizens, applications for admission[2]
1900	396	....
1901	540	....
1902	636	....
1903	1,058	....
1904	2,837	....
1905	2,168	....
1906	5,063	....
1907	19,918	....
1908	38,510	13,052
1909	51,941	24,118
1910	56,555	44,340
1911	56,830	44,439
1912	55,990	42,649
1913	73,802	44,701
1914	86,139	45,893
	452,383	259,192

[1] *U. S. Statistical Abstract.* Includes all arrivals of immigrants from Canada. Returned American citizens are not classed as immigrants.

[2] *Annual Reports* of the U. S. Commissioner of Immigration. Canadian citizens only. Includes about 4 per cent who were debarred from entry.

These figures do not appear confirmatory of the estimates made here. They are obviously defective, however, for the earlier years of the period at least, since it is inconceivable that, with the close relations which exist between the populations of Canada and the United States along 3,000 miles of common boundaries, less than 6,000 Canadians and alien residents of Canada should migrate to the United States during five years. For the later years these statistics and the present estimate can be reconciled.

Emigration from Canada of Natives of Countries other than the United States and Great Britain.—The census returns show an increase amounting to 311,826[1] in the population in Canada, of natives of foreign countries other than Great Britain and the United States. During the same period the total immigration of such persons into Canada, including 20 per cent of the total

[1] *Canada Year Book*, 1913, p. 73: 166,414 in 1901; 478,240 in 1911.

saloon immigrants [1] and including also 29.6 per cent of the total immigration from the United States,[2] amounted to 689,328. Subtraction, from this amount, of 311,826, the amount of increase of such persons in Canada from 1901 to 1911, leaves 377,502 such persons who left Canada or died in Canada between 1901 and 1911. Application of the Canadian death-rate, 13.9 per thousand, for ten years to the number of such persons already in Canada in 1901, and for three years to the total number of such persons immigrating into Canada during the period, gives 51,877 as the number of deaths in Canada,[3] leaving 325,625 as the total emigration of such persons from Canada during the period from 1901 to 1911.

Total Emigration from Canada. — The present calculation has accounted so far for: (1) the total emigration to the United States of natives of the United States from June 1, 1901, to June 1, 1911; (2) the total emigration to the United States of natives of Canada from 1900 to 1909 inclusive; (3) the total and annual emigration to Great Britain from 1900 to 1913 inclusive; (4) the total emigration of natives of Great Britain to other than their home country from June 1, 1901, to June 1, 1911; and (5) the total emigration of natives of countries other than Canada, Great Britain, or the United States from June 1, 1901, to June 1, 1911. There remain the tasks of estimating the emigration to countries other than Great Britain for the periods from January 1, 1900, to June 1, 1901, and from June 1, 1911, to December 31, 1913, and of distributing the totals for the period 1901 to 1911 among the individual years. There are no statistical data available to aid in building up estimates for the first period or for the distribution of the totals among the years from 1901 to 1911, and recourse must be had to arbitrary guesses. It is known that there was a heavy movement of population out of Canada following the depression of 1907 and again in the latter part of 1913, and weight will be given to this guide. For the later years of the period and especially for the period from June 1, 1911, to December 31, 1913, the United States statistics of immigration are of assistance. The

---

[1] See *supra*, p. 50.   [2] See *supra*, p. 48.

[3] $(166,414 \times 0.0139 \times 10) \times (689,328 \times 0.0139 \times 3) = 51,877$.

estimate of emigration, made on the basis of the preceding calculations and of what other information is available, is presented
in Table VIII.[1]

The estimate reached here for total emigration from Canada,
1,752,719, is higher than was expected. Coats [2] makes a rough
estimate of 1,262,994, for the total emigration from Canada for
approximately the same period. But the chief discrepancy between his estimate and the present one is in the figures of emigration to the United States, and Coats bases his estimate chiefly
on the American statistics for the earlier years of the period,
with a result in totals which are demonstrably too low.[3]

Capital taken out by Emigrants. — Coats accepts Paish's estimate of $200 as the amount taken with them by emigrants who
leave by ocean ports. On the assumption that the immigrants
from the United States into Canada are mainly agriculturists and
that those who return are therefore also mainly of the agricultural
class, he estimates that they take out with them $500 in cash.
For the remainder of the emigration to the United States, he
estimates that they take out on the average $50 each, based on
the amounts of money reported to the United States immigration
agents at the border. The first two of these estimates seem to
the writer to be too high. Over one half of the immigrants from
the United States are of the non-agricultural laborer class,[4] and it
is probable that these are much more migratory than farmers,
who can establish themselves in Canada only at considerable
expense and must make sacrifices to leave. Paish's estimate of
$200 as the average amount of money taken out per capita by
departing emigrants also appears to be too high, when due consideration is given to the fact that there is a smaller relative
movement into Canada than into the United States, of such

---

[1] See p. 57, *infra.*   [2] *Cost of Living Report*, vol. ii, pp. 897–900.

[3] *E.g.*, Coats, basing his calculation on an estimate for 1909 of the U. S. Commissioner of Immigration for Canada, takes 150,000 as the number of Americans
who returned to the U. S. from Canada from 1900 to early in 1914. The later U. S.
statistics, which are admittedly too low, give a total of 191,091 for the Americans
who returned from Canada to the United States during the five-year period from
June 30, 1909, to June 30, 1914 alone. See *supra*, p. 49.

[4] See *supra*, p. 43.

persons as the many Italians who come to stay only until their savings have reached a satisfactory amount. The bulk of the emigration from Canada is probably due to failure and unemployment in Canada, and not to the accumulation of what are, for persons of the immigrant class, modest fortunes in their home countries. In view of these considerations it is estimated that $100 per capita is a sufficiently generous estimate of the amount of money taken out of Canada by emigrants. This gives the results presented in the following table:

TABLE VIII

EMIGRATION FROM CANADA, AND CAPITAL TAKEN OUT OF CANADA BY EMIGRANTS, 1900 TO 1913

| Year | Emigration from Canada | | | | | | Capital taken out of Canada *thousands of dollars* |
| | Natives of United States | Natives of Canada | Natives of Great Britain | | Natives of other countries | Total emigration | |
			To Great Britain	To other countries			
1900	2,000	5,000	3,937	5,000	5,000	20,937	2,094
1901	3,000	5,000	3,196	5,000	5,000	21,196	2,119
1902	5,000	5,000	4,279	10,000	10,000	34,279	3,428
1903	10,000	10,000	5,101	10,000	10,000	45,101	4,510
1904	10,000	10,000	6,807	15,000	20,000	61,807	6,181
1905	20,000	15,000	7,376	20,000	20,000	82,376	8,237
1906	30,000	15,000	8,731	20,000	40,000	113,731	11,373
1907	35,000	20,000	12,467	35,000	50,000	152,467	15,247
1908	45,000	40,000	14,752	40,000	70,000	209,752	20,975
1909	40,000	50,000	12,400	35,000	50,000	187,400	18,740
1910	40,000	40,000	15,286	45,000	50,000	190,286	19,029
1911	40,000	40,000	18,537	50,000	50,000	198,537	19,854
1912	50,000	40,000	19,458	50,000	50,000	209,458	20,946
1913	50,000	40,000	25,392	60,000	50,000	225,392	22,539
Total...	380,000	335,000	157,719	400,000	480,000	1,752,719	175,272

NON-COMMERCIAL REMITTANCES FROM AND TO CANADA

Aliens in Canada remit each year important amounts of money to their relatives and friends in their native countries. In many cases the sole or chief wage-earner emigrates to Canada and supports the remainder of his family by his remittances. The most comprehensive study of such remittances is that made by C. F. Speare in 1908 for the United States.[1] He estimated that about 30 per cent of the remittances were made by postal money-orders, and the remainder through private banks, express companies, consular offices, charitable associations, and by sending currency through the mail. The illiterate or otherwise ignorant immigrants from eastern and southeastern Europe make least use of the facilities offered by the post office and prefer to make their remittances through private bankers of their own race and speaking their own language. Such immigrants form a much larger proportion of the alien population in the United States than in Canada. In the immigration into Canada the British and the Americans are in predominant numbers, and these are presumably able to use the less expensive services of the post office. On the other hand, remittances to the United States from Canada can be sent, by those who have banking accounts, by ordinary domestic check without any more formality than is involved in paying a domestic bill by check.

There are available for Canada, statistics of the amounts of postal money-orders issued in Canada and payable in other countries. Coats[2] uses these statistics as the sole basis of his estimate for remittances from Canada to other countries. He shows that there is a considerable degree of correlation between the annual immigration by countries of origin and the annual remittances in postal money-orders to these countries.[3]

Coats makes no reference to remittances other than by postal money-orders, and deducts 40 per cent from the amounts of postal money-orders payable abroad, to cover remittances for small business transactions. The Canadian imports of parcels and packages by post office and express, which would cover most of

[1] *North American Review*, January, 1908, pp. 106–116.

[2] *Cost of Living Report*, vol. ii, pp. 892–896.

[3] Coats shows that the remittances by postal money-order were much greater in proportion to immigration for those countries like Italy and Austria-Hungary, whose nationals make the highest per capita remittances, according to Speare. A much closer correlation would have been shown if, instead of comparing annual immigration into Canada with remittances, it had been possible to compare total population in Canada of persons of these nationalities year by year with remittances.

these small transactions, amounted in value for the period under study to only 13 per cent of the total issue of money-orders payable in other countries. Over 88 per cent of these parcels were imported from the United States, and a substantial portion of the payments therefor was unquestionably made by check drawn on Canadian banks.[1]

Beginning with 1911 there are available official statistics of the amounts of foreign money-orders issued by express companies in Canada. For the three years 1911 to 1913, these amounted to 7.3 per cent of the foreign money-orders issued by the post office. For the United States, Speare estimated at 28 to 35 per cent the proportion of remittances made by express companies to remittances made through the post office. This confirms the opinion expressed above that there is relatively greater use of the post office for making foreign remittances in Canada than in the United States. Further confirmation is furnished by the fact that the amount of foreign money-orders issued through the post office per capita of foreign born population was $7.38 in the United States in 1910 as compared with $11.50 in Canada in the same year.[2]

It is further to be noted that foreign money-orders are issued to cover such items as traveling expenses abroad of Canadians and the money taken from Canada by departing emigrants, which are accounted for elsewhere in this study. Taking all of these phases of the problem into consideration, it is estimated that the total remittances to friends abroad exceed by only 50 per cent the amount of foreign postal money-orders issued in Canada, including the amount remitted in settlement of small commercial transactions.

The remittances sent to Canada from abroad are much smaller in amount than the remittances sent abroad from Canada, as is to be expected in a country having a large immigrant population. The only data available for an estimate of the amount of

---

[1] The statistics of these imports are published in the *Annual Trade and Navigation Returns* of the Customs Department.

[2] Computed from Census and money-order statistics in *U. S. Statistical Abstract,* 1914, and *Canada Year Book* 1913.

such remittances are the statistics of postal money-orders issued in foreign countries payable in Canada. During the period under study, 74 per cent in amount of these money-orders was sent to Canada from the United States and 16 per cent from Great Britain. These remittances can be partly explained as funds sent to aid emigrants to Canada in making a start. A part of the remittances from the United States also consisted undoubtedly of funds sent by Canadians in the United States to their relatives at home. Shipments of parcels are not separately classified either in the Canadian export statistics or in the United States import statistics. The British trade-returns classify imports of parcels separately only for goods free of duty, but there are few commodities exported from Canada which are dutiable under the British tariff. The imports of such parcels from Canada from

TABLE IX

NON-COMMERCIAL REMITTANCES TO AND FROM CANADA, 1900 TO 1913

In thousands of dollars

Year	Postal money-orders issued in Canada payable abroad [1]	Remittances sent abroad from Canada [2]	Remittances to Canada sent from abroad [3]
1900	3,346	5,019	2,531
1901	4,379	6,568	3,084
1902	5,617	8,425	4,090
1903	7,027	10,540	4,900
1904	8,453	12,679	5,399
1905	10,081	15,121	6,067
1906	12,412	18,618	6,994
1907	17,003	25,504	7,814
1908	16,572	24,858	7,829
1909	18,542	27,813	7,984
1910	23,716	35,574	8,560
1911	29,914	44,871	8,815 [4]
1912	37,746	56,619	9,136 [4]
1913	42,498	63,747	7,950 [4]
Total		355,956	91,153

[1] *Canada Year Books.* Adjusted to calendar year basis from fiscal year statistics on the hypothesis of equal monthly distribution.

[2] 150 per cent of the amounts in the preceding column.

[3] *Canada Year Books*, Postal Money Orders issued in other countries, payable in Canada. Adjusted to calendar year basis from fiscal year statistics on the hypothesis of equal monthly distribution.

[4] Includes small amounts of British Postal Notes cashed in Canada, data obtained from Canada: Post Office Dept., *Annual Report*, 1914.

1902 to 1913 amounted in value to about 35 per cent of the amount of money-orders issued in Great Britain payable in Canada during the same period. The movement of parcels to the United States was probably in much greater volume, even relatively to the greater amount of remittances sent from the United States. A greater allowance has to be made, therefore, for remittances arising out of commercial transactions in the case of foreign money-orders payable in Canada than in the case of Canadian money-orders payable abroad. It is estimated that the non-commercial remittances to Canada from abroad by other methods than through the post office were offset by commercial remittances sent through the post office, and the figures of remittances by postal money-order will be taken as a measure of the total non-commercial remittances.

TABLE X

THE BALANCE OF NON-COMMERCIAL TRANSACTIONS, 1900 TO 1913

In thousands of dollars

Year	Debits			Credits			Balances	
	Capital taken out of Canada by emigrants	Non-commercial remittances sent abroad from Canada	Total	Capital brought into Canada by immigrants	Non-commercial remittances sent to Canada from abroad	Total	Debit	Credit
1900	2,094	5,019	7,113	7,631	2,531	10,162	....	3,049
1901	2,119	6,568	8,687	9,034	3,084	12,118	....	3,431
1902	3,428	8,425	11,853	16,840	4,090	20,930	....	9,077
1903	4,510	10,540	15,050	19,774	4,900	24,674	....	9,624
1904	6,181	12,679	18,860	18,507	5,399	23,906	....	5,046
1905	8,237	15,121	23,358	25,428	6,067	31,495	....	8,137
1906	11,373	18,618	29,991	29,665	6,994	36,659	....	6,668
1907	15,247	25,504	40,751	33,505	7,814	41,319	....	568
1908	20,975	24,858	45,833	30,372	7,829	38,201	7,632	....
1909	18,740	27,813	46,553	38,565	7,984	46,549	4	....
1910	19,029	35,574	54,603	45,668	8,560	54,228	375	....
1911	19,854	44,871	64,725	47,877	8,815	56,692	8,033	....
1912	20,946	56,619	77,565	45,038	9,136	54,174	23,391	....
1913	22,539	63,747	86,286	43,905	7,950	51,855	34,431	....
Total..	175,272	355,956	531,228	411,809	91,153	502,962	73,866	45,600

Table IX presents the estimated non-commercial remittances sent abroad from Canada and sent to Canada from abroad.

THE BALANCE OF NON-COMMERCIAL TRANSACTIONS

Table X summarizes the statistical results obtained in the foregoing discussion of the non-commercial items in the Canadian balance of international indebtedness, and strikes a balance between the debit and credit items.

CHAPTER IV

FREIGHT, INSURANCE. AND TOURIST EXPENDITURES

INTRODUCTORY

INTERNATIONAL transactions in services, although often overlooked or underestimated, are an important element in the international balance of indebtedness. The movement of physical goods in international commerce largely monopolizes public attention, not because sales of services are of little consequence in the volume of international transactions, but chiefly because of the practically universal limitation of official statistics to the "visible" items in the international trade balance.[1] For the purpose of determining the balance of international indebtedness, the purchase or sale of services is, dollar for dollar, of identical significance with the purchase or sale of goods.

In this section an estimate will first be made, year by year, for each item in the international balance of service transactions, dealt with under the following headings: freight payments, insurance payments, tourists' expenditures, interest payments, and sundries. All the partial balances then having been estimated, it will be possible to proceed to a computation of the total international balance of indebtedness, and to an analysis of this balance into its constituent elements of Canadian borrowings from abroad and Canadian loans abroad. In the calculation of the various items in the balance of service transactions, the same statistical difficulties are encountered and the same methods are used for their solution as in the calculation of the balance of non-commercial transactions.[2]

---

[1] Argentina offers the only instance known to the writer where continuous and comprehensive statistics of export and import services are officially collected and published. The British Board of Trade has recently begun the collection and publication of similar statistics for Great Britain.

[2] See p. 40, *supra*.

Freight Charges

Methods of Estimating Freight Charges. — Canada must make payment abroad for services rendered to her in connection with the transportation of imports to Canada, and per contra she receives payment from abroad for services which Canadian ships or railroads render in connection with the transportation of her own products to foreign countries.[1] The calculation of the amounts of these payments is beset with many complexities and difficulties. British economists have been struggling for many years with the task of ascertaining the amount of annual income derived by Great Britain from abroad through the services of her merchant marine.[2] The methods which they have developed are not applicable, however, to the Canadian situation, either because the nature of the problem is different or because the essential statistical data are lacking.

For Great Britain the main problem is to discover what are the earnings of British shipping used in carrying freight for other countries. In Canada the chief problem is to discover what are the payments made to other countries on account of transportation services performed for Canada, since only a small fraction of Canada's foreign trade is borne in Canadian vessels. One method followed by British writers is to apply to the entire British tonnage engaged in foreign trade the figures for earnings per ton ascertained for a few typical ships. But this method is not applicable to the present problem. No statistics exist of Canadian-owned vessels engaged in foreign trade. For Canada, moreover, overland transportation is important. Great Britain and Canada differ in their methods of computing import values: the British import statistics are based on c. i. f. values, and

[1] Including insurance charges and commissions for brokers' services on imports, but not on exports, because most of these services are rendered by non-Canadian, chiefly British, companies. Payments for passenger transportation are not dealt with separately in this study, but are sufficiently accounted for, it is believed, in the estimates of tourists' expenditures and of capital carried with them by migrants.

[2] Cf. especially: Sir Robert Giffen, "On the Use of Import and Export Statistics," *Journal of the Royal Statistical Society*, June, 1882; C. K. Hobson, *The Export of Capital*, 1914, pp. 171–187; "The Measurement of the Balance of Trade," *Economica*, May, 1921.

therefore cover insurance and freight added to the invoice value of the imports; the Canadian import statistics are based on f. o. b. values, and therefore leave unaccounted for the insurance and freight which Canadians must pay on such of their imports as are carried by foreign vessels.

Another method used to ascertain the amount of freight and insurance charges rests on the reasoning that "since the imports and exports of the whole world are, for the most part, the same goods valued at the point of arrival and departure respectively, the excess of value of imports should give a rough measure of the difference of valuation due to the cost of ocean carriage, including freight, insurance, and other charges." [1]

If this reasoning be accepted, the percentage of freight and insurance charges to total imports can then be calculated, and if the further assumption is made that the freight and other charges for the country under consideration and for the world at large form an approximately uniform percentage of the total imports of the two respectively, the amount of freight and other charges on imports for that country can then be readily calculated from the statistics of imports.

Sir Robert Giffen, in the essay referred to, uses this method for ascertaining the total earnings of the world's shipping from the transportation of freight, and also the other charges connected with ocean transportation. He then obtains an estimate of the British share of these earnings by using the percentage of British shipping tonnage to world tonnage, after having made an allowance for the amount of the difference between world imports and exports to be attributed to miscellaneous charges. He fails to allow, however, for shipments by land transportation and for the large fraction of the world's shipping engaged in internal trade which should have been excluded from the calculation. Giffen, however, tests his estimate by other methods of calculation not adapted to the Canadian situation because of the absence for

---

[1] Edgar Crammond, *The British Shipping Industry*, London, 1917, p. 27. The excess of value of the imports should also cover the cost of transportation from the point of departure to the point of arrival, where transportation is wholly or partly by rail or inland shipping.

Canada of the abundance of information available in dealing with British shipping.

C. K. Hobson [1] follows the method described above of ascertaining the world's freight bill and finds the British share therein by applying the percentage of clearances and entrances of British ships to total clearances and entrances at the principal ports of the world. He also checks his estimate by methods not available for a Canadian study because of the absence of the necessary statistics.

In the study of the balance of trade of the United States made for the Harvard University Committee on Economic Research in 1919,[2] the shipping freight charges payable to and paid by the United States are also calculated in part by the same method of deducting world exports from world imports. But instead of dividing the figure thus obtained by the total world *imports* to obtain the percentage of freight charges to imports, the percentage which the difference between world imports and world exports was in 1907 of the total world foreign trade, *export and import*, is used as an index of the ad valorem percentage of freight charges for both imports and exports. Granting the validity of the general method, this departure from the usual procedure cannot be justified. The total world imports and the total world exports are the same goods valued both at the points of departure and destination. Taking the world as a whole, freights are paid only on the imports. To take the percentage of the total freight charges to the total of exports and imports is to divide by almost two [3] the true burden of freight costs. If any American shipping was engaged in the commerce between countries other than the United States, this method is defective also in that it does not account for the earnings from this commerce. Moreover, this study makes no allowance for the transportation charges on trade with Canada and Mexico by land routes.

[1] *Op. cit.*, p. 174.

[2] C. J. Bullock, J. H. Williams, and R. S. Tucker, "The Balance of Trade of the United States," The Harvard *Review of Economic Statistics*, Preliminary Vol. No. 3, p. 231.

[3] Almost two, and not exactly two, because world imports, including as they do freight costs, are greater than world exports.

All these writers agree in using as the primary basis for their estimates of freight charges the differences between total world imports and total world exports. It is a necessary presupposition of this method that export statistics cover f. o. b. values and import statistics are for c. i. f. values. While nothing but a rough estimate is possible by any method, with statistics as inadequate as they are, there are too many serious defects in the primary data used in this method to justify its use. There are no authoritative compilations of the necessary statistics.[1] There are important divergencies in the methods of computing commerce statistics used by various countries. The United States, Canada, British South Africa, Cuba, Mexico, and the Philippines collect import statistics on the basis of f. o. b. values, and the total imports of these countries comprise an appreciable percentage of the total world imports; the freight charges on the imports of these countries would not be taken into account in a calculation of this sort. In many cases, commerce statistics are collected on the basis of arbitrary valuations. Different fiscal years and different definitions for statistical purposes of imports and exports render non-comparable the commerce statistics of different countries. Even if all these shortcomings were absent, the lack of justification in applying a percentage true for the world, to individual countries varying widely in the degree to which their trade is bulky or comes from close-by regions or is frontier traffic, leaves little ground for any confidence in the value of such computations.[2]

No easy solution of the problem has been found for Canada. The only guide is Mr. Coats' guess that from 1900 to 1914 the excess of Canada's freight payments to other countries, over pay-

[1] This is confirmed by the strikingly different results obtained by different writers using this method for years not far apart. See p. 78, *infra*.

[2] To be consistent with itself, the method criticized here should divide the difference between world imports and world exports by the world imports to obtain the ad valorem percentage of freight charges to import values for any country and by the world exports to obtain a similar percentage for the freight earnings on carriage of exports. The freight charges should be a smaller percentage of c. i. f. import values than of f. o. b. export values. None of the writers using this method seems, however, to have made use of this refinement.

ments to Canada by other countries, was $60,000,000.[1] The fact
that the calculation of balances of trade has received greatest
attention in Great Britain, an insular country, has led all the
writers into the error of neglecting all except ocean freight
charges.[2] For Canada in particular the overland and Great
Lakes freights on the imports of cotton from the American south,
coal, coke, and steel from Pennsylvania, corn from the Middle
West, tobacco from Virginia and Kentucky, and fruit from Cali-
fornia and Florida, represent long and expensive freight hauls,
the charges for which must be settled abroad, alike with the
charges on the less bulky water-borne imports from Great Britain.
This further complicates the problem of reaching a satisfactory
estimate.

The method used in the present study to ascertain the freight
charges on imports is admittedly inadequate, but appears to the
writer to be the best available under the circumstances. The
first step taken was to collect for 1907, a normal year in about
the middle of the period studied, freight rates and import values
by weight or measurement on a few representative commodities,
including both bulky and light articles, and including railroad
rates and import values for goods imported from the United
States, and ocean freights and import values for goods imported
from Great Britain. In order to make the necessary calculation,
it was essential to obtain freight quotations: (1) to Montreal, as
the chief point of import in Canada; (2) by weight, or, if by
measurement, for commodities for which the conversion rate
from a measurement to a weight basis could be calculated; and
(3) for commodities for which the official import statistics reported imports both by quantities and by values. These restrictions on the data which could be used still left remaining
representative data from which could be roughly computed the
ad valorem percentage of freight charges to import values for

[1] *Cost of Living Report*, vol. ii, p. 901. This figure seems to the writer a serious
underestimate.

[2] *E.g.*, Coats' study for Canada; for the United States, the studies of Sir George
Paish for the National Monetary Commission, 1910 (61st Cong. 2d Sess., *Sen. Doc.*
579), and of the Harvard group referred to above; Edgar Crammond, Sir Robert
Giffen, and C. K. Hobson, for Great Britain.

the iron and steel and the cotton textile groups for imports from both Great Britain and the United States. These groups comprise the bulk of the imports from Great Britain but are not closely representative of the imports from the United States. The next step taken was to assume that the results obtained for the iron and steel and the textile groups were adequately representative for all bulky and for all light commodities, respectively, and from the import statistics for 1907 to calculate the percentages of the imports from Great Britain and the United States which were bulky and light respectively, and thus to obtain weighting factors to be used in applying these results to the total imports from these countries. The results obtained are presented in Table XI.

At first glance the higher ad valorem percentage indicated for freight charges on imports from the United States appears to discredit the accuracy of the index. But it should be noted that rail rates are higher on the same commodities than ocean freights, and that bulky articles predominate in the imports from the United States, whereas this is not true of imports from Great Britain. Over 75 per cent of the imports from Great Britain consist of textiles and manufactures of iron and steel, which are the groups represented in the index presented above. The remainder of the imports from Great Britain consist, to a predominant degree, of expensive manufactured products on which the ad valorem rates would probably be even lower than the average reached on the basis of the commodities here chosen. Among the imports from the United States not directly represented in the index, but which are of considerable importance, are coal, coke, oil, fruits, cotton, books and periodicals,[1] corn, drugs and chemicals, binder twine, lumber, meat, and a wide range of other commodities of relatively small value per unit of weight or bulk; and some of these imports come from parts of the United States at a great distance from the point of entry into Canada.[2]

---

[1] Generally sent by express or post at higher rates than the freight rates.

[2] "Canada imports very large quantities of various classes of both raw and manufactured goods from the United States, some of which are freighted but a few miles from the International border, while in other cases they are conveyed thousands of miles, the freight ranging from less than half a dollar to more than $20 a

The imports from countries other than the United Kingdom and the United States must come by ocean routes. These imports come on the average from greater distances than British imports, and they also consist to a larger degree of bulky com-

ton; or on a percentage basis, from less than 1 per cent to more than 100 per cent in value." *Final Report*, Dominions Royal Commission, 1917, p. 166. Great Britain: *Parliamentary Papers*, Cd. 7971.

TABLE XI

IMPORT VALUES AND FREIGHT RATES, 1907

Ocean

Commodity group	Unit	Average import value [1]	Average freight rate [2]	Percentage of freight charges to import value	Weights [3]	Final results
Great Britain:						
Manufactures of						
Iron and Steel ...	long ton	$53.83	$2.60	5.6	40	224
Cotton Textiles....	1000 yds.	94.63	2.18 [4]	2.3	60	138
Total..............	....	....	....	....	100	362
Per cent..........	....	....	....	....	....	3.6

Rail

United States:						
Manufactures of						
Iron and Steel ...	short ton	$50.30	$3.06	5.8	90	522
Cotton Textiles....	100 lbs.	33.11 [4]	0.36½	1.1	10	110
Total..............	....	....	....	....	100	632
Per cent	....	....	....	....	....	6.3

[1] Computed from Canada: *Trade and Commerce Report*, for fiscal year ending March 31, 1908.

[2] Computed from data in *Report of British Trade Commissioner to Canada on the Trade of Canada in 1907* (Great Britain: *Parliamentary Papers*, Cd. 3868).

[3] Weights are according to the relative importance in the imports of 1907, of bulky and light commodities. It is assumed in using these weights that rates on iron and steel commodities are representative of rates on all bulky commodities and that rates on cotton textiles are representative of rates on all light commodities.

[4] Based on conversion rate from measurement to weight basis, 1 lb. tare = 3.5 yards. Conversion rate computed from data in *Cost of Living Report*, vol. ii, p. 46 and U. S. Dept. of Commerce, *Miscellaneous Series*, No. 92, "Stowage of Cargoes," pp. 283, 287.

modities. Of the imports in 1907 from these countries, 60 per cent were relatively bulky, 40 per cent light, as compared with 40 per cent and 60 per cent respectively for the imports from Great Britain. On the assumption that the rates for bulky and for light commodities from these countries were the same as for similar imports from Great Britain, the percentage of freight charges to imports would be 4.3. After allowance for the greater distances, it is estimated that for imports from countries other than Great Britain and the United States, the percentage of freight charges to imports was 4.6 per cent in 1907.

Freight Charges on Imports from Great Britain. — From the payments for freight charges on imports into Canada in foreign vessels must be deducted the portion of these payments expended in Canada. C. K. Hobson, from an examination of the accounts of two tramp steamers, estimates that 30 per cent of the gross receipts of British vessels are expended by the owners of the vessels in foreign ports.[1] This estimate is based on the accounts of British vessels either engaged in the trade between Great Britain and countries more distant than Canada or not trading from Great Britain. Hobson's estimate is probably too high for the relatively short voyage between Great Britain and Canada, which permits of bunkering and laying in supplies in England for the round trip and involves stays of only a few days in Canadian ports. Deduction should also be made, however, for the expenditures of the crews in Canada. On the other hand, something should be added for the payments to be made by importers on account of insurance, interest, and forwarding agents' charges. It is customary for British exporters to Canada, in making out their invoices for purpose of entry through the Canadian customs, to deduct a 2½ per cent discount for cash payment. In some cases, the actual terms made with the Canadian buyers do not stipulate immediate payment and the discount for cash is not received by the importer. Something is therefore to be added for this item also. Giffen estimated that these miscellaneous items amounted

---

[1] *The Export of Capital*, p. 173. Giffen, in 1882, estimated that one sixth of the total receipts were expended abroad. (*Journal of the Royal Statistical Society*, June, 1882, p. 208.)

to $2\frac{1}{2}$ per cent of the value of British exports and imports.[1]
Canada's import trade, however, was financed by her own banks
more largely than was the case in the Continental European and
the smaller British colonies, or even in the United States before
1914, and this estimate seems excessive.   The best final estimate
which can be made is that the deductions for expenditures in
Canada of ship owners and crew were largely offset by the additional charges for insurance, interest, etc., and that a reduction
of the percentage of charges to imports from 3.6 to 3.5 will adequately account for the remainder.

Theoretically, also, deduction should be made for the imports
from Great Britain carried by Canadian-owned vessels, in order
to obtain a final figure for the payments to be made for freight
charges on imports from Great Britain. But the Canadian official
statistics of imports according to nationality of the vessel [2] show
that only a very small fraction of the imports from Great Britain
are carried in Canadian vessels. In the fiscal year ending March
31, 1914, less than 18,000 tons out of a total of 906,000 tons were
brought in Canadian vessels, and in other years even smaller
percentages. The fact that some of the imports from Great
Britain are carried by Canadian vessels is therefore disregarded.

In reaching an estimate for other years based on the percentage estimated for 1907, three sets of facts must be considered;
changes in freight rates, changes in prices, and changes in the
character of the goods imported. There was no change of significance in the character of the imports from Great Britain during
this period. In 1900, 47 per cent, and in 1914, 45 per cent of the
total imports from Great Britain consisted of textiles and textile
products; in 1900, 19 per cent, and in 1914, 15 per cent, of the
total imports consisted of metals and manufactures thereof.[3]
No adjustment need therefore be made for changes in the character of the imports. But the period was marked both by a rise
in prices and a rise in freight rates.

---

[1] Giffen, *op. cit.*, p. 219.

[2] *Annual Shipping Reports* of the Department of Customs.

[3] Fiscal years; computed from Canada: *Trade and Commerce Reports*, 1900 and
1914.

From quotations available for west-bound freight from British ports to Montreal for 13 representative commodities for the years 1907, 1910, and 1913, a roughly weighted index number was obtained which, taking 1907 as 100, indicated an increase of 5.8 per cent from 1907 to 1910 and 33.2 per cent from 1907 to 1913.[1] For the years before 1907 no Canadian quotations were obtainable. In the opening year of the 20th century, freights were unusually high because of the South African war, but they declined sharply after the conclusion of the war, with little recovery until 1906. By the use of British indices for outward freights (that is,

[1] Quotations given in reports of British Trade Commissioners on Trade of Dominion of Canada, British *Parliamentary Papers*, Cd. 3868 (1908); Cd. 5591 (1911); Cd. 6870 (1913). The quotations used in making the index were for: crockery, hardware, iron bars, iron sheets, iron girders, bolts and nuts, tinplate, cutlery, heavy cottons, all other dry goods, machinery (average of four quotations). Weighting done on the basis of relative importance of the commodities in the imports.

TABLE XII

INDICES FOR FREIGHT CHARGES ON IMPORTS FROM GREAT BRITAIN, 1900 TO 1913 (1907 = 100)

Year	British outward freight indices			Canadian inward freights present calculation	Index used in present study
	C. K. Hobson [1]	Board of Trade [2]	Dominions Royal Commission [3]		
1900	....	117.6	....	....	117.6
1901	....	95.0	....	....	95.0
1902	....	89.5	89.5	....	89.5
1903	78.9	....	77.6	....	77.6
1904	78.0	....	71.3	....	71.3
1905	83.7	....	80.6	....	80.6
1906	100.0	....	100.0	....	100.0
1907	100.0	....	100.0	100.0	100.0
1908	85.0	....	94.0	....	101.9
1909	83.2	....	101.5	....	103.8
1910	99.0	....	103.0	105.8	105.8
1911	116.0	....	123.9	....	114.9
1912	156.0	....	159.7	....	124.0
1913	....	....	....	133.2	133.2

[1] From C. K. Hobson, *The Export of Capital*, p. 182.

[2] *Ibid.* Recomputed to 1907 as base year by putting the figure for 1902 at 89.5, as in the Dominions Royal Commission Index.

[3] Dominions Royal Commission, *Final Report*, Appendix C, p. 109. (Great Britain: *Parliamentary Papers*, Cd. 7971, 1917.) Figures read from chart and recomputed to 1907 as 100.

outward from Great Britain) to all countries, a guide can be obtained of the trend of Canadian inward freights to 1907.

Table XII presents the freight indices which have been found. For the years 1900 to 1902 the British Board of Trade index is used. In the absence of more satisfactory data, the Dominions Royal Commission index [1] is used for the years 1903 to 1907, and the present calculation for the years 1907, 1910, and 1913 is used as the index for these years and also as the basis of an index for

[1] The report of the Dominions Royal Commission, in which this index was found, does not explain its source or the method used in its construction. It was probably obtained by the Commission from the British Board of Trade.

TABLE XIII

FREIGHT PAYMENTS BY CANADA ON IMPORTS FROM GREAT BRITAIN, 1900 TO 1913

In thousands of dollars

Year	I Imports from Great Britain [1]	II Percentage of freight charges to imports, 1907	III Freight rate index (Table XII)	IV Price index [2]	V Percentage of freight charges to imports (II×III÷IV)	VI Freight payments on imports from Great Britain (I × V)
1900	43,550	..	117.6	94.3	4.4	1,916
1901	45,921	..	95.0	91.2	3.6	1,653
1902	53,908	..	89.5	90.9	3.4	1,833
1903	60,259	..	77.6	91.4	3.0	1,808
1904	60,984	..	71.3	92.6	2.7	1,647
1905	64,713	..	80.6	92.1	3.1	2,006
1906	77,536	..	100.0	95.1	3.7	2,869
1907	92,285	3.5	100.0	100.0	3.5	3,230
1908	76.616	..	101.9	97.1	3.7	2,835
1909	89,173	..	103.8	98.2	3.7	3,299
1910	106,285	..	105.8	102.6	3.6	3,826
1911	115,163	..	114.9	103.2	3.9	4,491
1912	113,284	..	124.0	108.4	4.0	5,331
1913	113,642	..	133.2	109.9	4.2	5,613
Total..						42,357

[1] *Canada Year Book*, 1913, p. 230. Imports entered for consumption. Adjusted to calendar year basis from fiscal year statistics.

[2] Great Britain: Labor Dept. Board of Trade, recomputed to 1907 as 100. Data from *Cost of Living Report*, vol. ii, p. 149.

the intermediate years constructed on the assumption that there were uniform increases in each year from 1907 to 1910, and from 1910 to 1913, respectively.

The ad valorem percentage of freight charges to total imports from Great Britain, for 1907, multiplied for each year by the freight index and also by the reciprocal of the price index, will give the ad valorem percentage of freight charges to imports from Great Britain for each year in the period. The amount of freight charges for each year can then be obtained by multiplying the amount of imports for each year by the percentage, for that year, of freight charges to imports. Table XIII presents the final calculation of the payments made abroad for freight charges on imports from Great Britain.

TABLE XIV

FREIGHT PAYMENTS BY CANADA ON IMPORTS FROM THE UNITED STATES, 1900 TO 1913

In thousands of dollars

Year	I Imports from the United States.[1]	II Percentage of freight charges to imports, 1907	III Price index [2]	IV Percentage of freight charges to imports (II ÷ III)	V Freight charges on imports from the United States (I × IV)
1900	104,615	..	85	6.2	6,486
1901	110,947	..	84	6.3	6,990
1902	121,767	..	91	5.8	7,062
1903	135,900	..	91	5.8	7,882
1904	147,721	..	92	5.8	8,568
1905	160,615	..	91	5.8	9,316
1906	183,465	..	94	5.6	10,274
1907	203,019	5.3	100	5.3	10,760
1908	178,704	..	97	5.5	9,829
1909	205,641	..	103	5.1	10,488
1910	260,509	..	106	5.0	13,025
1911	316,533	..	101	5.2	16,460
1912	409,434	..	107	5.0	20,472
1913	405,616	..	106	5.0	20,280
Total..					157,892

[1] *Canada Year Book*, 1913, p. 230. Adjusted to calendar year basis from fiscal year statistics.
[2] U. S. Dept. of Labor, Bureau of Labor Statistics, *Wholesale Prices Index*, Bull. No. 181, p. 16. Recomputed from 1914 as base to 1907 as base.

Freight Charges on Imports from the United States. — It was estimated above that the ad valorem percentage of freight charges to imports from the United States was 6.3 per cent in 1907. An addition of at least $\frac{1}{2}$ of one per cent should be made for cash discounts deducted from the invoice for purposes of customs entry, but not actually received by the importer. Deductions must be made for freight charges on imports from the United States carried by Canadian vessels, and for the portion of overland freight charges which covers the carriage of goods from the Canadian boundary to their destination. Based on scanty data, an allowance of $1\frac{1}{2}$ per cent ad valorem is made for these two items, leaving 5.3 per cent as the net ad valorem percentage of freight charges to import values for 1907. Railroad freight rates remained practically constant during the period under study, whereas prices rose steadily. Assuming that no change occurred in railroad freights during the period, the payment to be made by Canada on account of freight charges on imports from the United States will be estimated as equal for each year

TABLE XV

FREIGHT PAYMENTS BY CANADA ON IMPORTS FROM COUNTRIES OTHER THAN GREAT BRITAIN AND THE UNITED STATES, 1900 TO 1913

In thousands of dollars

Year	Imports [1]	Freight payments by Canada [2]
1900	26,939	808
1901	30,222	907
1902	34,972	1,049
1903	38,043	1,141
1904	38,849	1,165
1905	42,071	1,262
1906	47,133	1,414
1907	51,852	1,556
1908	48,813	1,464
1909	54,602	1,638
1910	64,468	1,934
1911	72,327	2,170
1912	90,211	2,706
1913	92,010	2,760

[1] *Canada Year Book*, 1913, p. 230. Adjusted to calendar year basis from fiscal year statistics.
[2] Based on the estimate that freight charges after deductions were 3 per cent of the value of imports.

to 5.3 per cent of the value of the imports for that year multiplied by the reciprocal of the price index for that year. Table XIV presents the calculation of freight charges paid by Canada on imports from the United States.

Freight Charges on Imports from other Countries. — There remain to be considered the freight charges on imports from countries other than the United States and the United Kingdom. The estimate for 1907, of 4.6 per cent as the ad valorem percentage of freight and other charges to imports, will be used for all the years, on the assumption that increases in freight rates offset increases in prices. Canadian vessels carry an appreciable proportion of these imports, especially of those coming from Newfoundland, the West Indies, the Far East, and Australia. Deduction of 20 per cent of the charges for expenditures of vessels and crews in Canada and 20 per cent of the remainder for imports brought by Canadian vessels results in approximately 3 per

TABLE XVI

FREIGHT PAYMENTS BY CANADA ON IMPORTS FROM ALL COUNTRIES, 1900 TO 1913

In thousands of dollars

Year	On imports from Great Britain	On imports from United States	On imports from other countries	On imports from all countries
1900	1,916	6,486	808	9,210
1901	1,653	6,990	907	9,550
1902	1,833	7,062	1,049	9,944
1903	1,808	7,882	1,141	10,831
1904	1,647	8,568	1,165	11,380
1905	2,006	9,316	1,262	12,584
1906	2,869	10,274	1,414	14,557
1907	3,230	10,760	1,556	15,546
1908	2,835	9,829	1,464	14,128
1909	3,299	10,488	1,638	15,425
1910	3,826	13,025	1,934	18,785
1911	4,491	16,460	2,170	23,121
1912	5,331	20,472	2,706	28,509
1913	5,613	20,280	2,760	28,653
Total	42,357	157,892	21,974	222,223

cent as the ad valorem percentage of net freight payments to be made by Canada to imports from these countries. Table XV presents the calculation of these payments. Table XVI presents the estimates for total freight charges on imports from all countries.

The results obtained in this way may be compared with the figures which would have been available if the method discussed earlier in this section had been adopted. Table XVII is constructed on the assumption that the carrying charges for the world equal the difference between world imports and exports. The percentage of these charges to the amount of world imports is taken as the ad valorem percentage of import freight charges to imports. The percentages obtained by this method are uniformly higher than those found to hold for the selected commodities imported into Canada in 1907, and than those estimated, for corresponding years, in the present calculation.

TABLE XVII

RATIO OF FREIGHT CHARGES TO VALUE OF WORLD IMPORTS

Year	World imports	World exports	Excess of imports over exports	Ratio of freight charges to world imports: Hobson's method	Ratio of freight charges to Canadian imports. Present calculation.[4]
	In thousands of pounds sterling			Per cent	
1901 [1]	2,516	2,292	224	8.9	5.1
1904 [2]	2,628	2,446	182	6.9	4.6
1906 [1]	3,253	3,052	201	6.2	4.7
1907 [3]	3,737.2	3,383.6	353.6	9.5	4.5
1909 [1]	3,611	3,377	234	6.5	4.4
1912 ${1 \atop 2}$ {	4,403	4,061	342	7.8	} 4.5
	4,390	4,050	340	7.7	

[1] Edgar Crammond, *The British Shipping Industry*, 1917, p. 27.

[2] *Report of Committee to Chamber of Shipping of the United Kingdom and Liverpool Steam Ship Owners' Association*, July, 1917, vol. ii, pp. 76, 77.

[3] C. K. Hobson, *The Export of Capital*, p. 174; as quoted from *Manchester Guardian*, February 10, 1911. Comparison with the results obtained by the same method by other writers for nearby years suggests that this is an overestimate.

[4] Ratio of total freight charges, after allowances, to total imports from all countries.

Freight Charges on Exports. — The freight charges on exports sold f. o. b. are paid by the purchaser of the goods. The Canadian exports are shipped to their destination mainly by foreign carriers, but Canada receives payments for the purchases in Canada of vessels and crew. On the exports to the United States, Canada receives payment for the charges for transportation from the point of origin in Canada to the point where the exports cross the boundary, but in most cases the distances to the boundary are short. It is estimated that 2 per cent of the value of the exports will cover the payments to be made to Canada: for railroad transportation to the boundary on exports to the United States, and to the ocean ports on exports by sea sold f. o. b. producing point and not f. o. b. the port of export; for water transportation on exports carried in Canadian vessels; and for expenditures in Canada of foreign vessels and crews. Table XVIII presents the estimate of payments to Canada on account of export freight charges.

TABLE XVIII

FREIGHT PAYMENTS TO CANADA ON EXPORTS, 1900 TO 1913

In thousands of dollars

Year	Exports [1]	Freight payments to Canada [2]
1900	181,493	3,630
1901	200,548	4,011
1902	216,629	4,333
1903	227,470	4,549
1904	196,566	3,931
1905	222,864	4,457
1906	253,110	5,062
1907	254,037	5,081
1908	265,146	5,303
1909	288,685	5,774
1910	295,415	5,908
1911	296,568	5,931
1912	362,966	7,259
1913	460,519	9,210
Total	3,722,016	74,439

[1] Total Merchandise Exports, calendar year statistics, from Dept. of Customs, *Unrevised Monthly Statements of Imports and Exports.*

[2] Based on the estimate that freight payments, etc., to Canada were 2 per cent of the value of the exports.

Insurance Payments sent Abroad from Canada

To ascertain the amount of fire- and life-insurance payments
sent abroad from Canada, use is made of the official statistics for
the excess of premium income over expenditures in Canada of
foreign companies. For an estimate of the payments made to
foreign companies for insurance other than life and fire, including
casualty, sickness, employers' liability, and sundry other kinds

TABLE XIX

Insurance Payments by Canada to Foreign Companies, 1900 to 1913

In thousands of dollars

Year	I Foreign life-insurance companies [1]	II Foreign fire-insurance companies [1]	Other foreign insurance companies –		V Total insurance payments by Canada (I + II + IV)
			III Premium receipts in Canada [2]	IV Excess of premium income over expenditure in Canada [3]	
	Excess of premium income over expenditure in Canada				
1900	985	1,712 [4]	1,002	200	527 [4]
1901	665	67 [4]	555	112	710
1902	1,285	2,862	691	138	4,285
1903	1,055	1,851	864	173	3,079
1904	556	3,874 [4]	830	166	3,152 [4]
1905	859	3,611	1,087	217	4,687
1906	1,130	3,299	1,275	255	4,684
1907	634	2,284	1,458	292	3,210
1908	827	1,872	1,764	353	3,052
1909	929	2,869	2,000	400	4,198
1910	871	2,483	2,500	500	3,854
1911	1,279	3,012	3,481	636	4,927
1912	1,851	3,666	3,802	840	6,357
1913	2,169	3,636	3,162	595	6,400
Total..	15,095	25,792	24,471	4,877	45,764

[1] Computed from data in Canada: Superintendent of Insurance, *Annual Reports;* total income in
Canada exclusive of interest, minus total expenditures in Canada.

[2] 1900–1904, *Canada Year Books,* premium receipts in Canada of all foreign insurance companies
minus premium receipts in Canada of foreign fire- and life-insurance companies. 1905–1908, compiled
from annual reports to Superintendent of Insurance of individual companies. 1909–1910, estimates,
based on incomplete data. 1911–1913, *Canada Year Books.*

[3] 1911–1913, *Canada Year Books.* 1900–1910, 20 per cent of premium receipts in Canada, which
was the average percentage to premium income of excess of premium income over expenditure for all
Canadian companies engaged in miscellaneous insurance during the same period.

[4] Excess of expenditures over premium income, due to conflagrations in these years.

of insurance, less satisfactory data are available. The amount of premium income received in Canada by foreign companies dealing in insurance other than life and fire was obtained or estimated on the basis of complete or partial data, derived from various official sources, and the excess of income over expenditures was then estimated on the basis of the proportion which premium income bore to excess of income over expenditure during several selected years within the period under study for all the Canadian companies dealing in sundry insurance. The interest income of foreign insurance companies from investments in Canada will be accounted for when interest payments are estimated.

Table XIX presents the estimated amounts of the insurance payments sent abroad from Canada during the years 1900 to 1913.

INSURANCE PAYMENTS BY OTHER COUNTRIES TO CANADA

Canadian life-insurance companies, and to a smaller extent Canadian fire-insurance companies, operate in countries other than Canada. The official reports indicate that only one Canadian company dealing in insurance other than fire and life operates outside of Canada, and its foreign business is not important enough to justify consideration here.

There are available official data covering the amount of life-insurance risks of Canadian companies in other countries for the years 1902 to 1913. For the period 1909 to 1913, the annual excess of income over expenditure for Canadian companies on both domestic and foreign business averaged 2.8 per cent of the amount of policies in force. A little over 22 per cent of the total income consisted of interest on investments, presumably almost wholly in Canada. After allowance for interest on investments and for the greater relative cost of doing business abroad than at home, 2 per cent is taken as the percentage, for the years 1902 to 1913, of excess of premium income over expenditure to the total amount of insurance in force outside of Canada.

The data available relating to the operations outside of Canada of Canadian fire-insurance companies give the premium receipts and the losses on business outside of Canada for the entire period covered. The official data given in the Annual Reports of the Superintendent of Insurance indicate that on the total business done by Canadian fire-insurance companies in Canada and elsewhere during the years from 1900 to 1913, the excess of income over expenditure amounted to a little over 12 per cent of the excess of premiums over losses. The income from investments is a relatively small fraction of the total income of fire-insurance companies. Making a small allowance for income from investments and for the greater cost of operating abroad than at home, 10 per cent is taken as the percentage of excess of income over expenditure to the excess of premiums over losses for the business of Canadian fire-insurance companies outside of Canada.

TABLE XX

INSURANCE PAYMENTS TO CANADA BY OTHER COUNTRIES, 1900 TO 1913

In thousands of dollars

Year	Life insurance		Fire insurance		Total payments to Canada
	Canadian policies in force in other countries [1]	Net income [2]	Excess of premiums over losses in foreign business [3]	Net income [2]	
1900	......	585 [4]	836	84	669
1901	......	806 [4]	1,179	118	924
1902	51,389	1,028	1,345	134	1,162
1903	64,219	1,284	1,787	179	1,463
1904	76,358	1,527	1,196	120	1,647
1905	89,667	1,793	1,604	160	1,953
1906	99,711	1,994	289	29	2,023
1907	110,756	2,215	981	98	2,313
1908	120,952	2,419	779	78	2,497
1909	131,295	2,626	1,634	163	2,789
1910	141,832	2,837	1,427	143	2,980
1911	157,115	3,142	1,194	119	3,261
1912	175,141	3,503	1,428	143	3,646
1913	194,721	3,894	1,027	103	3,997
Total..		29,653		1,671	31,324

[1] *Cost of Living Report*, vol. ii, p. 906.
[2] The method used in obtaining the figures given in these columns is explained in the text.
[3] *Annual Reports* of the Superintendent of Insurance.
[4] Estimated from incomplete data.

Table XX presents the estimated amounts of the insurance payments to Canada by other countries.

Coats,[1] basing his estimate on a different method of calculation whose details are not given, and using only data for the years 1902 to 1913, estimates at $20,000,000 the excess of income over expenditure on the business of Canadian life-insurance companies outside of Canada, as compared with the present estimate of $29,600,000. He presents no estimate for fire-insurance companies.

EXPENDITURES BY TOURISTS IN CANADA

The only method available for reaching an estimate of the expenditures by tourists in Canada is to make an estimate of the average expenditures by each tourist in Canada and to multiply that estimate by the number of tourists recorded as having entered Canada. No statistics are collected for tourists entering Canada from the United States.[2] Their expenditures, which are unquestionably of considerable importance,[3] can only be guessed at. It has been estimated by Canadian newspapers that in the summer of 1920, $50,000,000 was spent by American tourists in Canada. Allowance being made for the rise in prices and for the increase in tourist traffic, this figure has been used as a rough guide in making the estimate. For ocean tourists holding cabin tickets on the steamers, it is estimated that the average expenditure is

[1] *Cost of Living Report,* vol. ii, p. 906.

[2] "During the year ended June 30, 1909, more than 9,000,000 people entered the United States over the northern border. No doubt the number crossing from the United States to Canada was equally great." U. S. Commissioner of Immigration's *Report* for 1911, p. 158. If only 5 per cent of these were tourists to Canada and if each tourist spent in Canada on the average only $30, the total expenditure would exceed the estimate made in Table XXI. The American consul at Halifax, after a careful study of the available data, estimated that 60,000 American tourists in Nova Scotia spend, during the four summer months, on the average at least $42.50 each. (U. S. Dept. of Commerce, *Monthly Consular and Trade Reports* [Dec. 1909], No. 351, pp. 245 seq.)

[3] "Many of the wealthier classes of the Southern States spend their entire summers across the border, and from Nova Scotia to Vancouver the Canadian borderlands and islands along the waterways are dotted with the summer homes of Americans." H. S. Van Sant, U. S. consul at Kingston, Ontario, in U. S. Dept. of Commerce, *Monthly Consular and Trade Reports* (June, 1909), No. 345, p. 207.

$1,000. This is the estimate made by Paish in 1910 for the average expenditure of *all* tourists in the United States, and followed by the study of the American balance of trade made for the Harvard University Committee on Economic Research, and by Coats in his study of the Canadian balance of trade.[1]

One thousand dollars seems an unreasonably high estimate for expenditures in Canada by those tourists whose standard of expenditure is low enough to induce them to travel to Canada in the steerage, especially when it is considered that any one who states that he comes to Canada on a visit and not for permanent residence is classed as a tourist by the immigration authorities, and that children as well as adults are included in the statistics. Three hundred dollars is taken as a sufficiently generous estimate of the average expenditures in Canada of tourists who arrived steerage.

Statistics of tourist arrivals at ocean ports and the estimated expenditure of all tourists in Canada are given in Table XXI.

Coats[2] estimates that tourists other than American spent in Canada $125,000,000 during a period approximately the same as that studied here, and that American tourists spent about $15,000,000 more in Canada during the period than was spent by Canadian tourists in the United States. His estimate for the expenditures of tourists in Canada other than Americans exceeds the one reached in this study by about $55,000,000. But Coats estimates the number of saloon tourists arriving in Canada at a higher number than the official statistics used here,[3] and esti-

---

[1] Sir George Paish, *The Trade Balance of the United States*, National Monetary Commission, 1910 (61st Cong., 2d Sess., *Sen. Doc.* 579), pp. 180–182; Bullock, Williams, and Tucker, "The Balance of Trade of the United States," Harvard *Review of Economic Statistics*, Preliminary Volume No. 3, p. 230; *Cost of Living Report*, vol. ii, p. 905.

[2] *Ibid.*, pp. 896, 897, 904, 905.

[3] The official statistics of saloon tourists are not included in any of the general tables compiled by the Immigration Branch, and are buried in an inconspicuous part of the text of the annual reports of the Commissioner of Immigration. Mr. Coats seems to have been unaware of their existence. He divides the total number of saloon arrivals into returned Canadians and tourists, overlooking the fact that some immigrants travel on first-class tickets. He thus reaches an overestimate of the number of saloon tourists, and an underestimate of the number of immigrants.

mates at $1,000 the expenditures of both saloon and steerage tourists, whereas $300 is the figure used here for expenditures by steerage tourists.

EXPENDITURES BY CANADIAN TOURISTS

The expenditures of Canadian overseas tourists are estimated on the basis of $1,000 spent abroad, including transportation charges, by each Canadian who travels on a first-class ocean ticket, and $300 spent abroad by each Canadian who travels steerage. The figures of Canadian tourists are obtained from

TABLE XXI

TOURIST EXPENDITURES IN CANADA, 1900 TO 1913

In thousands of dollars

Year	Saloon tourist arrivals at ocean ports		Steerage tourist arrivals at ocean ports		Expenditures of American tourists	Total expenditures
	Number [1]	Expenditures ($1000 each)	Number [2]	Expenditures ($300 each)		
1900	1,978	1,978	253	76	5,000	7,054
1901	2,896	2,896	312	94	5,000	7,990
1902	3,439	3,439	362	109	7,500	11,048
1903	2,902	2,902	414	124	7,500	10,526
1904	2,405	2,405	1,262	379	10,000	12,784
1905	2,576	2,576	2,562	768	10,000	13,344
1906	3,345	3,345	3,170	951	12,500	16,796
1907	2,223	2,223	4,902	1,471	12,500	16,194
1908	2,695	2,695	5,023	1,507	15,000	19,202
1909	2,952	2,952	5,338	1,601	15,000	19,553
1910	5,194	5,194	6,833	2,050	17,500	24,744
1911	6,543	6,543	7,244	2,173	17,500	26,216
1912	6,398	6,398	10,016	3,005	20,000	29,403
1913	7,088	7,088	11,229	3,369	20,000	30,457
Total..		52,634		17,677	175,000	245,311

[1] Canada: Dept. of the Interior, Immigration Branch, *Annual Reports.* Adjusted to calendar year basis from fiscal year statistics. From 1900 to 1904 the data are compilations from the reports of separate ports. The figures for 1909 and 1910 are estimates based on incomplete data. Arrivals via United States ocean ports are included.

[2] Canada: Department of Immigration and Colonization, *Immigration Facts and Figures,* 1920. Adjusted to calendar year basis from fiscal year statistics. Arrivals via United States ocean ports are included.

the official statistics for returned Canadians arriving at ocean
ports, including United States ports. The "returned Canadians"
who travel steerage consist in large part of alien residents of
Canada who return from a visit to their native country. For
expenditures of Canadian tourists in the United States, there is
no information upon which to base an estimate. The number
of American tourists who visit Canada is probably much greater
than the number of Canadian tourists who visit the United
States.[1] But Canadians do a considerable amount of shopping
in the United States and only a small fraction of their purchases
is declared to the customs inspectors, whereas the expenditure
of tourists in Canada is almost wholly for transportation, hotel,
and other services. On the other hand, the average standard of

[1] Cf. *Cost of Living Report*, vol. ii, p. 905.

TABLE XXII

EXPENDITURES ABROAD BY CANADIAN TOURISTS, 1900 TO 1913

In thousands of dollars

Year	Saloon returned Canadians [1]	Expenditures ($1000 each)	Steerage returned Canadians [2]	Expenditures ($300 each)	Expenditures in United States	Total expenditures
1900	3,154	3,154	937	281	2,500	5,935
1901	3,523	3,523	1,273	382	2,500	6,405
1902	3,290	3,290	1,623	487	3,750	7,527
1903	3,011	3,011	2,177	653	3,750	7,414
1904	2,754	2,754	3,919	1,176	5,000	8,930
1905	3,964	3,964	8,133	2,440	5,000	11,404
1906	5,623	5,623	11,652	3,496	6,250	15,369
1907	4,672	4,672	16,337	4,901	6,250	15,823
1908	4,469	4,469	20,538	6,161	7,500	18,130
1909	4,405	4,405	25,589	7,677	7,500	19,582
1910	6,426	6,426	32,874	9,862	8,750	25,038
1911	8,544	8,544	37,746	11,324	8,750	28,618
1912	9,443	9,443	45,207	13,562	10,000	33,005
1913	11,264	11,264	53,153	15,946	10,000	37,210
Total..		74,542		78,348	87,500	240,390

[1] See note 1 to Table XXI, which applies also to the data in this column.

[2] Canada: Dept. of Immigration and Colonization, *Immigration Facts and Figures*, 1920. Adjusted
to calendar year basis from fiscal year statistics.

expenditure is probably much higher for the American tourists who visit Canada than for the Canadian tourists who visit the United States. The best guess possible in the absence of any statistical data is that Canadian tourists spend one half as much in the United States as is spent by American tourists in Canada.

Table XXII presents the statistics of expenditures by Canadian tourists abroad, as estimated.

SUNDRY ITEMS

There are a number of minor items of purchases and sales abroad of services by Canadians, for most of which statistical data are not available. Over 300 consuls and vice-consuls are maintained in Canada by foreign countries, and a number of trade commissioners by Great Britain, and their expenditures in Canada — to the extent to which they are met by remittances from their home countries and not by fees collected in Canada — should be considered as a credit item in the balance of international indebtedness. The expenditures of customs and immigration officials maintained by the United States in Canada should be similarly accounted for. There are always a considerable number of American and British commercial travelers and other agents in Canada, and their expenditures in Canada should also be considered as an export of services.

The only items of any importance on the other side of the balance are the expenditures in foreign countries of the Immigration Branch of the Department of the Interior in propaganda, office expenses, etc., and the mail and other subsidies paid to foreign steamship lines by the Canadian government. For these two items official statistics are collected. Canadian grants to missions abroad should also be mentioned, but no data as to their amount are available.

The expenditures of the immigration service in foreign countries during the period under study amounted approximately to a total of $7,750,000.[1] The mail and other subsidies granted during the same period amounted approximately to a total of $19,450,000.[2] Of this total, approximately 15 per cent went to

[1] *Immigration Facts and Figures*, 1920, p. 22.
[2] Canada: *Public Accounts*, 1920, p. 75.

steamship lines engaged in internal trade,[1] leaving 85 per cent, or approximately $16,500,000, as the payments on vessels sailing between Canada and other countries. Of this amount a minor fraction was paid to Canadian companies. The total amount of the payments made to foreign countries on account of the two items here considered may be taken to be roughly $20,000,000. There are no statistical data for the expenditures in Canada of officials of other countries or of commercial travelers and other agents of foreign business companies, but the amount of such expenditures is unquestionably at least as great as the payments by Canada discussed above. In the absence of data, it will be assumed that these two groups of items offset each other, and no further account will be taken of them in the final tabulation of the balance of international indebtedness.

The consideration of interest payments to and by Canada is postponed to the next chapter, where they will be dealt with in connection with capital investments. It is not yet possible, therefore, to strike a balance of the imports and exports of services.

[1] Computed from detailed data given in Canada: Dept. of Trade and Commerce, *Annual Report*, 1913, Part IV, pp. 28, 29.

CHAPTER V

CAPITAL INVESTMENTS, INTEREST PAYMENTS, AND THE CANADIAN BALANCE OF INTERNATIONAL INDEBTEDNESS

CANADIAN INVESTMENTS ABROAD AND INTEREST RECEIPTS THEREFROM

OWING to the almost complete absence of statistical data concerning the interest receipts from Canadian investments abroad, it is necessary to reach an estimate of the amount of such investments as a basis for estimating the interest payments to Canada from abroad.

There were during the period under study practically no public issues of foreign securities in Canada. Canadian financiers, it is true, have in recent years specialized in the promotion of light and power and tramway enterprises, and a number of public utilities in the United States, Cuba, Mexico, Porto Rico, Brazil, and Spain are controlled by Canadian interests. But the bulk of the capital actually invested in these enterprises is British. The Canadian control rests on ownership of common stock, consisting in large part of promoters' shares, and in most cases representing only a small fraction of the actual capital invested in the undertaking. The financing of these enterprises was done mainly through bond issues floated in London. Bonds issued by corporations operating under Canadian charters in foreign countries amounted from 1909 to 1913 inclusive to $120,500,000, of which only $7,200,000 were taken up in Canada.[1]

Private investments by Canadians in foreign securities, especially high-grade American investment securities, were, however, substantial in amount. The *Monetary Times*, of Toronto, in a recent issue commented on these holdings as follows:

Notwithstanding the liquidation that has taken place in three and a half years of war, it is said that there is still a considerable amount of high-grade

---

[1] E. R. Wood, *Annual Reviews of the Bond Market in Canada*. (Published by Dominion Securities Corporation, Ltd., Toronto.)

United States investment stocks held in the Dominion. Before the war the
business in Wall Street stocks transacted by Montreal and Toronto brokers
probably exceeded the business done in Canadian stocks. Many Canadian
capitalists and financiers were accustomed to carry considerable lines in
the United States stocks; also the wealthy American residents in Canada
and the highly paid executive officials of large United States branch indus-
trials located in this country, naturally leaned towards United States
securities in making their investments.[1]

Canadian railways owned or controlled 7,197 miles of road in
the United States in 1912.[2] These were largely roads acquired
before 1900, but some investment in expansion of lines, equipment, and terminal facilities was made during the period under
study. The Canadian insurance companies operating abroad
also had investments abroad in conformity with the insurance
laws of the countries in which they operated, but no statistics
relating to them are published. It is conservatively estimated,
on the basis of the scanty information available, that the miscellaneous foreign investments of Canadian capital made in the
period under study amounted to $50,000,000, distributed fairly
evenly through the period.

In addition to the miscellaneous investments, there are important investments abroad by the Canadian banks. The Canadian
banks hold substantial amounts of foreign securities, largely railway securities. Eckardt has estimated that, of the total holdings
of railway securities by the Canadian banks on February 28, 1901,
amounting to $27,496,000, at least $18,000,000 were foreign
securities.[3] It will be estimated here that two thirds of the holdings of railway securities by the Canadian banks consisted,
throughout the period, of foreign securities. But more important
than the holdings of foreign securities by the banks were their

[1] *Monetary Times* (Toronto), May 3, 1918. Canadian holdings of United States
Steel stocks in 1914 amounted to $7,892,000. (*Ibid.*, January 3, 1919.) A Montreal
capitalist, James Ross, at his death in 1913 left American securities amounting to
over $3,000,000. (*Ibid.*, December 27, 1913.) In the lists of the Montreal and
Toronto Stock Exchanges for 1912 and 1913 were included the securities of 14
non-Canadian enterprises, in 8 of which the annual transactions were substantial
in amount.

[2] *Canadian Annual Review*, 1912, p. 633.

[3] H. M. P. Eckardt, *Journal of the Canadian Bankers' Association*, vol. x, No. 2
(January, 1903), p. 4.

direct banking investments in foreign countries. The Canadian banks have a large number of branches abroad, and they also keep a considerable amount of funds in call loans abroad or on deposit with foreign banks. Tables XXIII and XXIV present the estimates of investments abroad by Canadian banks.

The bulk of the Canadian banking investments abroad consisted of call loans in New York, and on these the interest rate averaged 3.6 per cent throughout the period under study.[1] The net income would, of course, be substantially less, as banking expenses would have to be deducted therefrom. The interest on other Canadian investments abroad should average higher, probably somewhere between 4 and 5 per cent. It will be estimated that the average return on all Canadian investments abroad was 4 per cent. On December 31, 1899, the investments

[1] *Cost of Living Report*, vol. ii, p. 904.

TABLE XXIII

INVESTMENTS OF CANADIAN BANKS IN FOREIGN SECURITIES, 1900 TO 1913

In thousands of dollars

Year as of December 31	Holdings of railway securities by Canadian banks Total [1]	Holdings of railway securities by Canadian banks estimated foreign [2]	Increase in holdings of foreign securities over preceding year
1899	14,663	9,775	....
1900	25,507	17,005	7,230
1901	31,994	21,329	4,324
1902	36,925	24,617	3,288
1903	38,351	25,567	950
1904	38,744	25,829	262
1905	39,649	26,433	604
1906	41,455	27,637	1,204
1907	41,971	27,981	344
1908	44,213	29,475	1,494
1909	50,051	33,367	3,892
1910	59,519	39,679	6,312
1911	64,889	43,259	3,580
1912	68,840	45,893	2,634
1913	71,108	47,405	1,512
Total			37,630

[1] *Canada Gazette*, Monthly Bank Supplements. [2] Two thirds of preceding column.

abroad of Canadian banks, including both security and banking investments, amounted to $69,309,000. It is estimated, on the basis of what data have been found, that Canadian capital abroad in 1899 amounted to $100,000,000. Table XXV presents the final estimates of Canadian capital investments abroad, and interest receipts therefrom.

PRELIMINARY BALANCE OF INTERNATIONAL INDEBTEDNESS

Estimates have now been made for all the important classes of international transactions, with the exception of interest payments by Canada on its capital borrowings from abroad. The Canadian balance of international indebtedness in each year represents Canada's *net* borrowing or lending of capital, or the difference

TABLE XXIV

BANKING INVESTMENTS BY CANADIAN BANKS OUTSIDE OF CANADA, 1900 TO 1913 [1]

In thousands of dollars

| Year as of Dec. 31 | Assets in foreign countries | | | | | |
| | Due from banks in | | Call loans outside of Canada | Current loans outside of Canada | Specie held outside of Canada [2] | Total assets |
	United Kingdom	Foreign countries				
1899	12,078	22,291	25,303 [3]	13,896 [3]	2,797	76,365
1900	5,249	11,677	27,234	20,079	3,475	67,714
1901	6,883	11,456	45,263	32,160	5,330	101,092
1902	9,023	13,694	43,704	34,131	6,324	106,876
1903	9,258	12,703	34,991	18,616	5,861	81,429
1904	9,041	20,849	48,782	17,344	6,598	102,614
1905	8,308	14,344	61,010	30,882	7,491	122,035
1906	7,844	15,512	58,958	36,475	10,912	129,701
1907	6,074	16,308	43,509	22,928	9,079	97,898
1908	14,662	34,929	97,136	30,351	11,374	188,452
1909	7,295	24,114	138,505	40,072	12,765	222,751
1910	13,823	24,486	90,710	40,400	11,998	181,417
1911	20,740	25,667	92,106	37,970	13,703	190,186
1912	10,119	23,435	105,952	40,990	14,798	195,294
1913	9,312	25,601	115,984	58,305	19,478	228,680

[1] Data compiled from *Canada Gazette*, Monthly Bank Supplements.

[2] Separately reported only since July, 1913. Estimated to be 17 per cent of deposits outside of Canada, which was the average for July, 1913, to January, 1914.

between its borrowings and loans. If the basic items so far considered be tabulated and the balances between the debit and the
credit items struck for each year, and if there be added to these
balances the amounts of Canadian capital invested abroad, or
deducted from them the amounts of Canadian capital withdrawn
from abroad in each year, the resulting figures should represent
for each year the amounts of foreign capital invested in Canada
in that year, minus the interest payments by Canada in that year
on the total foreign capital invested in Canada.[1] This calculation
is made in Table XXVI.

[1] Minus the interest payments by Canada, because the interest charges have
not yet been added to the debits as imports of services, and the debit balances are
too low by the amounts of such charges.

TABLE XXIV

BANKING INVESTMENTS BY CANADIAN BANKS OUTSIDE OF CANADA,
1900 TO 1913[1]

In thousands of dollars

| Year as of Dec. 31 | Liabilities in foreign countries | | | | Excess of assets over liabilities | |
| | Due to banks in | | Deposits outside of Canada | Total liabilities | Amount | Increase or decrease over preceding year.[4] |
	United Kingdom	Foreign countries				
1899	4,360	908	16,451[3]	21,719	54,646	......
1900	4,190	526	20,442	25,158	42,556	*12,090*
1901	3,754	1,052	31,355	36,161	64,931	22,375
1902	5,611	1,157	37,199	43,967	62,909	2,022
1903	2,884	1,830	34,479	39,193	42,236	*20,673*
1904	2,452	1,224	38,814	42,490	60,124	17,888
1905	4,098	1,569	44,063	49,730	72,305	12,181
1906	8,207	1,716	64,191	74,114	55,587	*16,718*
1907	10,336	4,742	53,407	68,479	29,419	*26,168*
1908	2,186	2,979	66,903	72,068	116,384	86,965
1909	2,011	3,558	75,088	80,657	142,094	25,710
1910	1,573	4,374	70,574	76,521	104,896	*37,198*
1911	4,350	5,364	80,606	90,420	99,766	5,130
1912	8,312	7,982	87,050	103,344	91,950	7,816
1913	12,810	8,267	103,403	124,480	104,200	12,250
Total.						49,554

[3] As of July 31, 1900; not reported separately before this date.   [4] Decreases in italics.

Interest Rates on Foreign Capital invested in Canada

The final results of the calculation made in Table XXVI represent the amounts of foreign capital invested in Canada minus the interest payments by Canada on these investments. If estimates are made of the rates of interest paid on foreign capital invested in Canada, and of the total amount of foreign capital in Canada at the beginning of the period, it will be possible from the results of Table XXVI to calculate the amounts of the interest payments made by Canada and of the investments of foreign capital in Canada during the period of this study.

As the interest on foreign capital invested in Canada was an important item in the Canadian balance of international indebted-

TABLE XXV

CANADIAN CAPITAL INVESTMENTS ABROAD AND INTEREST RECEIPTS
THEREFROM, 1900 TO 1913

In thousands of dollars

Year	Investments by Canadian banks in		Miscellaneous Canadian investments abroad	Total [1]	Total Canadian capital abroad	Interest receipts therefrom [2]
	Foreign securities	Banking abroad [1]				
1899	....	....	....	....	100,000	....
1900	7,230	*12,090*	2,000	*2,860*	97,140	4,000
1901	4,324	22,375	2,000	28,699	125,839	3,886
1902	3,288	*2,022*	2,000	3,266	129,105	5,034
1903	950	*20,673*	3,000	*16,723*	112,382	5,164
1904	262	17,888	3,000	21,150	133,532	4,495
1905	604	12,181	3,000	15,785	149,317	5,341
1906	1,204	*16,718*	3,000	*12,514*	136,803	5,973
1907	344	*26,168*	4,000	21,824	114,979	5,472
1908	1,494	86,965	4,000	92,459	207,438	4,599
1909	3,892	25,710	4,000	33,602	241,040	8,298
1910	6,312	*37,198*	5,000	25,886	215,154	9,642
1911	3,580	*5,130*	5,000	3,450	218,604	8,606
1912	2,634	*7,816*	5,000	*182*	218,422	8,744
1913	1,512	12,250	5,000	18,762	237,184	8,737
Total..	37,630	49,554	50,000	137,184		87,991

[1] Withdrawals of capital from abroad in italics.
[2] Four per cent of amounts, one year preceding, of total Canadian capital abroad.

TABLE XXVI

PRELIMINARY BALANCE OF INTERNATIONAL INDEBTEDNESS, 1900 TO 1913

In thousands of dollars

Year	Debits						Credits							Preliminary Balances		
	Commodity imports (Table III)	Non-commercial debits (Table X)	Freight payments by Canada (Table XVI)	Insurance payments by Canada (Table XIX)[1]	Tourist expenditures by Canadians (Table XXII)	Total debits	Commodity exports (Table III)	Non-commercial credits (Table X)	Freight payments to Canada (Table XVIII)	Insurance payments to Canada (Table XX)	Tourist expenditures in Canada (Table XXI)	Interest payments to Canada (Table XXV)	Total credits	Excess of debits over credits[2]	Canadian capital invested abroad[3] (Table XXV)	Total of two preceding columns[4]
1900	180,276	7,113	9,210	527	5,935	211,007	184,940	10,162	3,630	669	7,054	4,000	210,455	552	2,860	2,308
1901	192,646	8,687	9,550	710	6,405	217,998	205,169	12,118	4,011	924	7,990	3,886	234,008	*16,100*	*28,699*	*12,599*
1902	212,830	11,853	9,944	4,285	7,527	246,439	215,900	20,930	4,333	1,162	11,048	5,034	258,407	*11,068*	3,266	*8,702*
1903	265,282	15,050	10,831	3,079	7,414	301,056	226,799	24,674	4,549	1,463	10,526	5,164	273,175	28,481	16,723	11,758
1904	256,827	18,860	11,380	3,152	8,930	292,845	198,059	23,006	3,931	1,647	12,784	4,495	244,822	48,023	21,150	60,173
1905	260,237	23,358	12,584	4,087	11,404	321,270	229,098	31,495	4,457	1,953	13,344	5,341	285,688	35,582	15,785	51,367
1906	320,560	29,991	14,557	4,684	15,369	394,161	267,737	36,659	5,062	2,023	16,796	5,973	334,250	59,911	12,514	47,397
1907	392,539	49,751	15,540	3,210	15,823	467,869	271,326	41,319	5,081	2,313	16,104	5,472	341,705	126,164	21,824	104,340
1908	312,575	45,833	14,128	3,052	18,130	393,718	268,057	38,201	5,303	2,497	19,202	4,599	337,859	55,859	92,459	148,318
1909	361,862	46,553	15,425	4,198	19,582	447,620	288,669	46,549	5,774	2,789	19,553	8,298	371,632	75,988	33,602	109,590
1910	450,371	54,603	18,785	3,854	25,038	553,051	296,648	54,228	5,908	2,980	24,744	9,642	304,150	158,501	25,886	132,615
1911	534,168	64,725	23,121	4,027	38,618	655,550	301,611	56,692	5,031	3,261	26,216	8,606	402,317	253,242	3,450	256,602
1912	651,232	77,565	28,509	6,357	33,005	706,668	375,724	54,174	7,259	3,646	29,403	8,744	478,950	317,718	*182*	317,536
1913	694,205	86,286	28,653	6,400	37,210	852,754	471,401	51,855	9,210	3,997	30,457	8,737	575,657	277,097	18,762	295,859
Total	5,112,610	531,228	222,223	45,764	240,390	6,152,215	3,801,138	502,062	74,439	31,324	245,311	87,991	4,743,165	1,409,050	137,184	1,546,234

[1] Excess of expenditures in Canada over premium receipts in italics.
[2] Excess of credits over debits in italics.
[3] Withdrawals of capital from abroad in italics.
[4] Credit balances in italics.

ness, it is important to secure as accurate an estimate as possible
of the rate of interest actually paid. Sir George Paish stated in a
speech in Toronto on December 4, 1913, that Great Britain had
lent £500,000,000 to Canada at only slightly over 4 per cent,
but that the capital borrowed by Canada from the United States
had been charged for at a higher rate.[1] Sir Edmund Walker, an
eminent Canadian banker, estimated at 4½ per cent the average
rate of interest on foreign investments in Canada.[2] Coats takes
the average interest rate on British capital in Canada at 5 per
cent throughout the period from 1900 to 1914.[3] More direct information is available bearing on the rates at which issues of
securities were sold and the average yield of various securities
at their market prices during the period under study.

Lehfeldt, from a careful study of the primary records, obtained
the following as the average rates of interest at which colonial
fixed-income stocks were issued in Great Britain: [4]

AVERAGE RATE OF RETURN ON LARGE COLONIAL INVESTMENTS ISSUED
TO PAY A FIXED RATE OF INTEREST

Year	Per cent	Year	Per cent
1900	3.20	1907	3.99
1901	3.40	1908	4.04
1902	3.21	1909	3.96
1903	3.21	1910	4.19
1904	3.78	1911	4.03
1905	3.78	1912	4.30
1906	3.85	1913	4.44

These averages cover bond and preferred stock flotations, but
do not include common stock issues. Lehfeldt found, however,
that common stock issues are only 10 per cent of the total British
investments in large issues, and the percentage of common stock
issues to total British investments outside of Great Britain would
undoubtedly be even lower. He found, also, that the yield of
common shares of large companies did not exceed by much the

[1] *Canadian Annual Review*, 1913, p. 28.

[2] Reported by T. H. Boggs, "Capital Investments and Trade Balances within
the British Empire," *Quarterly Journal of Economics*, vol. xxix, p. 786.

[3] *Cost of Living Report*, vol. ii, p. 891.

[4] R. A. Lehfeldt, "The Rate of Interest on British and Foreign Investments,"
Journal of the Royal Statistical Society, January and March, 1913.

interest paid on "loan money," the difference being roughly $\frac{1}{2}$ of one per cent in favor of shares.[1]

Lehfeldt's study shows that there was a steady trend throughout the period toward higher interest rates, but that not until 1908 did the average rate on new issues reach 4 per cent, and at no time during the period did it reach as high as 4.5 per cent. It was a matter of general comment in the financial press during this period that Canadian issues were being floated in London at more favorable rates than the issues of any other foreign or colonial countries. Lehfeldt's calculations, since they do not separate Canadian from other colonial capital flotations, and, moreover, do not cover the investments of the United States in Canada, which to only a very slight extent take the form of purchases of fixed-income securities, cannot be used as an index of the rate of interest paid on foreign capital invested in Canada. They are useful, however, as a check on other calculations.

Table XXVII presents some data, obtained from Canadian sources, bearing on the rate of interest yielded by Canadian investments. Also included in the table is an index of average annual interest rates yielded by investments in Canada for the period from 1900 to 1913, as computed from the data presented. The figures presented in this table for the average rate of interest yielded by various investments in Canada require a further note of explanation. With two exceptions, the data used in computing the final index were based on current market prices. The figures for the average rate of interest on the bonded debt of Canada were based on the par value of the debt. The figures for the average yield of the security investments of insurance companies were based on the book values, which, it may be supposed, were the cost prices less a depreciation reserve or less current deductions for depreciation in value. Because of the general upward trend of interest rates during the period, fixed-income securities fell in price.[2] The indices for yields of bonds in terms of current market prices therefore overestimate the rate of interest actually paid on the original investments. On the other hand, prices of in-

---

[1] *Op. cit.*, March, 1913, p. 415.
[2] Cf. *Cost of Living Report*, vol. ii, pp. 622, 709.

dustrial and other common shares rose considerably, and of preferred shares rose moderately, during the period.[1] The indices for the yields of these securities in terms of current market prices underestimate, therefore, the rate of yield of the original investments. A crude allowance has been made for the greater relative importance of bonds in the foreign investments in Canada, and also for the magnifying influence on the index, of interest yields if computed in terms of actual current prices, by giving to the index

[1] Cf. *Cost of Living Report*, vol. ii, pp. 602 seq.

TABLE XXVII

RATE OF INTEREST YIELDED BY INVESTMENTS IN CANADA, 1900 TO 1913

Year	Municipal bonds. Average interest yield at current market prices [1]			Industrial, railroad, and financial stocks and bonds. Interest yield at current market prices [2]			Average rate of yield on securities and loans of all fire insurance companies in Canada [3]	Average rate of interest of preceding items	Government of Canada. Average rate of interest paid on bonded debt [4]	Average rate of interest yielded by foreign investments in Canada
	Provincial governments	Large cities and Ontario counties	Large Ontario towns and townships	Common stocks	Preferred stocks	Bonds				
1900	3.56	3.81	4.06	5.3	5.5	4.99	3.51	4.39	3.67	4.03
1901	3.75	3.93	4.19	5.2	5.5	5.00	3.51	4.44	3.67	4.05
1902	3.75	3.93	4.19	5.1	5.5	4.94	3.64	4.43	3.67	4.05
1903	3.75	3.93	4.19	5.2	6.3	5.20	3.84	4.63	3.67	4.15
1904	3.75	3.93	4.19	5.3	6.5	5.33	3.94	4.71	3.63	4.17
1905	3.56	3.93	4.06	4.9	6.3	5.04	3.90	4.53	3.63	4.08
1906	3.56	3.93	4.06	5.0	6.7	5.00	4.22	4.64	3.66	4.15
1907	4.12	4.62	5.00	5.6	7.0	5.22	4.12	5.09	3.57	4.33
1908	4.12	4.62	5.00	5.6	7.3	5.29	4.32	5.18	3.56	4.37
1909	3.87	4.12	4.31	5.2	6.5	5.06	4.29	4.76	3.56	4.16
1910	3.90	4.21	4.56	5.3	6.4	5.04	4.36	4.83	3.53	4.18
1911	3.95	4.29	4.67	5.6	6.1	5.06	4.50	4.88	3.49	4.18
1912	4.12	4.75	5.12	5.5	5.9	5.06	4.61	5.01	3.47	4.24
1913	4.30	5.37	6.25	5.7	6.0	5.21	5.43	5.47	3.43	4.45

[1] C. H. Burgess, "Review of the Municipal Bond Market, 1896–1913," in *Monetary Times Annual*, January, 1914, pp. 80, 81.

[2] *Cost of Living Report*, vol. ii, p. 625; 55 common stocks, 5 preferred stocks, and 9 bonds used in making up these averages.

[3] Computed from statistics in *Canada Year Books* and *Annual Reports* of the Superintendent of Insurance, covering the amounts of income-earning assets in Canada and the interest and dividends from stocks, etc.

[4] Canada: *Public Accounts*, 1914, p. 75; based on par value of bonded debt, and exclusive of domestic loans.

for the yield of Canadian government bonds on a par value basis equal weight with the seven other indices combined.

Canada was obliged to pay interest, during the period under study, on foreign capital invested in Canada before 1900 as well as on the capital invested subsequent to 1900. Unless the loans matured and were converted to new loans on a different interest basis, the rates of interest payable on the investments made before 1900 would be those current at the time such investments were made.

Interest rates were relatively high before 1890 but were at an unusually low level in the last decade of the nineteenth century. In 1898 the Canadian government placed a large-sized loan at a price to yield only slightly over $2\frac{1}{2}$ per cent. Foreign investments made in Canada prior to 1900 consisted to a great extent of government and municipal loans and low-yield railroad and public utility bonds. Some important share investments had failed to yield dividends. It is estimated that on investments of foreign capital in Canada made before 1900 the average yield was 3 per cent until 1907, and, to make allowance for later conversion of old loans at higher rates, 4 per cent after 1907.

Sir Frederick Williams-Taylor, for many years the manager of the Bank of Montreal in London, in 1902 estimated at £205,405,-100 the total investments of British capital in Canada to date, through public flotations of securities.[1] In 1900 and 1901 the total public issue in London of new Canadian securities amounted to £2,282,000,[2] making the total public investment of British capital in Canada amount, at the end of 1899, to £203,123,100, or $989,209,497. Adding $150,000,000 for United States investments in Canada,[3] and $60,000,000 for British investments privately made and for investments in Canada of all other countries, gives a total investment, of foreign capital in Canada at the beginning of 1900, of approximately $1,200,000,000.

[1] F. Williams-Taylor, "Canadian Loans in London," *United Empire*, December, 1912.

[2] *Economist* (London), November 16, 1912, p. 1013.

[3] The estimate made by N. T. Bacon, "American International Indebtedness," *Yale Review*, November, 1900. It conforms fairly well in its total figure, although not in details, to estimates made by other writers for later years. See Chapter VI, pp. 127 seq.

INVESTMENTS OF FOREIGN CAPITAL IN CANADA, AND
INTEREST PAYMENTS BY CANADA

Interest on $1,200,000,000 at 3 per cent gives $36,000,000 as
the amount of interest paid by Canada in 1900 on investments of
foreign capital in Canada. Table XXVI presented for each year
the investments of Canadian capital abroad and the Canadian
net balances of indebtedness, but with interest payments by
Canada unaccounted for. Subtraction from the interest payments by Canada, in 1900, of the preliminary *credit* balance for
1900, as shown in Table XXVI, gives as a result the amount of
investment of foreign capital in Canada in that year. For each
subsequent year there must be included, in the statement of the
interest payments by Canada, interest on foreign capital invested
in Canada from the beginning of 1900 to the end of the year preceding, as well as interest on foreign capital invested in Canada
before 1900. The net investment of foreign capital in Canada in
each year can be ascertained by adding as debits the total interest payments by Canada in the corresponding year, to the
preliminary balances of indebtedness shown in Table XXVI.

In Table XXVIII the procedure explained in the foregoing
paragraph is used to ascertain the amounts of both the annual
payments of interest by Canada and the annual net [1] investments
of foreign capital in Canada. In the calculation of the amount of
interest payments, the index presented in Table XXVII is used
for interest payments on capital invested subsequent to January
1, 1900, and the estimate of 3 per cent until 1907 and 4 per cent
after 1907 is used for investments made prior to 1900.

The total interest and dividend payments to be made in or by
Canada were estimated for 1912 by the *Financial Post* of Toronto,
on the basis of the January payments through Canadian banks,
of company reports and of the government loan statement, at
$190,313,704. Of this total, $70,313,704 were accounted for by
interest and dividends on listed securities payable in Canada,
leaving $120,000,000 as the interest on foreign investments in

---

[1] *I. e.*, the excess of new investments over liquidation of old investments.

Canada.[1] In the present calculation the interest payments on foreign investments in Canada were estimated for 1912 as $117,466,000, which is under the circumstances a very close agreement.

It should be noted that foreign investments in Canada are the only item for which a direct estimate was not made, and that the estimate for the amount of such investments was obtained on the *a priori* assumption that immediate obligations must approximately balance each other each year and that any debit surplus remaining after the Canadian investments of capital abroad, plus

[1] Reported in U. S. *Commerce Reports*, February 1, 1912.

TABLE XXVIII

CAPITAL INVESTMENTS IN CANADA AND INTEREST PAYMENTS THEREON

In thousands of dollars

Year	I Total debit balance from Table XXVI[1]	Interest payments by Canada on capital invested in Canada			V Capital invested in Canada in given year (I + IV)	VI Total capital invested in Canada from 1900 to year previous to given year, inclusive	VII Average rate of interest (Table XXVII) *per cent* [2]
		II Before 1900	III From 1900 to year previous to given year, inclusive	IV Total			
1900	*2,308*	36,000	....	36,000	33,692	....	....
1901	12,599	36,000	1,365	37,365	49,964	33,692	4.05
1902	8,702	36,000	3,388	39,388	30,686	83,656	4.05
1903	11,758	36,000	4,741	40,741	52,499	114,242	4.15
1904	69,173	36,000	6,957	42,957	112,130	166,841	4.17
1905	51,367	36,000	11,382	47,382	98,749	278,971	4.08
1906	47,397	36,000	15,675	51,675	99,072	377,720	4.15
1907	104,340	36,000	20,645	56,645	160,985	476,792	4.33
1908	148,318	48,000	27,871	75,871	224,189	637,777	4.37
1909	109,590	48,000	35,858	83,858	193,448	861,966	4.16
1910	132,615	48,000	44,116	92,116	224,731	1,055,414	4.18
1911	256,692	48,000	53,510	101,510	358,202	1,280,145	4.18
1912	317,536	48,000	69,466	117,466	435,002	1,638,347	4.24
1913	295,859	48,000	89,226	137,226	433,085	2,073,349	4.45
Total	1,546,234	576,000	384,200	960,200	2,506,434		

[1] Credit balances in italics.   [2] Used in computing estimates in column III.

all the debit items, had been set off against all the credit items, must represent Canadian debit obligations whose settlement was deferred, that is, foreign investments of capital in Canada. By this method the estimate of the final balance when presented will bear an unearned air of exactitude. On the other hand, if direct evidence with regard to the amount of foreign capital in Canada approximately bears out the estimates reached here indirectly, it may be justly regarded as a satisfactory verification of the calculations made in this chapter, including the estimates for all the other items. The comparison of the estimate reached here of the amount of foreign capital invested in Canada with the direct evidence dealing with these investments is postponed to the next chapter.

TABLE XXIX

The Balance of Service Transactions, 1900 to 1913

In thousands of dollars

Year	Debits				
	Freight payments by Canada (Table XVI)	Insurance payments by Canada (Table XIX)[1]	Tourist expenditures by Canadians (Table XXII)	Interest payments by Canada (Table XXVIII)	Total debits
1900	9,210	527	5,935	36,000	50,618
1901	9,550	710	6,405	37,365	54,030
1902	9,944	4,285	7,527	39,388	61,144
1903	10,831	3,079	7,414	40,741	62,065
1904	11,380	3,152	8,930	42,957	60,115
1905	12,584	4,687	11,404	47,382	76,057
1906	14,557	4,684	15,369	51,675	86,285
1907	15,546	3,210	15,823	56,645	91,224
1908	14,128	3,052	18,130	75,871	111,181
1909	15,425	4,198	19,582	83,858	123,063
1910	18,785	3,854	25,038	92,116	139,793
1911	23,121	4,927	28,618	101,510	158,176
1912	28,509	6,357	33,005	117,466	185,337
1913	28,653	6,400	37,210	137,226	209,489
Total..	222,223	45,764	240,390	960,200	1,468,577

[1] Excess of expenditures over premium income in italics.

The Balance of Service Transactions

Before proceeding to the tabulation of the final balance of Canadian indebtedness, there can be presented, now that the interest payments by Canada have been estimated, the balance of service transactions (Table XXIX).

The Canadian Balance of International Indebtedness, 1900 to 1913

The Canadian balance of international indebtedness can now be computed from the three partial balances. In the calculation of international balances of indebtedness, usage is fairly evenly divided between, on the one hand, the practice of adding imports of services to imports of commodities, and, on the other hand, the

TABLE XXIX

The Balance of Service Transactions, 1900 to 1913

In thousands of dollars

Year	Credits					Debit balances
	Freight payments to Canada (Table XVIII)	Insurance payments to Canada (Table XX)	Tourist expenditures in Canada (Table XXI)	Interest payments to Canada (Table XXV)	Total credits	
1900	3,630	669	7,054	4,000	15,353	35,265
1901	4,011	924	7,990	3,886	16,811	37,219
1902	4,333	1,162	11,048	5,034	21,577	39,567
1903	4,549	1,463	10,526	5,164	21,702	40,363
1904	3,931	1,647	12,784	4,495	22,857	37,258
1905	4,457	1,953	13,344	5,341	25,095	50,962
1906	5,062	2,023	16,796	5,973	29,854	56,431
1907	5,081	2,313	16,194	5,472	29,060	62,164
1908	5,303	2,497	19,202	4,599	31,601	79,580
1909	5,774	2,789	19,553	8,298	36,414	86,649
1910	5,908	2,980	24,744	9,642	43,274	96,519
1911	5,931	3,261	26,216	8,666	44,014	114,162
1912	7,259	3,646	29,403	8,744	49,052	136,285
1913	9,210	3,997	30,457	8,737	52,401	157,088
Total..	74,439	31,324	245,311	87,991	439,065	1,029,512

practice of subtracting, as an offsetting factor, the imports of services from the exports of commodities. If the ascertainment of the balance of indebtedness is the only object sought, both usages bring identical results, and the divergence is to be regarded merely as a difference in bookkeeping methods. But logically the addition of imports of services to imports of commodities appears to have greater claim to validity. If what is sought is the total volume of international trade, including the trade in both commodities and services, the only valid method is to total all imports, whether of commodities or of services, on the one side, and all exports, whether of commodities or of services, on the other.

Non-commercial transactions cannot, however, be logically handled in the same manner. They are unilateral in character and, in so far as the total volume of international trade is concerned, they exhaust their effect in bringing about an import or export of commodities or services already accounted for in the commodity and service balances of trade. To add the non-commercial debits to the other debits, and the non-commercial credits to the other credits, is to exaggerate the volume of international transactions. To subtract non-commercial debits from commercial credits, and non-commercial credits from commercial debits, on the other hand, is to underestimate the volume of international transactions. In order to make the statement of the balance of international indebtedness represent also as closely as is practicable the total volume of international transactions, the method used will be to add to total commodity and service debits the debit *balances* of non-commercial transactions, and to add to commodity and service credits the credit *balances* of non-commercial transactions. As these *balances* were small, the total debits and the total credits will not appreciably exaggerate nor underestimate the actual volume of international transactions.

Tables XXX and XXXI, which follow below, summarize in tabular form the material presented so far in Part I of this study. Table XXX presents the Canadian balance of international indebtedness for the period of this study. Table XXXI shows that this balance was the result of a corresponding excess of Canadian borrowings from abroad over Canadian loans abroad.

TABLE XXX

The Canadian Balance of International Indebtedness, 1900 to 1913

In thousands of dollars

Year	Debits			
	Commodity Imports (Table III)	Debit service transactions (Table XXIX)	Non-commercial debit balances (Table X)	Total debits
1900	189,276	50,618	....	239,894
1901	192,646	54,030	....	246,676
1902	212,830	61,144	....	273,974
1903	265,282	62,065	....	327,347
1904	256,827	60,115	....	316,942
1905	269,237	76,057	....	345,294
1906	329,560	86,285	....	415,845
1907	392,539	91,224	....	483,763
1908	312,575	111,181	7,632	431,388
1909	361,862	123,063	4	484,929
1910	450,371	139,793	375	590,539
1911	534,168	158,176	8,033	700,377
1912	651,232	185,337	23,391	859,960
1913	694,205	209,489	34,431	938,125
Total....	5,112,610	1,468,577	73,866	6,655,053

Year	Credits				Debit balances of indebtedness
	Commodity exports (Table III)	Credit service transactions (Table XXIX)	Non-commercial credit balances (Table X)	Total credits	
1900	184,940	15,353	3,049	203,342	36,552
1901	205,169	16,811	3,431	225,411	21,265
1902	215,900	21,577	9,077	246,554	27,420
1903	226,799	21,702	9,624	258,125	69,222
1904	198,059	22,857	5,046	225,962	90,980
1905	229,098	25,095	8,137	262,330	82,964
1906	267,737	29,854	6,668	304,259	111,586
1907	271,326	29,060	568	300,954	182,809
1908	268,057	31,601	....	299,658	131,730
1909	288,669	36,414	....	325,083	159,846
1910	296,648	43,274	....	339,922	250,617
1911	301,611	44,014	....	345,625	354,752
1912	375,724	49,052	....	424,776	435,184
1913	471,401	52,401	....	523,802	414,323
Total..	3,801,138	439,065	45,600	4,285,803	2,369,250

Comparison of Present Calculation with Coats's Calculation

Table XXXII presents a comparison of the results of the present calculation for the entire period 1900 to 1913 with Coats's calculation for approximately the same period. In general the calculations are not in close agreement either as to total results or as to the constituent items. The divergencies are due in part to the varying periods covered by the data used by Coats,[1] and to his use of the uncorrected statistics of imports and exports. In the main, however, they are due to the use, in the two calculations, of different statistical data and of different methods of

[1] His study in some of its details covers the years 1900–1913; in others, 1900–1914; in a few instances the period covered is less than fourteen years.

TABLE XXXI

The Balance of International Indebtedness and Capital Investments, 1900 TO 1913

In thousands of dollars

Year	I Foreign investments of capital in Canada (Table XXVIII)	II Canadian investments of capital abroad (Table XXV)[1]	III The Canadian debit balance of international indebtedness (I–II)
1900	33,692	*2,860*	36,552
1901	49,964	28,699	21,265
1902	36,686	3,266	27,420
1903	52,499	*16,723*	69,222
1904	112,130	21,150	90,980
1905	98,749	15,785	82,964
1906	99,072	*12,514*	111,586
1907	160,985	21,824	182,809
1908	224,189	92,459	131,730
1909	193,448	33,602	159,846
1910	224,731	25,886	250,617
1911	358,202	3,450	354,752
1912	435,002	*182*	435,184
1913	433,085	18,762	414,323
Total	2,506,434	137,184	2,369,250

[1] Withdrawals of capital from abroad in italics.

estimating where statistical data were lacking. Coats does not make estimates for the individual years, and as, for our purpose, the figures for individual years are of much more importance than those for the total period, it would have been impossible in any case to rely wholly on the analysis made by Coats of the Canadian balance of indebtedness. In the next chapter, verification of the present calculation is sought by comparing the estimate reached here for foreign investments in Canada with the available data bearing directly on the amounts of such investments.

TABLE XXXII

COMPARISON OF PRESENT CALCULATION OF CANADIAN BALANCE OF
INTERNATIONAL INDEBTEDNESS WITH COATS'S CALCULATION
FOR THE ENTIRE PERIOD, 1900 TO 1913

In thousands of dollars

	Present calculation	Coats's calculation [1]
Debits		
Commodity Imports.............	5,112,610	5,359,700
Service Transactions.............	1,468,577	1,815,000
Non-Commercial Debit Balances....	73,866	....
Total Debits....................	6,655,053	7,174,700
Credits		
Commodity Exports.............	3,801,138	4,031,400
Service Transactions.............	439,065	160,000
Non-Commercial Credit Balances ..	45,600	305,000
Total Credits....................	4,285,803	4,496,400
Debit Balance of Indebtedness	2,369,250	2,678,300
	6,655,053	7,174,700
Foreign Capital Invested in Canada..	2,506,434	2,713,300
Canadian Capital Invested Abroad ..	137,184	35,000
Debit Balance of Indebtedness......	2,369,250	2,678,300

[1] *Cost of Living Report*, vol. ii, p. 906. Coats's results are rearranged to correspond to the method of presentation followed in the present study.

CHAPTER VI

INVESTMENTS OF FOREIGN CAPITAL IN CANADA
A VERIFICATION OF ESTIMATES MADE
IN CHAPTER V

THE NATURE OF THE PROBLEM

IN the preceding chapter the amount of foreign capital invested in Canada during the period 1900 to 1913 inclusive was estimated at $2,506,434,000. The estimate was reached indirectly, on the assumption that there must be each year an equal balance between immediate debit and credit obligations, and that, if all items affecting the international balance of indebtedness except foreign investments in Canada are accounted for, any apparent debit excess shown must be explained as due to and measuring the amount of such investments. It should not be necessary here to offer a justification of the fundamental principles upon which this assumption is based. But this is a roundabout way of reaching the amount of foreign investments in Canada, and, moreover, it is the only estimate presented in the preceding chapter which is not based on an examination of the available statistical data bearing directly upon the point under consideration. In this chapter an attempt is made to verify this estimate by an examination of the direct statistical evidence bearing upon the amount of foreign capital invested in Canada.

There is available a considerable quantity of data bearing on the investment of foreign capital in Canada during the period under study. Unfortunately, much of it is of questionable accuracy and all of it together fails to cover the entire field. Moreover, statistics of international investments have certain characteristics which invariably render it difficult, if not impossible, to obtain complete and accurate measurements of the amount of such investments. In the last resort, after special classes of investments have been more or less accurately compiled on the basis of fairly complete and accurate data, use must be made of conjectural material for those classes of investments for which equally satisfactory data cannot be secured.

BRITISH INVESTMENTS IN CANADA

British Public Investments in Canada

The term "public" is commonly applied to capital investments made through the issue of securities for public sale after advertisement in financial journals. For such part of the foreign investments in Canada as took this initial form there are available a number of compilations claiming completeness. But even within this restricted field, statistical compilations must be used with caution. Public issues of securities almost invariably are made through brokers or agents in the buying market. Compilations of such issues may be based on the nominal or par values, or on the actual issue prices of the securities, and for common shares the results obtained will vary appreciably as one or the other method is used. To ascertain the actual investment of capital in Canada, compilation on the basis of the issue price is preferable for both fixed-income securities and common stocks. To ascertain the actual indebtedness of Canada to other countries, compilations on the basis of the par value are certainly preferable for bonds and debenture stocks; for share securities, which involve no contractual obligations to repay a specified principal at some future date, it appears to be a debatable question which method of compilation is preferable. For our present purpose, which is to ascertain the actual movement of capital into Canada, compilations only on the basis of the issue price are admissable, and the estimate reached in the previous chapter, if it be accurate, is a measure on this basis of the amount of foreign capital invested in Canada from 1900 to 1913. But even from the compilation based on the issue price, there should be deducted vendors' or promoters' shares.

Where an issue is simultaneously floated in more than one foreign money market, the total issue may be recorded in the compilations of two or more of these markets. Or a foreign market may be credited with taking all of an issue, although part of it was subscribed for in the domestic market. The writer has found several instances where a Canadian security issue partly subscribed for in Canada has been credited to London for its total amount, with a consequent overestimate of the amount of Canadian borrowings. Moreover, a part of an issue floated in one market may eventually find its way to another market through private purchase on the stock exchange, and may enter into the estimates both for the public investments in Canada of one country and the private investments of another.

Canadian issues, if floated in foreign markets, are usually, although not invariably, made payable both as to principal and interest in the currency of the lending country. Theoretically, conversion to Canadian currency should be made at the current rate of exchange, but as, under the normal conditions ruling on the foreign markets during the period under study, the current quotations never varied substantially from the mint pars of exchange, the latter are a satisfactory basis for conversion. In this particular instance the awkwardness, for purposes of easy calculation, of the mint par of exchange between the £ sterling and the Canadian dollar — $4.8665 to the £[1] — has led to frequent use, for ease in conversion, of $5 Canadian as the equivalent of £1 sterling, with a consequent overestimate from this factor alone of almost 3 per cent of the amount of British capital invested in Canada.

A further source of possible error lies in the confusion between the amount authorized and the amount actually issued. Occasionally, also, when an issue is greatly undersubscribed, the unsubscribed part of the issue is withdrawn to be replaced later by a new issue on more favorable terms to the investor. Care must be taken in such instances to avoid double inclusion of the amount reissued.

Finally, what is sought here is the amount of net investment of foreign capital in Canada, or the excess of new investments over liquidation of old investments. The period under study, however, was marked by a constantly growing capital indebtedness of Canada to foreign countries, and there was little or no liquidation of old debts upon maturity, except through conversion into a new security issue or from proceeds of a new issue.[2] Some of

---

[1] The legal par of exchange is $4.86⅔, but the actual mint par is as stated in the text.

[2] In the course of a careful examination of a great mass of data bearing on the

the compilations exclude conversion loans and new issues made to liquidate maturing obligations. The possibility of serious error from this source can, therefore, be guarded against.

Annual Compilations

Table XXXIII on page 112 presents for purposes of comparison four annual compilations, two English and two Canadian, of the amounts of Canadian securities publicly issued in London.[1] One of the compilations covers bond issues only.

These statistics, it should be made clear, are not estimates in the ordinary sense of the term, but are actual compilations made each year from the notices of issue. The substantial disagreements between the four compilations, in the field of foreign investments where the obstacles to accurate measurement are least formidable, indicate the difficulties which face any attempt to secure reliable statistics of the amount of international capital investments. Some of the discrepancies in the figures for individual years can be explained as due to the use of different bases for allocation of issues to particular years. Choice lies between the dates of announcement of issue, of payment of the first instalment, and of final payment, and anywhere from three to fifteen months commonly elapses between the first and the last dates. Most of the discrepancy must be explained, however, as due either to incompleteness of compilation or to one or more of the possible sources of error discussed above.

Wood's compilation, it is important to note, covers only bond issues.[2] It is sufficient comment on the need for caution in using statistics of international investments that for the seven years, 1907 to 1913, which are covered by all four of the original compilations presented in Table XXXIII, Wood's total for bond issues alone, $1,187,161,000, is in excess of the *Economist's* and

details of foreign investments in Canada, the writer has not found a single instance, during the period under study, of the liquidation upon maturity of a Canadian issue other than by conversion into a new security or by use of the cash proceeds of a new issue.

[1] Shares sold only to shareholders, if publicity is given to such issues, are included in the two English compilations.

[2] Including so-called "debenture stocks."

of Field's totals for both stocks and bonds, \$1,105,262,000 and \$1,152,239,000, respectively, and is only slightly less than the *Statist's* total, \$1,217,927,000, for both stocks and bonds. Although, in the public issues of Canadian securities in London,[1] bonds predominate, the close agreement of the three totals for bonds and stocks with Wood's total for bonds alone cannot be explained as due to smallness of the stock issues, since these amounted during this period to at least \$300,000,000.

[1] Canadian public issues in Great Britain outside of London, all authorities agree, are negligible, if not actually zero.

TABLE XXXIII

Public Issues of Canadian Securities in Great Britain, 1900 to 1913

In thousands of dollars

Year	Compilations of			
	London *Economist*[1]	London *Statist*[2]	F. W. Field[3]	E. R. Wood[4]
1900	3,068	. . . . . .	. . . . . .	. . . . . .
1901	8,045	. . . . . .	. . . . . .	. . . . . .
1902	4,641	. . . . . .	. . . . . .	. . . . . .
1903	21,652	. . . . . .	. . . . . .	. . . . . .
1904	21,934	. . . . . .	. . . . . .	. . . . . .
1905	51,456	. . . . . .	65,892	85,621
1906	42,656	. . . . . .	31,302	26,564
1907	25,256	37,020	54,562	63,095
1908	133,944	152,478	142,957	165,455
1909	124,687	183,538	182,195	176,107
1910	176,990	160,903	187,270	183,170
1911	200,717	179,184	194,096	177,769
1912	228,808	182,140	160,499	166,481
1913	214,860	322,664	230,660	255,084
Total..	1,258,714	1,217,927	1,249,433	1,299,346

[1] *Economist* (London), July 8, 1911, and June 13, 1914. Converted from £ sterling at \$4.87 = £1.

[2] *Statist* (London), Supplement, February 14, 1914. Converted from £ sterling at \$4.87 = £1.

[3] *Capital Investments in Canada* (1914 ed.), Appendix. Pp. 259–282. Converted from £ sterling at \$4.87 = £1.

[4] For 1908 to 1913, from E. R. Wood, *Annual Reviews of the Bond Market in Canada.* For 1905 to 1907, from *Monetary Times Annual*, January, 1919, p. 50, based on compilations by Wood. Figures for 1905 to 1908 may include small amounts of British subscriptions to issues of Canadian companies operating abroad. For the later years, these have been deducted from the totals as given by Wood.

The *Statist* and the *Economist* compilations, in so far as information regarding the methods used in constructing them is given, have essentially the same basis. They both tabulate the issues at their issue price; they both exclude conversion issues and vendors' or promoters' shares; they both make deductions from new issues for proceeds used to meet maturities of old obligations, where information is given. The marked discrepancy between the two compilations for 1913, amounting to $107,804,-000, is partly accounted for by the inclusion of a large issue of Canadian Pacific Railway common shares in 1912, the announcement year, by the *Economist*, and in 1913, the subscription year, by the *Statist*. This still leaves important discrepancies between the two compilations, with an excess, amounting to $112,665,000 for the common period 1907-1913, for the *Statist* over the *Economist* compilation, apparently to be explained only by incomplete compilation on the part of the *Economist*.

The Wood compilation for bond issues is constructed in terms of Canadian currency, generally — although apparently not uniformly — on the basis of an arbitrary conversion value from English currency to Canadian of $5 to the £ sterling, and of par instead of issue prices, but with more care than any of the other compilations, where issues were made in more than one market, in distributing the issues among the markets in accordance with the subscription thereto in each market. There probably results from the first two factors an overestimate greater than the downward correction made by the third but not sufficient, nevertheless, to explain the size of the total reached, if the English compilations based on both bond and stock issues are substantially accurate. Wood's compilation, however, unlike the English ones, makes no reduction for conversion issues and for new issues used to redeem maturing obligations. These amount to substantial figures, sufficient, it appears from an examination of the available data, substantially to explain the remaining discrepancies between Wood's compilation and those of the *Statist* and the *Economist*.

The *Statist* total for the years 1907-1913 exceeds Field's total for the same period by $65,688,000. Field uses par values in compiling his total. For share securities the difference between par and issue prices is often very great; and in most cases where Canadian shares were not issued at par they were issued at less than par,— in some cases at as low rates as 25 and 50 per cent of par,—so that errors in one direction are not substantially offset by errors in the other direction.[1] This, of course, operates to exaggerate the amount of foreign capital invested in Canada. Moreover, Field makes no reduction for conversion issues and redemptions of maturities from the proceeds of new issues. That the *Statist* compilation should nevertheless present higher totals than the Field compilation suggests, therefore, that there are important omissions from Field's lists of issues. The British subscriptions to Canadian Pacific issues of ordinary shares to shareholders amounted during this period to only $116,000,000 at the par values and to at least $153,000,000 at the actual issue prices.[2] Field included some of these issues in his compilation and excluded others, but upon what principle he does not indicate. But there are other important omissions from Field's compilation, particularly of bond issues, which can be explained only as due to oversight or to incomplete facilities for gathering information regarding such issues.

For the four years 1909 to 1913 both Wood and Field presented, in connection with their compilations, the complete data from which these were compiled, including in most instances both the par and the issue prices, but not including for Wood's compilations the details of municipal issues. From the material thus made available and from materials obtained from other sources such as the official annual reports on Canada's funded debt [3] and the files of Canadian and English financial journals, extensive — although not complete — information bearing on the amount of

[1] The conspicuous and important instance of the issue of Canadian share securities at higher than par is in the case of the Canadian Pacific Railway issues of ordinary shares to shareholders only at premiums of 25 to 75 per cent. Most of these issues are not included, however, in the Field compilation. (See text.) Canadian bank shares are commonly issued at a premium, but, with minor exceptions, they are floated in the Canadian market.

[2] F. W. Field, *Capital Investments in Canada*, 1914 ed., pp. 22 and 125.

[3] Canada: *Public Accounts*.

issues floated for conversion purposes or to redeem maturities
was obtained. From this material the issues of Canadian securities
in the British market were recompiled, as far as possible on the
basis of: issue prices, the exclusion of conversion and redemption
loans, the inclusion of 60 per cent of the Canadian Pacific issues to
shareholders,[1] the conversion of sterling to dollars at the rate of
$4.87 to £1 sterling, and the allocation to Great Britain, wherever
information as to issues distributed in several markets was available, of only such portions of the issues as were subscribed for
in Great Britain. Both the details and the final results showed
that Field's compilation was carelessly made and that, apart
from arithmetical and other errors, there were serious omissions
and mistaken attributions to Great Britain of all or part of issues
largely subscribed for elsewhere. Wood's compilation of bond
issues, however, apart from the points made above, withstood the
detailed examination without disclosing any important errors or
omissions. The results obtained from this compilation, as compared with the other compilations for the corresponding years,
are given in Table XXXIV.

The present compilation, it will be noted, is in closest agree-

[1] This is the proportion in which Canadian Pacific Railway common stock was
held in Great Britain in 1913. (F. W. Field, *Capital Investments in Canada,* 1914
ed., p. 125.)

TABLE XXXIV

Public Issues of Canadian Securities in Great Britain, 1910 to 1913

In thousands of dollars

Year	Compilations of				Present compilation
	London *Economist*	London *Statist*	F. W. Field	E. R. Wood	
1910	176,990	160,903	187,270	183,170	177,926
1911	200,717	179,184	194,096	177,769	218,095
1912	228,808	182,140	160,499	166,481	187,140
1913	214,860	322,664	230,660	255,084	324,235
Total..	821,375	844,891	772,525	782,504	907,396

ment with that of the *Statist*, and in fact is in almost exact agreement for the last two years of the period. The discrepancies between these two compilations for 1910 and 1911 are to be explained either by more complete deduction by the *Statist* for conversion and redemption issues, or by fuller compilation by the writer, or by both factors. It is the belief of the writer that the second factor is the more important source of disagreement, and that a detailed comparison of the *Statist* and the present compilations, if it were possible, would reveal some omissions even from the present compilation. Where totals are reached by enumeration from data appearing in scattered sources and irregularly, and no improper inclusions are made, some degree of underestimate must almost inevitably result. On these grounds it is believed that the figures presented in the present compilation are the nearest to accuracy.[1]

For the years 1900 to 1904 the *Economist* figures are the only ones available; for 1905 and 1906 the *Economist* figures are preferable to those of Field and Wood for the reasons given above; for the years 1907 to 1909 the *Statist* figures are chosen for similar

[1] Annual compilations of British investments abroad made by the *London Times* and the *London Financial Times* were not available for comparison. The *London Daily Telegraph* of December 11, 1913, gave the amount of Canadian public borrowings in London in 1912 and in 1913 up to the date of publication, without deductions of conversion issues, as $204,915,000 and $310,041,020 respectively, which is in fair agreement with the present calculation. (*Canadian Annual Review*, 1913, p. 27.) No other compilations are known to the writer.

TABLE XXXV

BRITISH PUBLIC INVESTMENTS IN CANADIAN SECURITIES, 1900 TO 1913

In thousands of dollars

Year		Year	
1900 [1]	3,068	1908 [2]	152,478
1901 [1]	8,045	1909 [2]	183,538
1902 [1]	4,641	1910 [3]	177,926
1903 [1]	21,652	1911 [3]	218,095
1904 [1]	21,934	1912 [3]	187,140
1905 [1]	51,456	1913 [3]	324,235
1906 [1]	42,656		
1907 [2]	37,020	Total	1,433,884

[1] *Economist*.　　　[2] *Statist*.　　　[3] Present compilation.

reasons; and for the years 1910 to 1913 the results of the present compilation are used. The figures chosen as representing the amount of British capital publicly invested in Canada during the period under investigation are given in Table XXXV.

Total British Holdings of Canadian Securities

The calculations made so far with respect to the amount of British public investments in Canada were based altogether on compilations of the *annual flow* of capital to Canada. There is available another body of data dealing not with the amount of British capital publicly invested in Canada year by year, but with the *total amounts* of British holdings of Canadian securities at different periods. Such estimates can be reached by two different methods: (*a*) the compilation, from available sources, of the total issues in Great Britain of Canadian securities up to the date of compilation, less the amount of redemptions, maturities, repudiations, and bankruptcies; (*b*) the compilation of the Canadian securities listed on the day of compilation on the British stock exchanges. The first method is much more likely to yield results comparable to those obtained by compilations of the annual public issues in Great Britain of Canadian securities. The estimates based on the second method may include British investments in Canadian securities which were never issued publicly in Great Britain; may not make proper allowance for parts of issues held in other countries; and may not include British holdings of Canadian securities which were publicly issued on the British market, but are nevertheless not listed on any British stock exchange. If allowance is made for these possible causes of inconsistency with statistics of public issues such as those examined above, estimates of British holdings of Canadian securities at different dates make possible the testing of the figures given above for the public investments of British capital in Canada during the periods between these dates.

What appears to be for our purposes the most satisfactory estimate of British holdings of Canadian securities is that made for the end of 1902 and for the latter part of 1912 by Mr. (later Sir) Frederick Williams-Taylor, Manager throughout this period of the Bank of Montreal branch in London.[1] His estimates are based on a compilation of issues, less redemptions and conversions, and cover only borrowings through the medium of public issues, but are inclusive of Canadian Pacific Railway issues of common stock to shareholders only. Whether par or issue prices are used is not indicated. His totals are £205,405,100 for the end of 1902 and £410,449,000 for late in 1912, indicating a total net public investment in Canada of £205,043,900, or $998,563,793, between the two dates. This compares with the estimate made above for the years 1903 to 1912 inclusive, of $1,093,895,000. Even closer agreement would be shown if to Williams-Taylor's total for 1912 be added the issues made between the date on which it was compiled and December 31, 1912.[2] Moreover, there are undoubtedly some omissions, especially of minor issues, from Williams-Taylor's compilation.[3] His compilation may be taken, therefore, as a substantial verification of the present estimate.

Edgar Crammond [4] has made similar estimates for 1906 and 1910, based, however, on compilations from the lists of active securities of all British stock exchanges and from additional data given in the (London) *Stock Exchange Official Intelligence*.[5] His figures for total British holdings of listed Canadian securities as of December 31, 1906, and 1910,[6] are £251,900,000 and £365,000,000, respectively, indicating a total net investment in

---

[1] In a paper on "Canadian Loans in London," read before the Royal Colonial Institute (London), on November 14, 1912, and published in *United Empire*, the Journal of the Institute, for December, 1912. Sir Williams-Taylor's fitness for this task may be indicated by the fact that over 50 per cent of the British public investments in Canada are effected through the London branch of the Bank of Montreal.

[2] Williams-Taylor made his estimate public on November 14, 1912. During November and December, 1912, there were public issues of Canadian securities in Great Britain amounting to at least $15,000,000. (Cf. Field, *Capital Investments in Canada*, 1914 ed., p. 277.)

[3] I have been able to identify two omissions of security issues by small municipalities and three omissions of security issues by small railways. One of these omitted railway issues was made early in October, 1912, which may mean that the compilation under consideration did not cover the issues of this month, which amounted to at least $25,000,000 (*ibid.*).

[4] During this period, Secretary of the Liverpool Stock Exchange.

[5] "British Investments Abroad," *Quarterly Review*, July, 1907, and July, 1911.

[6] The *Economist* published for the same date, December 31, 1910, an estimate of

Canadian securities during the four-year period, 1907 to 1910, of £113,100,000, or $550,797,000. The figure for the same period reached by the present estimate is almost identical, namely, $550,962,000. The data covered by the two estimates are probably not precisely identical, especially because there are probably included, in Crammond's totals, portions of listed issues held elsewhere than in Great Britain and so accounted for in the present estimate, but his omissions of publicly issued Canadian securities not listed on any of the British exchanges may well offset the error arising from this source. The close agreement between Crammond's and the present estimate may, therefore, be regarded as further verification of the calculations made above.

Sir George Paish, one of the editors of the London *Statist*, estimated at £373,541,000 the total amount of British capital publicly invested in Canada at the end of 1910. He based his estimate for government issues on a capitalization of the income received by British holders of Canadian federal and provincial government loans as reported to the British income tax authorities, and for corporation issues, on an examination of the individual company reports.[1] Early in 1914 he estimated the total British public capital investments in Canada as of December, 1913, at £514,870,000.[2] This last-cited figure corresponds closely, however, to his estimate for 1910 plus the *Statist* annual figures of Canadian public issues in London for the three subsequent years,[3] and is probably not independent of the annual compila-

£365,368,800 for the amount of British capital in Canada, compiled from the *Official List* of the London Stock Exchange and, for mining stocks, from figures given in *Mathieson's Mining Handbook*. The London Stock Exchange *Official List* it was explained, contained no defunct or redeemed issues, and included "practically every important colonial issue which had been offered in London " (*Economist*, June 21, 1911). Although the method of compilation used by the *Economist* appears to have varied somewhat from that used by Crammond, it brought identical results.

[1] *Journal of Royal Statistical Society*, September, 1909, pp. 465–480; January, 1911, pp. 167–187.

[2] *Statist*, Supplement, February 14, 1914.

[3] According to the *Statist* series, the capital publicly issued in London for Canada from 1911 to 1913 inclusive amounted to £140,449,447. According to Paish's estimates of the total amounts of British capital publicly invested in Canada, the net increase during these three years in such investments amounted to £141,329,000.

tion. As the *Statist* series has already been considered, no further confirmation can be derived from this estimate.

British Private Investments in Canada

It is much more difficult to secure satisfactory estimates of private than of public investments in Canada. Private investments take a great number of forms; in most cases they receive little publicity; and no comprehensive and systematic efforts have ever been made to compile annual totals for such investments from actual information. Resort must necessarily be had, therefore, to estimates of a very rough sort, based upon whatever information is available. The most comprehensive estimate for Canada is that of F. W. Field, formerly editor of the *Monetary Times* of Canada. But the material upon which he bases his estimates contains duplications; part of it covers only the period from 1905 to 1913; important classes of private investment are omitted; and some of the guesses made in the absence of better statistical facilities appear of questionable worth. Field's estimates must therefore be used with great caution.

Private Sales to Great Britain of Canadian Securities

In addition to the public issues of Canadian securities in Great Britain, substantial amounts of Canadian securities are privately sold in Great Britain. These private sales may in a rough way be divided into two classes: first, sales by issuing governments or corporations, of entire issues or large blocks of new issues at the time of issue, direct to investment companies or to syndicates of private-investors; and, second, the transfer of small lots of Canadian securities from Canadian to British ownership in the ordinary course of security broker or stock exchange transactions.

For sales of securities of the first class, the following quotation is of interest: [1]

In addition to Canada's public borrowings in London, many blocks of Canadian securities are sold there privately. That is, they are not taken by public subscription, but are purchased by financial houses for distribution to their clients or by investors direct. In some cases public issues are subsequently made.

[1] *Monetary Times Annual*, January, 1914, p. 85.

Search through the files of the *Monetary Times* from 1910 to 1913 produced data accounting for $6,563,000 of such sales in 1910, $3,500,000 in 1912, and $8,692,000 in 1913, a total for the four years, of $18,755,000. This is unquestionably an incomplete compilation for these years, and leaves similar sales in the earlier years altogether unaccounted for, but there is no source providing more complete information. Field has estimated the total private sales of Canadian municipal securities to British shareholders, since 1905, at $10,000,000 by 1909,[1] $12,000,000 by early in 1911,[2] and $15,000,000 by the end of 1913.[3] It will be estimated here that private sales of municipal securities from 1900 to 1905 amounted to $5,000,000.

For private sales of securities of the second class, that is, small-lot sales through brokers to British investors, of securities originally issued in Canada, there is, and perhaps can be, no direct information. Two possible sources of information with regard to the British holdings of securities issued in Canada are: the annual lists of shareholders, with addresses and amounts held, which the Canadian banks are required by law to issue; and the British probate records, which might disclose holdings of such securities in the estates of British deceased. The British probate records are not available. The lists of shareholders in Canadian banks are issued annually as a government document, but they are bulky volumes with absolutely no attempt at classification or analysis of the data they contain.[4] Some of the banks have made public or private issues of their securities in Great Britain, but the bulk of their securities was issued in Canada. Sampling the data given in these reports, by taking the first six pages of the lists for each bank in 1899 and 1913, indicates that the British holdings of Canadian bank securities, exclusive of those banks which made issues in England, were at both dates somewhere between $7\frac{1}{2}$ and 12 per cent of the total issues. Analysis of a list of the holdings of the 41 largest individual shareholders in Canadian banks at the end of 1913 showed that, at the market prices in

---

[1] *Monetary Times*, November 13, 1909.

[2] *Capital Investments in Canada*, 1911 ed., p. 9.   [3] *Ibid.*, 1914 ed., p. 9.

[4] Canada: Dept. of Finance, *Annual Lists of Shareholders in Canadian Banks.*

1913, approximately 14 per cent of these holdings were in the
United States, 5 per cent in Great Britain, and 4 per cent in
other countries outside of Canada.[1] British shareholders undoubtedly comprised a larger percentage of the small than of the
very large holdings, but in the case of the United States the reverse was probably true. The estimate is made, based on this
and other information, that British investors from 1900 to 1913
placed $10,000,000 in Canadian bank capital through private
purchases in small lots of Canadian bank shares.

It is probable that Canadian bank shares, because of their
good reputation as investment securities, are held by foreign
investors in relatively larger amounts than other Canadian securities which are issued on the Canadian market and which are not
listed on any foreign exchange. On the other hand, the double
liability which attaches to Canadian bank shares has generally
been supposed seriously to injure their saleability in foreign countries. It is perhaps a conservative estimate, considering the great
amount of Canadian security issues, that British small-lot purchases of Canadian securities, including bank shares, amounted to
$25,000,000 from 1900 to 1913.

Treasury Bills

Canadian governmental bodies sometimes borrow in London
by means of Treasury Bills, to tide over a temporary period of
inadequate revenue, or in anticipation of the floating of a permanent bond issue to fund the floating debt. No attempt will
be made to account for such borrowings throughout the period
under study, partly because information bearing thereon is inadequate, partly because such loans are either redeemed or
funded shortly after their flotation. If they are redeemed, they
affect the flow of capital in reverse directions in the years of
flotation and redemption, respectively, but they were generally
not substantial in amount, and it is not possible to obtain the
data necessary to account for them here. If they are funded
through a bond issue, they are then accounted for, although
belatedly, in the compilation of public issues for that year.

[1] *Monetary Times Annual*, January, 1914. p. 42.

In 1912 and 1913, because of the unfavorable conditions then ruling for Canadian borrowers in the London market, both Canadian governments and private corporations resorted extensively to short-term loans to tide them over what was believed to be only a temporarily unfavorable money market. As the period under study ends on December 31, 1913, it would be proper to include as part of Canada's borrowings the amount of such loans which had not been redeemed by that date. Here again complete information is not available, but an incomplete compilation from data given in Canadian financial journals gives a total of $22,937,700 for such loans during 1913, exclusive of all note issues elsewhere accounted for.

The British private investments in Canadian securities are summarized in Table XXXVIII.[1] Where it was impossible to apportion the private investments to the individual years upon the basis of known data, they have been roughly distributed on the assumption that their proportion to public investments remained uniform throughout the period.

British Miscellaneous Investments in Canada

In addition to the British purchases of Canadian securities, there are important investments of British capital in Canada which take other forms. Among these should be included: the investments of British insurance companies in Canada; British purchases of Canadian mining, agricultural, timber, and urban properties; the investments of British shipping companies in Canadian coastwise and internal shipping; direct investments in Canadian industrial plants and mercantile establishments; British money lent on mortgage in Canada; and British capital used in financing Canadian import and export trade. The only comprehensive data covering such investments which are available are those presented by Field as the result of an extensive investigation.[2]

Field presents the following estimates for items not already accounted for above, and exclusive of investments in Canada by British insurance companies.[3]

[1] P. 126, *infra.*   [3] For these, see *infra,* p. 125.
[2] *Capital Investments in Canada,* 1914 ed., Chap. I, and passim.

TABLE XXXVI

MISCELLANEOUS BRITISH INVESTMENTS IN CANADA, 1905 TO 1913

(F. W. Field's Estimates)

In thousands of dollars

	1905–1909 [1]	1905–April, 1911 [2]	1905–December, 1913 [3]
Branch Plants......................	....	....	6,000
Investments with Loan and Mortgage Companies......................	5,720	8,725	12,000
Industrial Investments..............	22,500	26,375	29,000
Mining Investments................	56,315	57,555	59,000
Land and Lumber Purchases.........	19,000	34,000	40,000
Purchases of Town and City Property ..	....	8,525	25,000
	103,535	135,180	171,000

[1] *Monetary Times*, November 13, 1909.　　[3] *Ibid.*, 1914 ed., p. 9.
[2] *Capital Investments in Canada*, 1911 ed., p. 9.

Field's estimates cover only the nine years' period from 1905 to 1913. He states that his estimates, if anything, err on the conservative side.[1] If allowance be made for investments in mercantile and shipping enterprises and for British capital used in financing Canadian foreign trade, items which Field overlooked but which are of some importance, and also for miscellaneous investments in the five years, 1900 to 1904, not covered by Field's investigation, it is a conservative guess that the British miscellaneous investments other than by insurance companies for the period 1900 to 1913 amounted to at least $200,000,000.[2] These are apportioned to the individual years in Table XXXVIII largely upon the basis of data given by Field.[3]

[1] *Capital Investments in Canada*, 1914 ed., p. 19.
[2] See *infra*, p. 126.
[3] Cf. E. R. Wood, *Review of the Bond Market in Canada in 1911*: "The proceeds of Bond Sales are only a small part of the stream of capital that is pouring into Canada to assist in the proper development of our large areas and enterprises. . . . Investments from abroad in real estate and in our timber and mineral resources cannot accurately be determined, but are known to be of large amount, and there is every reason to suppose that capital through these sources is showing the same proportionate increase as is known to be the case in the sale of bonds."

British Insurance Company Investments in Canada

For the investments in Canada of British life- and fire-insurance companies, it is assumed, in the absence of other information, that they are measured by the increase in the assets in Canada of these companies.[1] For the years 1900 to 1913 these were as follows:

TABLE XXXVII

ASSETS IN CANADA OF BRITISH FIRE- AND LIFE-INSURANCE COMPANIES

In thousands of dollars

Year	Total assets in Canada [1]	Increases over preceding year
1900	40,453	1,000 (est.)
1901	41,493	1,040
1902	42,768	1,275
1903	43,949	1,181
1904	45,515	1,566
1905	45,750	235
1906	45,840	90
1907	48,364	2,524
1908	51,583	3,219
1909	55,063	3,480
1910	58,714	3,651
1911	63,948	5,234
1912	70,113	6,165
1913	71,932	1,819
Total		32,479

[1] Canada: *Annual Reports* of the Superintendent of Insurance. Data for 1899 not available.

The private investments of Great Britain in Canada, as estimated above, amounted to $319,234,000, or approximately 22 per cent of the public investments. In 1909, Sir George Paish, before the Royal Statistical Society, estimated that Great Britain's private investments in other countries were one third of her public investments, but some of the economists and statis-

[1] This is undoubtedly a gross overestimate, as the liabilities in Canada must have kept pace more or less with the assets in Canada, but no more satisfactory basis for reaching an estimate was available.

ticians present thought this too high.[1] Later, Paish estimated the British private investments in Canada from 1907 to 1913 at £50,000,000, or about 20 per cent of his estimate of the British public investments in Canada.[2] The present estimate for this period, probably based on a more complete canvass of the available data, is $275,000,000. The discrepancy between the estimates could be explained by Paish's omission of any one of the four minor classes of private investments dealt with here.

Table XXXVIII summarizes the British capital investments in Canada, 1900 to 1913.

TABLE XXXVIII

BRITISH INVESTMENTS IN CANADA, 1900 TO 1913

In thousands of dollars

Year	Securities				Miscellaneous		Total
	Public issues	Private sales by issuing governments and corporations	Individual sales	Treasury bills	Insurance companies	Other miscellaneous	
1900	3,068	1,000	1,000	....	1,000	4,000	10,068
1901	8,045	1,000	1,000	....	1,040	4,000	15,085
1902	4,641	1,000	1,000	....	1,275	4,000	11,916
1903	21,652	1,000	1,000	....	1,181	4,000	28,833
1904	21,934	1,000	1,000	....	1,566	4,000	29,500
1905	51,456	2,000	1,000	....	235	21,707	76,398
1906	42,656	2,000	2,000	....	90	21,707	68,453
1907	37,020	2,000	2,000	....	2,524	21,707	65,251
1908	152,478	2,000	2,000	....	3,219	21,707	181,404
1909	183,538	2,000	2,000	....	3,480	21,707	212,725
1910	177,926	8,563	2,000	....	3,651	26,317	218,457
1911	218,095	1,000	3,000	....	5,234	17,098	244,427
1912	187,140	4,500	3,000	....	6,165	14,025	214,830
1913	324,235	9,692	3,000	23,000	1,819	14,025	375,771
Total ..	1,433,884	38,755	25,000	23,000	32,479	200,000	1,753,118

[1] Sir George Paish, "Great Britain's Investments in other Lands," *Journal of the Royal Statistical Society*, September, 1909, pp. 465-480.

[2] *Statist*, Supplement, February 14, 1914.

AMERICAN INVESTMENTS IN CANADA

American capital investments in Canada do not take the form of purchases of Canadian securities to nearly as great an extent as do the British. To a large extent they consist of direct investments by American individuals or corporations in Canadian enterprises or properties. It is therefore even more difficult to obtain accurate estimates of the amounts of these investments, and after all available definite information has been canvassed the estimates must be rounded out by very conjectural approximations.

American Investments in Canadian Securities

The only annual compilation made for public issues of Canadian securities on the American market is that of E. R. Wood, for bonds only, and beginning with 1905 only.[1] His total for the years 1905 to 1913 is $134,213,117, whereas F. W. Field estimates at $123,742,455 the American purchases of Canadian bonds, including presumably private purchases, during the same period.[2] In the matter of statistics of Canadian bond issues, Wood is the accepted authority, and his figures will be used.

To the public sales of Canadian securities in the United States there should be added American public and private purchases of Canadian stocks and private purchases of bonds. A random sampling of the reports of shareholders in Canadian banks for 1899 and 1913 indicates that the American holdings of Canadian bank stocks increased between these two dates by at least $5,000,000. Americans hold approximately 12 per cent of the common stock of the Canadian Pacific Railway.[3] The issues of this stock since 1900, including premiums on the last three issues, and the American participation therein, were as follows: [4]

---

[1] *Annual Reviews of the Bond Market in Canada.*
[2] *Capital Investments in Canada*, 1914 ed., p. 25.
[3] *Ibid.*, p. 124.
[4] *Ibid.*, p. 22.

In thousands of dollars

Year	Total	Sold in the United States (12 per cent of total)
1902	19,500	2,340
1904	16,900	2,028
1906	20,280	2,434
1908	3,984	478
1909	37,500	4,500
1912	27,000	3,240
1913	105,000	12,600
Total		27,620

Field estimated the amount of Canadian municipal bonds sold privately in the United States during the five-year period from 1905 to 1909 at $25,000,000,[1] and in 1910 at $2,000,000.[2] According to Wood, the amount of Canadian municipal securities sold publicly in the United States in 1913, $22,135,000, "would no doubt be increased to over $30,000,000 by indirect transactions which it is impossible to record."[3] The *Monetary Times Annual* of January, 1914, lists $13,060,000 of various Canadian security issues in 1913 which were privately sold in the United States and which have not been already included in any of the above estimates. There is here accounted for approximately $80,000,000 of Canadian securities sold privately to the United States. If there be considered the incomplete character of the data, and especially: (1) the absence of any estimates for some of the years in the period, (2) the fact that Canadian securities cross the American border in individual sales in substantial amounts, and (3) the absence of any record of public issues in the United States of Canadian securities from 1900 to 1904, it may be conservatively estimated that the Canadian securities privately purchased by Americans and the unrecorded public issues in the United States amounted to at least $100,000,000 during the period under study.

[1] *Monetary Times*, November 13, 1909.
[2] *Capital Investments in Canada*, 1911 ed., p. 24.
[3] *Review of the Bond Market in Canada in 1913.*

American Industrial, Mining, Land, and Timber Investments in Canada

American investments in Canada are preponderantly in the form of either the purchase or establishment of manufacturing enterprises in Canada, generally subsidiary to main plants in the United States, or the purchase of urban, farming, and timber land, lumber rights, and mining properties. For such invest-

TABLE XXXIX

MISCELLANEOUS AMERICAN INVESTMENTS IN CANADA

(F. W. Field's Estimates)

In thousands of dollars

	November, 1909 [1]	September, 1911 [2]	December, 1913 [3]
Branch Companies [4]	105,000	125,400	135,000
British Columbia Mills and Timber	58,000	65,000	71,000
British Columbia Mines	50,000	60,000	62,000
Land Deals in Prairie Provinces	20,000	25,000	41,000
Lumber and Mines, Prairie Provinces	5,000	10,000	10,500
Theatrical Enterprises	....	....	3,500
Packing Plants	5,000	6,000	6,750
Agricultural Implement Distributing Houses	6,575	8,575	9,255
Land Deals, British Columbia	4,500	8,500	60,000 [5]
Miscellaneous Industrial Investments	....	10,000	13,300
City and Town Property	....	15,525	20,000
Investments in the Maritime Provinces	....	12,850	13,125
Fox Farm Investments, Prince Edward Island	....	....	1,000
	254,075	346,850	445,330

[1] *Monetary Times*, November 13, 1909. Published also in U. S. Dept. of Commerce, *Daily Consular and Trade Reports*, September 27, 1910. There are identifiable in Field's data for 1909 $122,500,000 of American capital invested in British Columbia. The American consul at Victoria, B. C., reported early in 1910 that "conservative estimates place the value of American investments in British Columbia at near $150,000,000." — U. S. Dept. of Commerce, *Monthly Consular and Trade Reports*, No. 353 (February, 1910).

[2] *Capital Investments in Canada*, 1911 ed., p. 24.

[3] *Ibid.*, 1914 ed., p. 25.

[4] 1909, 175 companies, average capital, $600,000; 1911, 209 companies, average capital, $600,000; 1913, 450 companies, average capital, $300,000.

[5] This figure appears excessive, and Field does not support it by adequate evidence. The period from 1911 to 1913 was marked, however, by wild speculation in British Columbia urban property, in which Americans undoubtedly participated extensively.

ments there are available estimates made by F. W. Field at three
different dates while he was editor of the *Monetary Times* of
Canada. He based his estimates on replies to questionnaires sent
to all enterprises in Canada known to be financed by American
capital, on information received from hundreds of correspondents, and on other sources of information. In Field's own
opinion, his figures, if anything, are underestimates rather than
overestimates.[1]

His estimates, for the years 1909, 1911, and 1913, but exclusive
of the items already considered above and exclusive of investments in Canada by American insurance companies, are given in
Table XXXIX.

These figures represent estimates of the total amount of capital
invested to date in the enterprises listed. They admittedly have
no claim to exact accuracy, but they appear to have been reached
after a careful survey of the situation, and in any case they are
the only comprehensive estimates available with regard to the
field they cover.[2]

As new information accrued in the process of collecting data for
his successive estimates, Field changed somewhat the basis of
his calculations. Chief among these revisions was his use, in 1913,
of $300,000 as the average capital of American branch factories
in Canada, instead of $600,000, the figure he used in the estimates
for 1909 and 1911. Field does not make clear to what extent this
change was due to the realization of an overestimate in the earlier
calculations and to what extent it was due to an increased proportion of small plants in the later years, but it is altogether probable that the change was made in some part as a correction of the
earlier estimates. If such was the case, it would result in the apportionment, to the earlier years of the period, of an unduly large
proportion of the total American investments in Canada. In

[1] Cf. *Capital Investments in Canada*, 1911 ed., p. 23.
[2] All the numerous estimates current in recent years as to the amount of American capital investments in Canada prior to 1914 fall into two classes: they are either
based on Field's data with or without acknowledgment, or they are blind guesses
without any attempt at the hard labor necessary to give an estimate a rightful
claim to being even a good guess.

some cases, branches in Canada of American enterprises are financed largely by Canadian capital, but Field believes that where, in the absence of specific information, he could not make the proper allowances for such Canadian investments, they are more than offset by American capital privately invested in Canadian companies controlled in Canada and not accounted for elsewhere in his calculation.

In order to make use of Field's estimates, it is necessary, first, to estimate how much of the total investment up to 1913, amounting to $445,300,000, was invested after 1899, and second, to apportion this amount to the individual years.

In 1900, N. T. Bacon estimated the total American investments in Canada at $150,000,000, of which $100,000,000 were in mines, $25,000,000 in railways, and $25,000,000 in timber lands and loans.[1] In 1909, Field estimated at only slightly over $50,000,000 the American investments up to that year in Canadian mines. American investments in railroads consist largely in holdings of Canadian Pacific common stock and in branches in Canada of American railroads. American holdings of Canadian Pacific shares have already been accounted for. Bacon's estimate overlooks some items, however. It will be estimated, therefore, that $100,000,000 will cover all American capital in Canada in 1900 other than that in Canadian securities or owned by insurance companies, and that $50,000,000 will cover these last-named items. There results $345,330,000 as the amount of American investments in Canada from 1900 to 1913 exclusive of purchases of securities and insurance-company investments. On the basis of Field's estimates for 1909 and 1913, $191,255,000 of this total can be attributed to the four years 1910 to 1913. There remains the problem of distributing the balance, $144,075,000, among the ten years from 1900 to 1909.

There is evidence to show that the early years of this decade were marked by comparatively heavy investments of American capital. By the middle of 1907 there were already in Canada 150 branch plants of American companies, although there were very

[1] "American International Indebtedness," *Yale Review*, November, 1900.

few before 1897,[1] and only 175 by the end of 1909.[2] Further
evidence to the same effect is presented by the reports of American consuls in Canada. The American consul at Toronto reported early in 1902 that "the already large list of American
concerns having branch establishments in Canada is constantly
receiving additions." [3] In October of the same year the American
consul-general at Montreal, in a detailed report on American
investments in Canada, listed American investments in new
Canadian industrial enterprises, made in the preceding year, or
about to be made, amounting to over $20,000,000. In addition
he cited a number of purchases of Canadian factories by Americans and of removals of American factories to Canada which had
occurred in the preceding year, and stated that "the investments
made by Americans in agricultural, grazing, and timber lands
amount to many millions of dollars." [4] In September, 1903, the
American consul at Sherbrooke, Quebec, reported that "American capital is rapidly invading this part of the Dominion, and
the near future will see the erection and equipment of many large
manufacturing plants." [5] Early in 1906 the American consul at
Victoria, British Columbia, reported: "American investors have
made and are now making purchases of lands in British Columbia
and are projecting enterprises of magnitude much more generally
than ever before. . . . There has been a great development of
the lumber industry in British Columbia during the past year,
largely by Americans." [6] British Columbia was an important
field for American investments,[7] so that this report is significant
as helping to locate the period of the investments.

[1] U. S. Dept. of Commerce and Labor, *Consular Reports, Annual Series*, No. 4,
"Canada: Trade for the Year 1907," p. 9. This document attributes this information to a report compiled by the Dominion government, which I have been unable
to trace. It also speaks of a report by the Illinois Manufacturers' Association to
the effect that in 1907, 122 "leading" United States concerns had branch plants
in Canada.

[2] F. W. Field, *Monetary Times*, November 13, 1909.

[3] (May 3, 1902) U. S. Dept. of Commerce, *Monthly Consular Reports*, No. 262,
p. 524 (July, 1902).

[4] *Ibid.*, No. 268, pp. 115, 121 (January, 1903).

[5] *Ibid.*, No. 278, p. 562 (November, 1903).

[6] *Ibid.*, No. 305, pp. 16, 17 (February, 1906).

[7] Cf. *supra*, p. 129, footnote 1 to Table XXXIX.

These reports of consuls, which were not specially selected but were the only ones which were found throughout the period under study directly reporting substantial investments of American capital in Canada, appear to justify the allocation to the early years of the period, of a substantial proportion of the American investments made up to 1909, although this was not found to be true for British investments. The $144,075,000 of American capital, exclusive of investments by American insurance companies and of purchases of Canadian securities, estimated above to have been invested in Canada from 1900 to 1909, will accordingly be apportioned evenly throughout the period.

Investments of American Insurance Companies in Canada

The official statistics with regard to the assets in Canada of American fire- and life-insurance companies from 1900[1] to 1913,

[1] Data for 1899 were not available.

TABLE XL

INVESTMENTS IN CANADA OF AMERICAN FIRE- AND LIFE-INSURANCE COMPANIES

In thousands of dollars

Year	Total assets in Canada [1]	Increase over preceding year
1900	29,435	1,500 (est.)
1901	31,367	1,932
1902	33,728	2,361
1903	36,914	3,186
1904	40,759	3,845
1905	43,002	2,243
1906	45,052	2,050
1907	45,357	305
1908	50,399	5,042
1909	50,776	377
1910	55,456	4,680
1911	59,924	4,468
1912	67,681	7,757
1913	78,186	10,505
Total		50,251

[1] Canada: *Annual Reports* of the Superintendent of Insurance.

which in the absence of other information are assumed to represent investments in Canada,[1] are given in Table XL.

Summary

The American capital investments in Canada from 1900 to 1913, as estimated above, are summarized in the following table:

TABLE XLI

AMERICAN INVESTMENTS IN CANADA, 1900 TO 1913

In thousands of dollars

Year	Securities		Miscellaneous		Total
	Public bond issues in the United States	Private sales of securities	Insurance companies	Other miscellaneous	
1900	....	1,000	1,500	15,407	17,907
1901	....	1,000	1,932	15,407	18,339
1902	....	5,590	2,361	15,407	23,358
1903	....	3,500	3,186	15,407	22,093
1904	....	6,528	3,845	15,407	25,780
1905	9,257	5,500	2,243	15,408	32,408
1906	4,118	7,934	2,050	15,408	29,510
1907	4,779	5,500	305	15,408	25,992
1908	6,316	5,978	5,042	15,408	32,744
1909	10,368	10,000	377	15,408	36,153
1910	3,634	2,500	4,680	61,850	72,664
1911	17,554	3,500	4,468	50,621	76,143
1912	27,466	7,120	7,757	39,392	81,735
1913	50,721	34,350	10,505	39,392	134,968
Total..	134,213	100,000	50,251	345,330	629,794

The American investments in Canada from 1900 to 1913, according to the estimates made above, amounted to approximately $630,000,000. Field estimated the total amount of American capital in Canada in 1913 at approximately $637,000,000, but in reaching his estimate he took no account, for some of the items, of investments made before 1905, and included investments prior

[1] This is undoubtedly a gross overestimate, as the liabilities in Canada must have kept pace more or less with the assets in Canada, but no more satisfactory basis for reaching an estimate was available.

to 1900 for only a few of the items.[1] Subtraction, from Field's estimate of the amount of American capital in Canada in 1913, of Bacon's estimate for 1900, gives $487,000,000 as the amount of the American investments in Canada from 1900 to 1913. The present estimate exceeds this figure by approximately $143,000,-000. The discrepancy is explained: by Field's omission, from his estimate for 1913, of insurance company investments in Canada made in that year, amounting to $10,500,000 as here estimated; by his omission of American subscriptions to Canadian Pacific Railway common stocks, estimated at $27,600,000, from 1900 to 1913; by his underestimate of American public and private purchases of other Canadian securities; and by the incomplete character of his estimates for the years 1900 to 1905.

INVESTMENTS IN CANADA BY CONTINENTAL EUROPE

Continental European countries have made investments in Canada to some extent, but these have been small, both relative to the total foreign investments of these countries and to the total foreign investments in Canada. As a consequence but little attention has been paid, in the Continental literature dealing with international movements of capital, to investments in Canada.[2] Practically the only information with regard to the amount of

[1] *Capital Investments in Canada*, 1914 ed., p. 25.

[2] The most comprehensive studies of the foreign investments of German capital are those contained in the series of official reports, and especially the reports of 1904 and 1907, issued by the German Navy Department (*Reichsmarineamt*) and entitled: *Die Entwickelung der deutschen Seeinteressen*. Unfortunately for our purposes, German investments in Canada are lumped in these reports with investments in the United States.

Neymarck reports at periodic intervals for the Institut International Statistique the amounts of international investments of capital by and in a large number of countries, but although the countries included are in most instances of much less importance than Canada as a field for foreign investments, he makes no mention of Canada. His reports are published in the *Bulletin* of the Institut. An official survey, made by the French Ministry of Finance in 1902, of the amounts of French capital invested abroad, gives some information regarding French investments in Canada, which will be made use of later. Émile Becqué, in his book, *L'Internationalisation des Capitaux* (Montpellier, 1912), makes a comprehensive survey of the French statistics dealing with foreign investments of capital, but he discloses no source of information dealing with French investments in Canada other than the French official report of 1902 mentioned above.

capital invested in Canada by Continental Europe is that collected by F. W. Field.

Continental Holdings of Canadian Securities

Canadian securities, and especially railroad securities, are held to some extent on the Continent. These holdings consist almost entirely either of Canadian Pacific Railway common stock, or of securities originally issued publicly in England and therefore already credited to Great Britain in this study. Continental holdings of Canadian securities will therefore be disregarded, except where, as in the case of issues of Canadian Pacific Railway common stock, the entire issue was not attributed above to Great Britain and evidence is available of Continental purchases. In 1913, 17 per cent of the Canadian Pacific Railway common stock was held outside of Canada, the United States,

TABLE XLII

MISCELLANEOUS INVESTMENTS IN CANADA BY CONTINENTAL EUROPE
(Field's Estimates)

In thousands of dollars

Country	1909 [1]	September, 1911 [2]	1913 [3]
France		47,250	67,250
Germany	54,450	21,725	21,725
Other Countries		11,175	18,675
Total	54,450	80,150	107,650
Character of Investment:			
Manufacturing and Industrial Enterprises	8,500	9,725	9,725
Lands, Mines, and Mortgage Loans	45,950	66,425	93,925
Railway	....	4,000	4,000
Total	54,450	80,150	107,650

[1] *Monetary Times*, November 13, 1909.
[2] *Capital Investments in Canada*, 1911 ed., pp. 35 seq.
[3] *Ibid.*, 1914 ed., pp. 66 seq.

or Great Britain, mainly, of course, in Continental Europe.[1] For the period under study, 17 per cent of the issues of such stock would amount to $43,285,000. Notice has been found in various sources, chiefly the files of the *Monetary Times*, of public issues of Canadian securities on the Continent, amounting to $14,450,-000 from 1910 to 1912. Continental holdings of Canadian bank stocks will be estimated to have increased by $5,000,000 from 1900 to 1913. The total Continental investment in Canadian securities not elsewhere accounted for will be estimated, therefore, at $62,735,000.

Miscellaneous Investments in Canada by Continental Europe

Field's estimates of the investments in Canada by Continental Europe, exclusive of investments in Canadian securities, are given in Table XLII.

A French official report estimated the amount of the French capital in Canada in 1902 at a minimum of 139,000,000 francs, or approximately $28,000,000, invested as follows:[2]

	Francs	
Land	5,000,000	
Crédit-Foncier Franco-Canadien	50,000,000	
Mines	2,000,000	
Industries	2,000,000	59,000,000
Dominion of Canada and Province of Quebec Bonds		80,000,000
Total		139,000,000

This was regarded as an underestimate,[3] and did not include, according to the report, the investment by Menier in the Island of Anticosti and the capital brought to Canada by the French religious orders upon their expulsion from France. It also fails to account for French holdings of Canadian railroad and bank

---

[1] F. W. Field, *Capital Investments in Canada*, 1914 ed., p. 125. This percentage represented an increase over previous years.

[2] France: *Bulletin de Statistique et de Législation comparée du Ministère des Finances*, 1902, tome II, p. 475.

[3] *Ibid.*: "Certainement très inférieur à la réalité."

securities, which have already been considered above. It will be estimated that the French capital in Canada in 1900, other than in securities, amounted to 75,000,000 francs or $15,000,000.

According to Alvo Von Alvensleven, a German member of a Canadian investment firm especially concerned with placing German capital in Canada, the amount of German capital in Canada at the end of 1913, not including capital invested in Canadian railroad securities or in other securities by way of London, exceeded $50,000,000.[1] Field placed the amount of these investments at $21,725,000. It will be estimated that $35,000,000, or approximately the mean of these two estimates, represents the amount invested in Canada by Germany since 1900. It will be estimated also that all but $5,000,000 of the investments in Canada by all other countries, as estimated by Field, were made since 1900. This makes the total amount of such investments approximately $120,000,000, of which $100,000,000 was invested after 1899.

[1] *Monetary Times Annual*, January, 1914, p. 146.

TABLE XLIII

INVESTMENTS OF CONTINENTAL EUROPE IN CANADA, 1900 TO 1913

In thousands of dollars

Year	Canadian Pacific Railway common shares	Bank shares	Other securities issued in Europe	Miscellaneous investments	Total
1900	....	300	....	3,445	3,745
1901	....	300	....	3,445	3,745
1902	3,315	300	....	3,445	7,060
1903	....	300	....	3,445	3,745
1904	2,873	300	....	3,445	6,618
1905	....	300	....	3,445	3,745
1906	3,448	400	....	3,445	7,293
1907	....	400	....	3,445	3,845
1908	4,137	400	....	3,445	7,982
1909	677	400	....	3,445	4,522
1910	6,375	400	600	14,690	22,065
1911	....	400	12,000	15,440	27,840
1912	4,590	400	1,850	17,710	24,550
1913	17,850	400	....	17,710	35,960
Total..	43,265	5,000	14,450	100,000	162,715

Summary

The table on page 138 summarizes the foreign investments in Canada by Continental Europe from 1900 to 1913. The apportionment of the miscellaneous investments to the individual years is made: on the basis of available information for public issues of securities and for Canadian Pacific Railway common stock; on the basis of Field's estimates for 1909 to 1913; and on the assumption that the amount invested other than in securities up to 1909 was evenly distributed during the nine preceding years.

SUMMARY OF FINDINGS OF CHAPTER VI

In the following table the results of this chapter are summarized and are compared with the corresponding estimates made in the preceding chapter:

TABLE XLIV

INVESTMENTS OF FOREIGN COUNTRIES IN CANADA, 1900 TO 1913

In thousands of dollars

Year	British	American	Other countries	Total	Total, as estimated in Chapter V
1900	10,068	17,907	3,745	31,720	33,692
1901	15,085	18,339	3,745	37,169	49,964
1902	11,916	23,358	7,060	42,334	30,686
1903	28,833	22,093	3,745	54,671	52,499
1904	29,500	25,780	6,618	61,898	112,130
1905	76,398	32,408	3,745	112,551	98,749
1906	68,453	29,510	7,293	105,256	99,072
1907	65,251	25,992	3,845	95,088	160,985
1908	181,404	32,744	7,982	222,130	224,189
1909	212,725	36,153	4,522	253,400	193,448
1910	218,457	72,664	22,065	313,186	224,731
1911	244,427	76,143	27,840	348,410	358,202
1912	214,830	81,735	24,550	321,115	435,002
1913	375,771	134,968	35,960	546,699	433,085
Total..	1,753,118	629,794	162,715	2,545,627	2,506,434

The estimate reached in this chapter for the total amount of foreign capital invested in Canada from 1900 to 1913 is greater by $39,193,000, or 1.6 per cent, than the corresponding estimate reached in Chapter V. Considering the incomplete character of the material available for a direct estimate of the amount of foreign investments in Canada, the complicated character of the indirect estimate made in the preceding chapter, and the necessary resort in both estimates to conjectural material, the two sets of total results are in remarkably close agreement.

For individual years the two sets of estimates exhibit much less harmony. The discrepancies are especially great for the years 1904, 1907, 1910, 1912, and 1913. It is probable that most of the excess in the present estimate for 1913 over the corresponding estimate in the preceding chapter is due to (1) the delayed influence on the present estimate of temporary borrowings made in 1912 and converted to permanent loans in 1913, and (2) heavy borrowings made late in 1913, but which did not actually reach Canada in the form of imports until 1914. This would also help to explain the excess of the present total estimate over the estimate for the entire period, made in the preceding chapter. The data upon which the present estimate was based were much more comprehensive for the period as a whole than for the individual years in the period, and the apportionment of the investments to individual years was perforce made largely on the basis of conjectural hypotheses. But even though all the data used were complete and accurate, some discrepancy should still be expected between the two sets of estimates for the individual years. A loan recorded in this chapter as made in one year may not have influenced until the following calendar year the data upon which the estimates made in Chapter III were constructed. A public issue made in one calendar year may represent the funding of a Treasury Bill issue or a bank loan made some time previously, or may have been anticipated by purchases abroad on a short-time credit basis, and may therefore have already influenced the Canadian balance of indebtedness in an earlier year. Imports may be financed by permanent loans either after or before the imports actually occur. Other factors similar in character may operate in like manner to make estimates based on the date of flotation of loans disagree with estimates based on the factors revealing the indebtedness. Discrepancies between the two estimates for the individual years, due to such causes, should offset each other in a series of years. The closeness of the two estimates for the entire period confirms, therefore, the hypothesis that the discrepancies between the estimates for individual years are due in large part to the differences in time between the flotation of a loan and its transfer to the borrowing country in the form of commodities.

PART II

THE MECHANISM OF ADJUSTMENT OF THE CANADIAN BALANCE OF INTERNATIONAL INDEBTEDNESS

INTRODUCTORY

PART II of this study deals with the mechanism of adjustment of the Canadian balance of international indebtedness. During the period of this study the great disturbing factor was the inflow of foreign capital into Canada, and the particular problem for explanation—in fact, what is here meant by the "adjustment" of the balance of international indebtedness—is the mechanism of the process whereby the Canadian borrowings, negotiated in terms of money, entered Canada in the form of goods and not in gold. The classical school and its followers have not been wholly in agreement in their explanation of the mechanism of adjustment of international balances of indebtedness. John Stuart Mill's exposition of the process of adjustment will be taken as a starting point for the present attempt at inductive analysis and verification, but some attention will later be given to the controversial phases of the *a priori* theory.

The mechanism of adjustment of the Canadian balance of international indebtedness to the Canadian borrowings from abroad, granting two assumptions — first, that the period of borrowings followed immediately upon a period of even balance between the Canadian debits and credits, and second, that the borrowings continued at an even and steady rate for an indefinite period [1] — would be explained by Mill as follows: [2]

Commerce being supposed to be in a state of equilibrium when the obligatory remittances begin, the first remittance is necessarily made in money. This lowers prices in the remitting country, and raises them in the receiving. The natural effect is that more commodities are exported than before, and fewer imported, and that, on the score of commerce alone, a balance of

---

[1] The first of these assumptions applies closely enough to the period under study, whose first three years were marked by a close approach to an even balance between debits and credits. The second does not apply, but is made in order to simplify the first stages in the treatment of the problem. The necessary corrections will be made in the course of the discussion.

[2] *Principles of Political Economy*, Bk. III, Chap. XXI, § 4. Read "loans" in place of "obligatory remittances" and "tribute."

money will be constantly due from the receiving to the paying country. When the debt thus annually due to the tributary country becomes equal to the annual tribute or other regular payment due from it, no further transmission of money takes place; the equilibrium of exports and imports will no longer exist, but that of payments will; the exchange will be at par, the two debts will be set off against one another, and the tribute or remittance will be virtually paid in goods.

Mill would agree also that the flow of gold from the lending to the borrowing country would be preceded in the lending country by a rise in the price of bills on the borrowing country to the gold export point, and that the price of the foreign bills would continue at that point during the continuance of the outward flow of gold. The process of adjustment, as explained by Mill, thus consists of five successive stages, occurring in the following order:

(1) A rise in the price of bills on the borrowing country;

(2) A flow of gold from the lending to the borrowing country, accompanied by exchange at the gold export point of the lending country (and at the gold import point of the borrowing country);

(3) Relative changes in price levels in the two countries, prices rising in the borrowing country, falling in the lending country;

(4) Changes in imports and exports, the borrowing country acquiring an unfavorable balance of trade and the lending country acquiring a favorable balance;

(5) After the unfavorable trade balance of the borrowing country had become exactly equal to the rate of borrowing, the return of the exchanges to parity, the cessation of gold movements, and the stabilization of relative prices in the two countries at their new levels.

The present analysis of the mechanism of adjustment of the Canadian balance of international indebtedness will take up for examination the operation of variations in the exchanges, gold movements, changes in relative price levels, and changes in commodity imports and exports, in the order given, and of course primarily from the point of view of the borrowing country.

CHAPTER VII

EXCHANGE RATES AND GOLD MOVEMENTS

EXCHANGE RATES

EXCHANGE rates, aside from their relationship to gold movements, operate in the adjustment of international balances through their influence on the profitability of export and import of commodities and of the transfer of securities and bank deposits from country to country. When bills on foreign countries are low, that is, when the foreign exchanges in terms of a given country's currency are high, foreign goods are cheaper by the amounts of the discounts on the foreign countries' currencies; conversely, when bills on foreign countries are high, foreign goods are dearer by the amounts of the premiums on the currencies of the foreign countries, comparison in each case being with the state of affairs when the exchanges are at mint parity. If Canada begins to borrow from Great Britain, bills on London will presumably be at a discount in Canada, imports from Great Britain will be stimulated and exports to Great Britain will be checked thereby, and the fall in London bills will operate to bring about at least a partial transfer to Canada of the borrowed funds in the form of commodities. But a proper understanding of the part played by variations in the exchanges in the adjustment of international balances requires a clear appreciation of the differences between the two major classes of disturbances to the equilibrium of international balances of indebtedness.

First, there are the merely temporary and casual fluctuations in the international balance of indebtedness about its normal *equal balance* of debits and credits. Even though the basic conditions were such as to bring about an even balance of international debits and credits for Canada in the course of a week or a month or a year, there would nevertheless be daily divergencies from this even balance, due simply to the fact that fine economic adjustments are not characteristic of complex social processes operating under individualistic motivation and control. Casual disturbances in one direction of the even balance of international indebtedness tend to be soon offset by disturbances in the opposite direction, so long as the basic conditions continue to be such as to bring about an even balance. And there is no reason to doubt that variations in the exchange rates, largely within the range of the gold points, are an important factor, and in many cases the dominant factor, in the day-to-day adjustments of balances of indebtedness to such disturbances. But even in the adjustment of casual disturbances, variations in the exchanges operate mainly through their influence on transfers of securities and bank balances, on the settlement or postponement of maturing obligations, and on international short-time loans, — that is, on the direction and volume of immediate obligations, — and only slightly, if at all, through their influence on the volume of imports and exports. The principal effect of the variations in the exchanges under such circumstances is to minimize the flow of gold where, in the absence of their regulatory influence, gold would move in opposite directions within short periods of time.[1]

Secondly, when the even balance of debits and credits is disturbed by a more or less permanent factor, such as, for instance, continued borrowings from abroad, adjustment of the balance of international indebtedness consists not in the reëstablishment of an even balance between all debits and all credits, immediate and deferred, but in the establishment of an even balance of payments through the creation of an excess of trade debits over trade credits equal in amount to the current borrowing, so that the borrowed capital will enter in the form of goods and not of gold. If the borrowing continues indefinitely, and if the rate of exchange is to operate continuously as a regulatory factor through its stimulus to imports and its check to exports, it must continue

[1] Cf. J. S. Mill, *Principles*, Bk. III, Chap. xx, § 3: " . . . what is called an unfavorable exchange is an encouragement to export, and a discouragement to import. And if the balance due *is of small amount, and is the consequence of some merely casual disturbance in the ordinary course of trade*, it is soon liquidated in commodities, and the account adjusted by means of bills, without the transmission of any bullion." (Italics mine.)

indefinitely to be favorable to the borrowing country. But exchange rates cannot be for a long time in favor of a given country, under normal conditions of the maintenance of the gold standard and freedom of gold movements from artificial restraint, without moving to the gold import point and thus giving rise to an inflow of gold.

It is true that the movements of the exchanges normally show a strong aversion to reaching the gold points. But this is wholly due to the necessarily temporary character of any disturbance in the balance of payments and to the consequent probability that any movement of the exchanges in one direction will soon be followed by a movement in the reverse direction. The exchanges are prevented from reaching the gold points in consequence of minor disturbances of the balance of payments by financial operations,—such as postponements of settlement of obligations, transfers of bank balances, sales of floating securities, — which either create payment obligations in one direction or temporarily lessen the volume of immediate obligations in the other direction. But such operations are limited in their volume, and they are financially attractive only as temporary transactions to be reversed in their direction when the exchanges move to the other side of parity. The stock of liquid capital engaged in such operations is used to buy in one form or another exchange on country A in country B at below par, with the expectation that there will soon be an opportunity to sell it above par. It is these speculative operations which serve to keep the exchanges from reaching the gold points when the variations in the exchanges are due to minor and temporary variations in the relation of the supply of to the demand for foreign bills. If the balance of immediate obligations aside from such speculative transactions is such that the flow of foreign bills will be even for a short time greatly in excess of the demand for such bills, the additional demand for foreign bills arising out of such transactions will be insufficient to keep the rate of exchange from moving to the gold import point. If the balance of international transactions is such that, aside from these exchange market operations, foreign bills will continuously flow into the exchange market at a rate in excess of the demand for such bills, these operations will appear financially unattractive and will cease to take place as soon as it becomes evident that no early reversal in the direction of the exchanges is to be expected; the important check on the movement of the exchanges to the gold import point will be removed; the surplus of foreign bills will be liquidated by the shipment of gold from abroad. Of the checks which operate to restrain the exchanges from moving to the gold points, the influence of small variations in the exchanges on the course of commodity trade is a minor factor and the financial operations in the exchange market are the important element; and the latter are inadequate or cease altogether when the basic conditions are such as to bring about in the absence of gold movements a substantial or a continued debit or credit balance of immediate obligations. If there is a long-continued excess of foreign bills arising out of commercial and long-time borrowing transactions, it will not be absorbed by the short-time loans stimulated by the low prices of foreign bills, and will be liquidated only by inward gold shipments.

But gold imports, if they occur, operate through their influence on price levels to bring about the needed adjustment of the international balance of indebtedness in such manner that there may be an even balance of payments, that gold movements may cease, and that exchange rates may return to par. Although, therefore, a favorable rate of exchange may be expected, at the inception of borrowings, to coöperate with the effect on prices of the import of gold in stimulating imports and checking exports, variations in the exchanges exhaust their direct influence, in adjusting the balance of indebtedness to continued borrowings occurring at an even rate, at the beginning of the borrowings, when a fall in the foreign exchanges is first a preliminary to the import of gold and then accompanies the import of gold. Once the prices in borrowing and lending countries have been adjusted to their proper relative levels, gold imports cease, and the exchanges return to parity. The balance of payments is equalized, but the balance of indebtedness is not. When writers insist, as does, for instance, Professor Hollander,[1] that variations in exchange rates

---

[1] J. H. Hollander, "International Trade Under Depreciated Paper: A Criticism" (of an article under this title by Professor Taussig), *Quarterly Journal of Economics,*

unaccompanied by gold movements and price changes are sufficient of themselves to bring about an excess of imports over exports in a borrowing country, equal to the volume of borrowings,
they not only overestimate the possible influence of variations in
exchange on the course of trade, but they fall into positive error
because of their failure to distinguish between what Mill called
the "self-adjusting" variations in the exchange, and those
"which can be rectified only through prices." [1]

To aid in making clear what is at issue, let us consider the trade
between only two countries, Canada and the United States, assuming, as was true for the period under study, that the currencies of the two countries are identical in denominations and
mint values. Before the Canadian borrowings begin, Canada
annually imports from the United States goods to a value to the
American exporters of $100,000,000, and annually exports in
payment goods to a value of $100,000,000 to the American im-
porters. The supply in Canada of bills on the United States
equals the demand for such bills; the rate of exchange is at the
mint par; no gold is shipped in either direction. Assume now
that Canadian borrowings begin at an annual rate of $50,000,000.
The increase in the American demand for bills on Canada unaccompanied by an increase in the American supply of such bills
will turn the rate of exchange against the United States. It is
presumably Professor Hollander's argument that the Canadian
demand for American products is necessarily so highly elastic —
or the American demand for Canadian products so highly in-
elastic — that an increase in the amount of American funds in
the United States purchasable with a given amount of Canadian

vol. xxxii (1918), p. 678. Cf. Taussig's reply, *ibid.*, p. 692: "Surely it cannot be
maintained that such transactions [*i.e.*, loans] would bring about a movement
of commodities from the lending country merely through the disturbances of
foreign exchange within the limits of the gold points. Fluctuations in exchange
rates within these limits are never more than a minor factor as regards commodity
exports and imports." This rejoinder brings to bear against Hollander only the
claim that he overestimates the possible weight of the exchange factor in affecting
the course of trade. I have tried to demonstrate in the text that the exchange
rates cannot operate *at all*, except at the beginning of the period of borrowing, in
the manner described by Hollander.

[1] *Principles*, Bk. III, Ch. xx, § 3.

funds in Canada, short of that which would result from exchange on Canada moving to the gold export point, will necessarily be sufficient to induce an annual excess of $50,000,000, in the importation of American goods by Canada, over the Canadian exportation of its own goods to the United States.

There is theoretically a very faint possibility that such may be the order of events. There is surely nothing in the theory of the exchanges which makes it the necessary or even the probable course of events. Were it not for the limitations on the extent of variation in the exchanges, resulting from the profitability of gold shipments when the gold points are reached, there would be no reason, other than the peculiar profitability of speculation in the exchanges because they frequently reverse their direction of movement, why the variations in the exchanges should be more limited in their range than the variations in, let us say, the relative prices of wheat and iron ore. Granted the effectiveness of the profitability of gold shipment at the gold points as a limitation on the range of possible variation in the exchanges, there is no fundamental reason why the continued and substantial excess at mint parity of the demand for over the supply of foreign bills should not take the exchange on the foreign country to the limit of that range of variation, that is, to the gold export point. On the contrary, it would be surprising if, under the circumstances stated, the price of foreign bills did not immediately rise to the gold export point, and then, after some gold had been exported, return to par.

Professor Hollander appeals to the high authority of Ricardo in support of his contention that the adjustment of the balance of payments to foreign borrowings is effected without gold shipments through the influence of variations in the exchanges within the gold points on the commodity balance of trade.[1] But Ricardo maintained that the adjustment of the commodity balance of trade to capital borrowings came about automatically and without the intervention of gold movements. He does not appear ever to have stated in any of his formally published writings that variations in the exchanges played any part in the adjustment of international balances to capital borrowings or similar dis-

[1] J. H Hollander, *op cit.*, p. 677.

turbing factors. In personal correspondence with Malthus, however, he conceded that variations in the exchanges were part of the mechanism of adjustment of the commodity balance of trade to a subsidy. But he also conceded that if a substantial subsidy were granted, gold movements would be necessary; that is, the rate of exchange on the subsidy-receiving country would move to the gold export point.[1]

Canadian Dealings in Foreign Exchange

Canadian transactions in foreign exchange and in monetary gold are carried on almost wholly by way of New York. A supply of bills on London in excess of the amount needed to meet current obligations in Great Britain would be sold in London or New York for American funds, and similarly a shortage of sterling bills in Canada would be met by purchases of sterling exchange in New York or by sale of New York funds in London rather than by direct dealings with London. The rates of exchange between Canada and England are governed more by the triangular relations of London and Canada with New York than by the direct relations between Canada and England. The New York exchange market carries the burden of the Canadian supply and demand of sterling bills, and the volume of sterling exchange transactions in New York on American account is so much greater than the volume of transactions on Canadian account that in all probability the New York rates of sterling-exchange are not appreciably influenced by the transactions on Canadian account. The Canadian rates for sterling exchange, therefore, do not accurately reflect the state of the balance of payments between Canada and Great Britain. The New York rate of sterling exchange swings the Canadian sterling rate along with it. Unless the American balance of payments with Great Britain always coincided with the Canadian balance of payments with Great Britain, the Canadian rates of sterling exchange would not always move in sympathy with the Canadian balance. Canadian exchange transactions with countries other than Great Britain and the United States are comparatively unimportant, and are

[1] *Letters of Ricardo to Malthus* (James Bonar, editor), Oxford, 1887, p. 20.

almost invariably handled through London or New York. The operation of variations of exchange rates as part of the mechanism of adjustment of international balances, whether of payments or of indebtedness, must be sought, therefore, in so far as Canada is concerned, in the exchange relations between Canada and New York.

Throughout the greater part of the period under study, New York funds were generally — although not continuously — at a discount in Montreal and Toronto, thus reflecting the general prevalence of an excess in the supply of over the demand for foreign bills in Canada. This was the result to be expected from the continued flotation of Canadian loans abroad, not at an even rate, but in *irregularly increasing* volume. The generally upward trend in the rate of borrowings abroad would explain the generally present discount on New York funds. The irregularity in the rate of increase, and especially the sporadic recurrence of decreases, in the volume of borrowings abroad, would explain the occasional appearance of premiums on New York funds in Canada. The exchanges may therefore be presumed to have fluctuated in conformity with the theoretical expectations under borrowings abroad in fluctuating volume. At the inception of foreign borrowings, and at each increase in the rate of foreign borrowings, New York funds should have dropped below par in Canada. When borrowings had been maintained for some time at an approximately even rate, New York funds should have been at or near par. When the volume of borrowings declined, New York funds should have been at a premium. Detailed inductive verification is not feasible, because the effect of the borrowings on the exchanges is inextricably bound up with the effect of the casual disturbances in the Canadian balance of payments with other countries, due to minor and temporary causes. In general, however, the trend of New York exchange in Canada was in conformity with the theoretical expectations.[1]

[1] E. L. Stewart Patterson and Franklin Escher, *Banking Practice and Foreign Exchange*, Canadian Edition (Alexander Hamilton Institute Series on Modern Business), 1914, p. 418: "Until 1912 New York funds in Canada were generally at a discount, averaging between 1/64 and 1/32 of 1 per cent, and this in face of the fact that the so-called 'balance of trade' was always against Canada. . . .

Nevertheless, the peculiar relations existing between the American and Canadian financial markets render it highly improbable that variations in the New York exchanges were an appreciable factor in stimulating Canadian imports or checking Canadian exports even at the inception of borrowings or at periods when the rate of borrowings increased. American gold coin is legal tender in Canada at its face value, and is the predominant element in the gold reserves of both the government and the banks. It can pass freely between the two countries as money. There is, therefore, no delay nor brassage charge, for reminting, nor any loss in value because of wear and tear of the coins, when American gold coin crosses the Canadian boundary. Gold shipped from New York after banking hours of one day reaches Montreal before banking hours of the next day, so that time lost in shipment is not a factor. As a consequence the difference between the mint par and the gold points is virtually equal to the bare transportation and insurance costs. During the period under study, a shipment of gold could be made between New York and Montreal at a cost of 70 cents per thousand dollars. A Canadian bank would import gold, therefore, as soon as a rate of 1/16 to 5/64 of 1 per cent discount on New York funds was quoted, and would ship gold to New York before a premium of 1/16 to 5/64 of 1 per cent was quoted.[1] So narrow was the normal range of variations before 1914 that market quotations were considered only for very large transactions, the banks charging a flat rate on small counter transactions irrespective of the market. It is inconceivable that variations in exchange rates within so limited a range could have exerted an appreciable influence on the relative volume of Canadian imports and exports.

This abnormal condition was due principally to the steady flow of British and foreign capital into Canada during the period referred to, the relative exchange operations being effected through New York. With the diminution of the volume of these investments and the constantly increasing remittances to Europe on account of dividends, interest, etc., the position is gradually reversing; since 1912 the tendency of the exchange market for New York funds has been more or less against Canada, and the average now would probably work out at par or a slight premium."

[1] *Banking Practice and Foreign Exchange*, p. 419.

GOLD MOVEMENTS

It has been shown above that variations in the exchanges could not have been a significant factor in the adjustment of the Canadian balance of international indebtedness. The restricted range of possible variation between the gold points in Canadian exchange rates on New York should have resulted, it may be supposed, in an accentuation of gold movements. Some economists, it is true, have denied that movements of gold and consequent changes in relative price levels are a necessary or even a usual phase of the adjustment of trade balances to borrowings. Their reasoning can be more conveniently examined in a later chapter when the relationship of changes in price levels to the adjustment of international balances is investigated. In the remainder of this chapter the actual movements of monetary gold into and out of Canada during the period under study will be analyzed with a view to testing the explanation offered by Mill of the part played by gold movements in the mechanism of adjustment. As a preliminary, it is necessary that there be presented the essential facts concerning the monetary use of gold in Canada.

Although Canada has a substantial annual production of gold, almost all of it during the period under study was sent out of Canada to be smelted and refined. Until 1908 no gold coin was minted in Canada, and from 1908 to 1913 the gold coin minted in Canada amounted only to $4,853,000.[1] With some minor exceptions of no material importance, gold is used in Canada, for monetary and reserve purposes, only in coined form. There is no relationship, therefore, direct or indirect, temporary or permanent, between the Canadian production of gold, and Canada's stock of monetary gold.[2]

There is no hand-to-hand circulation of gold as money in

---

[1] Cf. *supra*, p. 31, Table II.

[2] J. F. Johnson misinterprets the situation, therefore, when he supports his claim that exports and imports of monetary gold are of small consequence in Canada, by the statement that the output of Canada's own mines is more than sufficient to furnish the annual increment in the banking reserve. *The Canadian Banking System*, pp. 80, 81.

Canada. Its monetary uses are confined in Canada to the following: (1) as a reserve held by the government against its own issues of paper money and against deposits in the government and postal savings banks; (2) as a reserve held by the banks against their demand liabilities and to obtain the needed amounts of government currency; (3) in settlement of balances between banks; (4) in settlement of foreign transactions by the banks.

(1) The only form of government currency in Canada, other than silver and bronze subsidiary coinage and the small amounts of Canadian gold coin, is the "Dominion note" or "legal tender." Before 1903 the Minister of Finance was authorized to issue $20,000,000, and from 1903 to the end of the period under study $30,000,000, of these notes against a reserve in gold of 25 per cent of that amount. He could issue notes in excess of the stated maximum without limit, but only in exchange for gold, dollar for dollar. Over 75 per cent of the circulation was normally in notes of denominations of $500 or over, most of these being "special notes" valid only between banks and with the government itself when tendered by a bank. The government has a monopoly of the issue of $1 and $2 notes, and the circulation of Dominion notes outside of the banks is almost wholly confined to these denominations. The uncovered issue of Dominion notes was so small during this period that the notes were virtually gold certificates and were commonly regarded as such. Since July, 1903, the government has also held an additional gold reserve of 10 per cent against the deposits in the government and the postal savings banks. These deposits were comparatively small in amount and underwent little fluctuation, so that the gold reserves on this account never exceeded $8,000,000 nor fell below $5,000,-000 during the period under study.

(2) The Canadian chartered banks [1] are authorized to issue their own notes in denominations of $5 and multiples thereof to

[1] Practically all the banking in Canada is done by the "chartered banks," the only exceptions being the Government Savings Bank, the Postal Savings Bank, and two small savings banks with old charters. Savings banking is done by the chartered banks as a special department of their general banking business. Trust and loan companies accept deposits, but they are not required to maintain gold reserves.

the amount of their paid-up capital, except that from 1908 on they were authorized to exceed this maximum during the crop-moving season by 15 per cent of the amount of their paid-up capital and reserve, and from July, 1913, to the end of the period under study they were authorized to issue notes to any amount upon the deposit in a "Central Gold Reserve" of an amount of gold or Dominion notes equal to the amount of their excess issue above their paid-up capital. There is no statutory requirement as to the amount of reserve to be kept by the banks against their demand liabilities, but the banks are required to keep at least 40 per cent of their "cash reserves," that is, gold and Dominion notes, in the form of Dominion notes. The original purpose of this provision was to assure to the government the continued circulation of the uncovered part of its issue of Dominion notes, but in practice the banks find it convenient to keep a larger part of their reserves in Dominion notes than in gold.

(3) In settlements of balances between banks very little use is made of gold, because of the cost and risk connected with its transportation. Dominion notes serve the purpose better, especially as the "special notes" valid only between banks protect the banks against loss from theft. Theoretically the banks need not keep any gold in their reserves, in so far as Canadian transactions are concerned, except as a means of obtaining Dominion notes whenever they are needed, since the government will issue Dominion notes to the banks upon demand in exchange for gold.

(4) The banks, however, always keep a part of their reserves in the form of gold in order to be prepared to meet immediately any demand for payments outside of Canada. If all their reserves were in the form of Dominion notes, some delay might ensue at critical moments in exchanging Dominion notes for gold at the redemption stations of the Receiver-General.

The direct use of monetary gold in Canada is confined, therefore, to international payments and to the exchange, with the government, of gold for Dominion notes or of Dominion notes for gold. There is no open gold market in Canada, and foreign obligations or claims of Canadians are liquidated through the banks.

No Canadian ever has any need, or makes any call, for gold coin for domestic monetary use.[1] The coin in the reserves consists mainly of United States and British gold coins, both of which are legal tender in Canada, the sovereign at $4.86⅔ and United States gold coin at its face value in dollars.

The total stock of monetary gold in Canada on December 31, 1913, was as follows:[2]

	Thousands of dollars	
Held by Receiver-General:		
Reserve against issue of Dominion notes.........	108,687	
Reserve against savings bank deposits...........	5,486	
	114,173	114,173
Held by banks in Canada:		
"Specie" in vaults...........................	25,944	
Gold in Central Gold Reserve..................	1,197	
	27,141	27,141
Total...................................		141,314

On the same date the holdings of Dominion notes by the banks, including holdings in the Central Gold Reserve, amounted to $111,178,000, of a total issue of $131,187,000. The amount of Dominion notes in the hands of the public was therefore approximately $20,000,000, or slightly less than the maximum uncovered issue, $22,500,000.

The official Canadian statistics of imports and exports of gold coin, it has already been pointed out,[3] are too inaccurate to be usable. The official statistics of the amounts of gold held in government and banking reserves are issued at monthly intervals. As no gold circulates in Canada, these statistics provide an adequately accurate measure of net gold movements into and out of Canada.[4]

[1] "In theory ours is a gold standard with a Gold Currency. But in practice it is Gold Standard without the Gold Currency. . . . The currency used every day by ordinary folk consists of silver and bronze tokens, from one cent to fifty cents, Dominion notes, and the notes of the chartered banks." James Bonar, *Economic Journal*, June, 1914, p. 298.

[2] *Canada Gazette*, January and February, 1914.

[3] P. 33, *supra*.

[4] Not absolutely accurate, however, because: (*a*) until July, 1913, the banks in their reports to the Government did not separate specie held in Canada from specie

The table on page 161 presents the net changes from month to month in the monetary stocks of gold in Canada, the average monthly change in each year, and the average monthly Canadian debit balance of international indebtedness in each year.

The data presented in this table appear at first glance to be strongly confirmatory of the theory that borrowings from abroad enter the borrowing country in the form of goods only after a preliminary flow of gold. The absence of monthly statistics of the amount of borrowings abroad prevents a detailed comparison of the dates of the variations in the direction and quantity of gold movements as compared with the dates of the variations in the amounts of flotation of foreign loans and their entrance into Canada in the form of goods. Nevertheless, the table shows that in general the inflow of gold was greatest in the years in which the excess of the Canadian borrowings over Canadian loans was greatest. It is significant that, with the sole exception of 1909, every decrease in the rate of inward flow of capital was accompanied by an outflow of gold either in the same or in the preceding year, in spite of the fact that the general expansion of population and industry in Canada during the period under study made necessary a corresponding expansion in the gold reserves.

It is not to be expected that the preliminary gold import, necessary according to Mill if borrowings are to enter in the form of goods, should be as great or nearly as great as the amount of the borrowings. Nevertheless, the variations in Canadian gold stocks appear too small to have been the effective means of adjusting the Canadian balance of indebtedness to the borrowings from abroad, especially when the size of these borrowings, and the lack of important coöperation in the adjustment of balances from variations in exchange rates, are taken into consideration. The borrowings fluctuated considerably from year to year, and the monthly fluctuations were in all probability relatively much

held elsewhere, and resort to estimates is necessary in deducting from the total specie holdings of the banks the specie held outside of Canada; (*b*) the term "specie" used by the banks includes small amounts of subsidiary silver and bronze currency; (*c*) minor contributions to the Canadian gold reserves were made from 1908 to 1913 from coin minted at the Canadian mint for which there are no monthly statistics. The aggregate error arising from these three factors must, however, be small.

TABLE XLV

MONTHLY INCREASES AND DECREASES IN THE CANADIAN STOCKS OF MONETARY GOLD, 1900 TO 1913[1],[2]

In thousands of dollars

	1900	1901	1902	1903	1904	1905	1906	1907	1908	1909	1910	1911	1912	1913
January	[4]	237	465	499	*679*	218	1,429	1,713	2,032	1,838	1,502	229	1,583	744
February	[4]	21	*61*	*406*	*508*	*640*	913	1,212	122	1,984	2,100	688	*926*	3,046
March	[4]	448	212	395	1,452	104	597	1,305	149	1,051	1,589	146	*1,369*	166
April	[4]	603	403	*1,770*	1,175	244	10	1,747	2,999	458	1,483	1,702	398	1,454
May	[4]	219	2,536	*4,829*	852	1,219	2,910	2,363	1,043	902	1,591	8,126	492	1,782
June	[4]	*81*	*784*	700	1,266	*229*	*1,150*	1,411	12	1,784	*1,036*	677	*91*	3,505
July	[4]	74	332	392	1,336	1,560	1,951	1,489	2,713	262	3,982	2,392	3,857	4,663
August	550	*16*	72	*634*	*1,670*	767	1,019	1,444	6,304	3,593	943	1,970	1,519	374
September	301	441	309	1,284	2,124	623	319	727	5,090	1,321	943	1,018	789	2,170
October	895	1,213	2,577	1,151	564	1,657	4,933	2,356	1,549	149	4,225	13,054	*646*	438
November	32	1,152	1,028	528	330	233	543	172	2,708	8,715	2,404	3,223	6,710	15,485
December	380	182	923	696	148	2,179	3,415	5,298	1,017	3,509	1,260	10,484	10,484	519
Total Increase or Decrease	2,158	763	5,382	11,072	7,842	315	5,078	4,201	21,674	6,818	11,986	28,100	1,534	19,458
Average Monthly Variation	432	391	816	1,107	1,009	806	1,525	1,775	2,145	2,131	1,897	2,925	2,405	2,862
Average Monthly Increase or Decrease	432	64	449	923	654	26	423	350	1,806	568	999	2,349	112	1,622

AVERAGE MONTHLY DEBIT BALANCE OF INDEBTEDNESS[3]

	1900	1901	1902	1903	1904	1905	1906	1907	1908	1909	1910	1911	1912	1913
	2,808	4,164	2,557	4,375	9,344	8,229	8,089	13,415	18,682	16,121	18,728	29,850	36,250	36,090

[1] Decreases in italics.

[2] Computed from official reports of Receiver-General and of banks as published monthly in *Canada Gazette*. From the holdings of specie in Canada and elsewhere reported by the banks, deduction was made for each month, of 17 per cent of the amount of deposits outside of Canada. See p. 30, Table II, note 2, *supra*.

[3] Computed from Table XXX, p. 105, *supra*.

[4] Insufficient data published to make possible the present calculation for these months.

greater. If variations in exchange rates and in gold movements, operating, through their influence on relative prices, on the profitability of import and export, comprise the entire mechanism of adjustment of trade balances, should not the tremendous and irregular inflow of capital into Canada have been accompanied by gold movements much more substantial and marked by much greater fluctuations than are indicated in the above table? When consideration is given to the fact that most, if not all, of the gold movements can be adequately explained by reference to internal banking and currency conditions in Canada and without direct reference to the borrowings abroad, the question just raised acquires even greater significance. In the five-year period from August, 1901, to August, 1906, the only net monthly change in the Canadian stock of monetary gold which exceeded $3,000,000, namely, the increase in May, 1903, amounting to $4,829,000, was due to the coming into force of the Savings Bank Act of 1903, which for the first time required the government to keep a reserve in gold — 10 per cent — against the deposits in the Government Savings Bank, and cannot therefore be attributed to the influence of Canadian borrowings abroad. The general upward trend of the Canadian monetary stocks of gold during the period under study can reasonably be supposed to reflect nothing more than the fairly steady growth in the Canadian need for currency and banking reserves during a period of expanding population, industry, and commerce, and of world-wide buoyancy in prices. Further analysis is necessary, especially of the relation of gold to banking in Canada, before the data presented in Table XLV can be justifiably offered as a satisfactory inductive verification of the theory of gold movements as expounded by Mill and other writers of the classical school.

The government holdings of gold were strictly regulated by statutory requirements. The government reserves against government savings-bank deposits clearly were independent of the inward flow of capital into Canada, and may therefore be disregarded in the search for evidence of the influence of borrowings abroad on Canada's stocks of monetary gold. With the exception of the original issue of the uncovered portion of the Dominion notes, the government never takes the initiative in the issue of these notes but awaits the presentation of gold for notes before putting them out into circulation. The uncovered issue of Dominion notes during the period under study never exceeded by more than a few million dollars, and often fell below, the amount of total circulation of Dominion notes outside of the banks. With respect to its holdings of gold against the remainder of the Dominion notes, the government, therefore, was virtually acting as custodian for the gold of the banks. If the government holdings of gold are disregarded, and the bank holdings of Dominion notes are treated as if they were gold, analysis of the relationship between Canada's gold stocks and borrowings abroad may be confined to the bank holdings without any appreciable error. The next chapter deals with the relationship of the Canadian banks to gold movements into and out of Canada.

CHAPTER VIII

THE CANADIAN BANKS AND THE ADJUSTMENT OF INTERNATIONAL BALANCES

THE "CASH RESERVES" OF THE CANADIAN BANKS, AND GOLD MOVEMENTS

THE holdings of specie and Dominion notes of the Canadian banks are known as their "cash reserves" against demand liabilities. The monthly reports of the banks to the government have, since August, 1900, been sufficiently detailed to permit of the separation of the items relating to their operations in Canada from those relating to their operations outside of Canada.[1] The total demand liabilities in Canada include the note circulation of the banks, their "demand" and "time" deposits, and the deposits of the Dominion and provincial governments with the banks. The "demand" deposits represent non-interest-bearing commercial deposits payable on demand. The "time" deposits represent interest-bearing deposits of two classes, not separated in the returns: interest-bearing commercial deposits payable on a fixed date, and savings deposits payable only after notice. In practice the restrictions against free checking on time deposits are not strictly enforced. In addition to the "cash reserves," the larger banks maintain "secondary reserves" outside of Canada, in the form of loans on call, mainly in New York, and net balances due from banks outside of Canada. The official returns are made monthly as of the final day of the month.

Chart II presents for three-month intervals the amounts of the total demand liabilities in Canada of the Canadian banks, the

[1] This does not hold true of the bank returns of holdings of specie and Dominion notes, which did not separate holdings in Canada from holdings elsewhere than in Canada until July, 1913. For the method used in this study of estimating the amounts of specie holdings in Canada, see p. 30, *supra*. The holdings of Dominion notes outside of Canada were negligible in amount and may be safely disregarded. During the last six months of 1913, when they were separately reported, they averaged under $15,000.

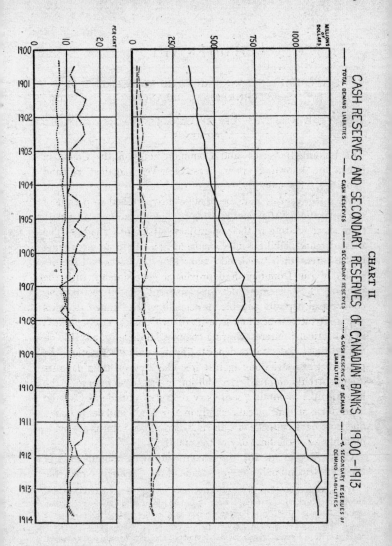

CHART II

CASH RESERVES AND SECONDARY RESERVES OF CANADIAN BANKS 1900–1913

—— TOTAL DEMAND LIABILITIES ·–·– CASH RESERVES —·— SECONDARY RESERVES ········ % CASH RESERVES OF DEMAND LIABILITIES —··— % SECONDARY RESERVES OF DEMAND LIABILITIES

MILLIONS OF DOLLARS

PER CENT

DATA OF CHART II

CASH RESERVES AND SECONDARY RESERVES OF CANADIAN BANKS,
1900 TO 1913 [1]

In thousands of dollars

Date (as of final day in month)	Total demand liabilities in Canada [2] Amount	Cash reserves in Canada [3]		Secondary reserves [4]	
		Amount	Per cent of total demand liabilities in Canada	Amount	Per cent of total demand liabilities in Canada
1900 September ..	340,876	26,702	7.8	42,389	12.4
December...	356,140	28,083	7.9	39,444	11.1
1901 March......	354,243	28,056	7.9	42,895	12.1
June	371,409	27,105	7.3	47,324	12.7
September ..	386,833	25,973	6.7	60,137	15.6
December...	397,798	27,646	6.9	58,796	14.8
1902 March......	391,500	28,215	7.2	51,717	13.2
June	407,800	30,025	7.4	59,751	14.7
September ..	427,654	29,179	6.8	64,973	15.2
December ..	440,301	31,312	7.1	59,653	13.5
1903 March......	437,802	32,153	7.3	47,731	10.9
June	445,806	37,396	8.4	47,250	10.6
September ..	462,409	39,041	8.4	55,428	12.0
December ..	470,231	41,181	8.8	52,238	11.1
1904 March......	473,395	40,341	8.5	51,021	10.8
June	493,507	42,734	8.7	49,569	10.0
September ..	511,655	47,227	9.2	69,183	13.5
December...	530,575	49,455	9.3	74,996	14.1
1905 March......	524,512	48,465	9.2	72,542	13.8
June	541,529	46,298	8.5	65,559	12.1
September ..	568,632	49,615	8.7	85,650	15.1
December...	593,762	50,213	8.5	77,995	13.1
1906 March......	601,206	48,633	8.1	73,843	12.3
June	620,588	49,669	8.0	69,690	11.2
September ..	644,820	50,960	7.9	82,625	12.8
December...	683,741	57,106	8.4	72,391	10.6
1907 March.......	661,508	54,670	8.3	52,389	7.9
June	680,610	59,595	8.8	62,268	9.2
September ..	685,181	62,556	9.1	68,041	9.9
December ..	656,157	66,003	10.1	50,819	7.8

See notes on following page.

DATA OF CHART II—*continued*

CASH RESERVES AND SECONDARY RESERVES OF CANADIAN BANKS,
1900 TO 1913[1]

In thousands of dollars

Date (as of final day in month)	Total demand liabilities in Canada[2] Amount	Cash reserves in Canada[3]		Secondary reserves[4]	
		Amount	Per cent of total demand liabilities in Canada	Amount	Per cent of total demand liabilities in Canada
1908 March......	631,731	61,039	9.7	65,304	10.3
June	648,264	63,564	9.8	78,015	12.0
September ..	687,017	76,261	11.1	116,356	16.9
December ..	728,922	81,849	11.2	141,562	19.4
1909 March......	733,723	81,686	11.1	145,173	19.8
June	774,509	81,600	10.5	150,473	19.4
September ..	814,984	83,325	10.2	168,752	20.7
December...	874,471	87,917	10.1	164,345	18.8
1910 March......	883,563	87,860	9.9	158,919	18.0
June	923,462	87,482	9.5	165,454	17.9
September ..	945,823	91,955	9.7	163,771	17.3
December ..	943,508	97,420	10.3	123,072	13.0
1911 March	947,442	98,524	10.4	121,208	12.8
June	998,292	107,177	10.7	145,322	14.6
September ..	1,023,532	107,467	10.5	147,538	14.4
December ..	1,061,209	121,418	11.4	128,699	12.1
1912 March	1,070,675	118,357	11.1	137,023	12.8
June	1,144,116	116,219	10.2	170,364	14.9
September ..	1,154,528	119,861	10.4	147,036	12.7
December ..	1,162,078	113,565	9.8	123,312	10.6
1913 March......	1,127,881	113,925	10.1	123,201	10.9
June	1,132,098	114,759	10.1	119,058	10.5
September ..	1,148,064	118,645	10.3	110,336	9.6
December ..	1,147,022	130,705	11.4	129,820	11.3

[1] Data from Monthly Bank Returns as published in *Canada Gazette*.

[2] Note circulation, demand deposits, time deposits, and deposits of Dominion and Provincial governments.

[3] Dominion notes and specie held in Canada. For method of estimating amount of specie held in Canada, see p. 30, Table II, note 2, *supra*.

[4] Call loans elsewhere than in Canada, and net balances due from banks outside Canada.

cash reserves and the secondary reserves against these liabilities, and also the percentages of each of these reserves to the total demand liabilities in Canada. The total demand liabilities, if allowance is made for seasonal fluctuations, rose constantly and at a fairly regular rate except for a temporary recession during the depression of 1907–1908 and again in 1913. The cash reserves also increased in about the same relative proportions, so that the curve indicating the percentage of cash reserves to total liabilities is nearly horizontal and is free from sharp fluctuations. Even without further analysis, the chart indicates an unusual degree of steadiness in the cash reserve ratio and, therefore, of power of control by the banks.

The data in the chart are drawn from the bank returns for single days at three-month intervals for the system as a whole, which included over twenty banks with an aggregate in 1913 of over 3,000 branches scattered over a great area and, in some cases, not in easy communication with the head offices. Casual or temporary variations in the inflow of deposits, the grant of loans, the withdrawals of cash, should be expected to bring about temporary fluctuations in the cash reserve ratio about the normal or desired ratio. The fact that the data are for *single* days should make the chart reflect fully these temporary fluctuations, where weekly or monthly averages would smooth them out. There would be a tendency, it is true, for variations in banking operations, if they are due to local or casual circumstances and not to some general factor operating throughout the country, to offset each other in the aggregate returns of the entire banking system. But the temporary fluctuations operating generally throughout the country should lead to fluctuations in the cash reserve ratio of the system as a whole. Also, since each bank has its own cash reserve policy and there are only relatively few banks, temporary fluctuations in the relative proportions of demand liabilities of the individual banks should tend to bring about fluctuations in the cash reserve ratio for the system as a whole, even though the aggregate demand liabilities of the system remained the same and even though each bank maintained its own reserve ratio unchanged. Many factors were operating, therefore, to make the cash reserve ratio of the system as a whole vary somewhat from day to day, even though it were the deliberate endeavor of each of the banks to maintain its own ratio at a constant level.

There were other factors which led the banks under certain circumstances deliberately and of their own accord to change their cash reserve ratios. The several items which make up the total demand liabilities of the banks differ in their reserve requirements, and variations in the relative proportions of the several items would therefore require compensatory variations in the reserve ratio. Slight variations in the reserve ratio from time to time are therefore consistent with the successful carrying-out by the banks of a policy of maintaining the reserves constantly at the minimum ratio to demand liabilities that is consistent with safety.

There is abundant evidence that even the general upward trend in the cash reserve ratio was due to deliberate adjustment of their reserves by the banks to the changing character of their demand liabilities. The safe minimum reserve ratio is higher for demand deposits than for time deposits and highest of all for note circulation.[1] Table XLVI shows that from 1908 on, time deposits were a decreasing percentage of the total demand liabilities of the banks and that therefore what would have been an adequate reserve ratio in the early part of the period would not have sufficed for the later part of the period.

Moreover, it appears that other changes were occurring in the character of the deposit liabilities of the banks, which made a higher reserve ratio expedient:

. . . The character of the bank liabilities in Canada has been changing in the past half-dozen years. [*I.e.*, 1907 to 1913.] The banks now hold a relatively larger amount of funds which must be considered as imminent liabilities. Among these are balances carried in current account by foreign

[1] It has been estimated that on the average the call on Canadian banks is twice per annum for time deposits, 25 times per annum for demand deposits, and 36 times per annum for notes. (B. E. Howard, "A Few Fundamentals — Credit Currency," *Monetary Times*, March 30, 1923.)

corporations, and special deposits on account of home corporations destined for meeting expenditures on works of one kind or another. When these items bulk so largely in the liabilities it is necessary to carry a larger ratio of reserve.[1]

In addition, the growth in population, and especially in urban population, the increase in the number of bank branches from 708 in 1900 to 3,140 in 1913, the improvement in means of communication, were all operating to increase the rapidity of circulation of bank notes and deposits and thus to raise the danger level for bank reserves. In Canada the banks regularly present each other's notes for payment either directly or through the clearing houses in the same manner as checks.[2] Canadian clearing-house

[1] H. P. M. Eckardt, "The Immediately Available Reserve," *Journal of the Canadian Bankers' Association*, vol. xx (July, 1913), p. 250.

[2] In periods of high currency demand, especially at crop-moving seasons, the statutory limitation of each bank's maximum note-issue to the amount of its paid-

TABLE XLVI

PERCENTAGE TO TOTAL DEMAND LIABILITIES IN CANADA OF NOTE, DEMAND DEPOSIT, AND TIME DEPOSIT LIABILITIES, 1900 TO 1913[1]

Date	Percentage of total demand liabilities			Date	Percentage of total demand liabilities		
	Note circulation	Demand deposits	Time deposits		Note circulation	Demand deposits	Time deposits
1900 September	14.7	29.9	53.7	1907 March	11.5	24.7	61.1
1901 March	13.4	25.6	59.3	September	11.6	24.7	61.5
September	14.5	25.0	58.7	1908 March ...	10.9	23.5	62.9
1902 March	13.4	23.7	61.2	September	11.1	26.7	59.7
September	14.3	26.2	57.9	1909 March ...	9.4	27.4	60.7
1903 March	13.3	24.6	60.4	September	9.7	29.4	58.2
September	13.8	25.2	59.5	1910 March ...	8.9	28.0	58.3
1904 March	12.6	22.5	62.9	September	9.2	28.9	57.7
September	12.5	24.5	61.3	1911 March ...	8.6	29.4	58.4
1905 March	11.2	24.6	62.3	September	9.5	30.6	56.4
September	12.3	24.8	60.9	1912 March ...	9.0	31.0	56.6
1906 March	11.0	25.4	61.1	September	9.0	32.4	55.5
September	12.0	26.0	60.0	1913 March ...	9.1	31.7	55.9
				September	9.7	33.2	54.1

[1] Computed from Monthly Bank Returns in *Canada Gazette*. The total demand liabilities include, also, small amounts of government deposits, percentages for which are not given in this table. The sums of the percentages in the table for each date therefore fall slightly short of 100.

statistics do not afford a reliable guide to the trend of the rapidity of circulation of bank notes and deposits. The branch-bank system reduces the need for inter-bank clearings, and intra-bank clearings are not made through the clearing houses. The relative increase in the number of branches of the larger banks, the decrease in the number of banks, and the decrease in the proportion of the total banking business done in the smaller banks with few branches, have all operated as a check on the growth of inter-bank clearings. On the other hand, the increase in the number of clearing houses in Canada, from eight in 1900 to sixteen in 1913, has operated to increase the proportion of inter-bank settlements made through the clearing houses. It is impossible to determine the relative importance of these two sets of counter tendencies, so that clearing-house statistics do not provide a reliable basis for an index of the rapidity of circulation of bank notes and checks.

It is possible, however, to derive from the Canadian banking statistics a satisfactory index, not precisely of the rapidity of circulation of bank deposits and liabilities, but what is of greater value for the present purpose, of the rapidity of inter-bank call for payment of bank notes and checks. The banks include, in their reports to the government of their condition on the last banking day of each month, a statement of the amounts of checks and notes of other banks which they have on hand. Normally these holdings represent the receipts from depositors in the course of the day's business which will be presented for clearance at ten o'clock the next morning. Theoretically a bank need keep a cash reserve only against demands for payment by other banks. If a bank's issue of notes or checks does not pass out of the hands of its own depositors, no demand is made upon its cash reserves, and the only effect of payments on its records is a shifting of deposits from one client to another, or of its liabilities from deposit to note account. The calls for cash by individuals, whether depositors or non-depositors, holding checks on the bank,

up capital operates to create a shortage of currency. At such times the banks do not always present each other's notes for payment, but use them as till money and pay them out over their counters, thus increasing their rapidity of circulation but reducing the liability of the banks to calls for payment in "cash."

can be met with the bank's own notes.[1] The ratio of the aggregate holdings by all the banks, of notes and checks other than their own, to the total demand liabilities of the banks should provide, therefore, an adequate index of the percentage of their demand liabilities for which demand for cash will be made daily.

Table XLVII presents a comparison of (1) the average yearly percentages of the holdings of notes and checks of other banks to the total liabilities of the banks with (2) the average yearly cash reserve ratio. The data presented in this table confirm the claim made above that a number of causes were operating relatively to increase the liability of the banks to daily calls for cash payments on account of their note circulation and deposits. To this extent

[1] Except for small change and for relatively small amounts of Dominion $1 and $2 notes.

TABLE XLVII

COMPARISON OF CASH RESERVE RATIOS AND INTER-BANK CALL RATIOS
AND INDEX OF BUSINESS CONFIDENCE, 1900 TO 1913

| Year | Percentage of total demand liabilities in Canada | | Index number of business confidence[2] |
	Cash reserve ratio [1]	Holdings of checks and notes of other banks [1]	1900 = 100
1901..........................	7.4	3.5	104.1
1902..........................	7.2	3.7	100.6
1903..........................	8.1	3.9	118.5
1904..........................	8.9	3.8	100.9
1905..........................	8.9	4.2	110.2
1906..........................	8.3	4.3	115.2
1907..........................	9.0	4.4	98.2
1908..........................	10.5	4.2	95.8
1909..........................	10.6	4.3	103.9
1910..........................	10.0	4.4	95.7
1911..........................	10.8	5.0	104.4
1912..........................	10.6	5.5	110.9
1913..........................	10.7	5.8	99.2

[1] Averages computed for each year from the aggregate totals of the monthly returns as of the last day of each month. Data from *Canada Gazette*.

[2] Computed by Coats from Dun's statistics of business failures in Canada: reciprocal of average of index numbers of (1) proportion of failures to the number of concerns in business, and (2) average liabilities of concerns failing. *Cost of Living Report*, vol. ii, p. 869.

the table supports the reasoning that the upward trend in the cash reserve ratio of the banks was the result of a deliberate adjustment to the changing character of the bank liabilities.

When a financial crisis appears to be approaching, and in fact whenever there is a lack of confidence in the soundness of business conditions, the banks as a safety measure should be expected to maintain, if they can, a higher reserve ratio. Similarly, when business confidence and optimism are widespread, the banks might decide that a lower reserve ratio would be adequate. There should be expected, therefore, some inverse correlation between the "barometer" of business confidence and the reserve ratio. In Table XLVII there is also given an index of business confidence for Canada, computed from statistics of business failures. Most of the years in which depression is indicated by a low index of business confidence were marked by substantial increases in the cash reserve ratio. The year 1910 is the only conspicuous exception, but monthly banking returns show that the cash reserve ratio rose sharply in the latter half of that year.

What has been demonstrated so far is that the Canadian banks always have their cash reserve ratio under close control, and that they always maintain it at what they decide to be the proper ratio under the circumstances of the moment. In general, the variations in conditions affecting the liability of the banks to be subjected to demands for cash funds are not so marked as to make the banks desire sharp fluctuations in the cash reserve ratio. Such constancy in cash reserve ratios is unusual in banking, but it has been a characteristic of the Canadian banking system since adequate statistics of its liabilities and cash reserves have been published.[1]

The demonstrated ability of the Canadian banks to maintain their cash reserve ratio under strict control has an important, if

[1] F. S. Mead, in 1907, in the course of a comparison of the cash reserves of various banking systems, presented a table showing the cash reserve ratio to total note and deposit liabilities of the Canadian banks from 1890 to 1906, and commented thereon as follows: "It will be noticed in the above table that the reserve in cash has been maintained at about the same percentage in a remarkably even way." "Bank Reserves in the United States, Canada, and England," *Quarterly Journal of Economics*, vol. xxi (May, 1907), p. 457.

not obvious, bearing upon the question of international gold movements. It will be remembered that practically all Canada's monetary gold comes from outside, that there is no gold in circulation in Canada, and that the entire Canadian stock of monetary gold is closely represented by the Dominion notes and specie in the cash reserves of the banks. The variations in the amounts of the cash reserves of the banks are virtually equivalent, therefore, to the movement of monetary gold into and out of Canada. The banks can maintain the constancy of the reserve ratio only if they have close control over one or the other terms of the ratio: cash reserves to total demand liabilities. If the cash reserve ratio is maintained at the desired level by adjusting the amount of the cash reserves to the amount of the total demand liabilities, and not vice versa, then the gold movements into and out of Canada are governed immediately by the reserve requirements of the banks, and not, as the *a priori* theory would explain it, by the state of the international balance of payments.

The money in circulation in Canada consists preponderantly of bank notes, and these in their own denominations, $5 and multiples thereof, had practically no competition from any other form of money during the period under study.[1] The country's supply of currency could not be appreciably altered by the banks without drastic curtailment or expansion of loans, and no appreciable shift from bank currency to other currency was possible. The banking system as a whole had little power of control, therefore, of the amount of its note issues, at least for short periods. The demand liabilities of the bank on account of note circulation were, therefore, not subject to close regulation by the banks, but were the resultant of general conditions largely independent of banking control.

Of the deposit liabilities, the volume of the deposits payable after notice or at a fixed date was equally clearly not subject to strict regulation by the banks. To a large extent the time deposits consist of savings deposits, that is, deposits payable after notice. Exactly to what extent this is the case is not ascertainable

[1] The only qualification to be made is that the Dominion government issued several million dollars of its own notes in $5 denominations during 1912 and 1913.

from the returns published by the banks. But the only recipients of savings deposits in Canada, other than the chartered banks, are the government savings and postal savings banks, two small savings banks with special charters, and the trust and loan companies, whose combined deposits throughout the period under study never amounted to as much as 10 per cent of the total time deposits in Canada. The savings deposits must, therefore, have been a large percentage of the total time deposits of the banks. The amount of these could not in practice be closely regulated. The banks are always glad to accept a substantial savings account. Moreover, they paid the same rate of interest on such deposits throughout the period, so that variations in the rate of interest were not used as a means of regulating the volume of savings deposits.

The amount of deposits payable on a fixed date, consisting chiefly of temporarily surplus funds of business concerns, could perhaps be regulated to a slight extent by varying the amounts of loans and discounts. An increase in loans would normally be accompanied by an increase in demand deposits. Withdrawals by check from these "created" deposits might in some cases be redeposited in time deposits by the payees of the checks.[1] Similarly a decrease in loans might indirectly reduce the amount of surplus funds available in the business community for time deposit.

A variation in the volume of loans granted by the banks, however, would operate primarily to bring about a corresponding variation in the volume of demand deposits. If the banks could freely expand or contract their loans, the dependence of demand deposits upon loans would give the banks the power to control their total demand liabilities.

But even the volume of loans granted by the banks, and consequently the volume of demand deposits, had only a very limited degree of flexibility. "The current loans of the Canadian banks are, to a large extent, an aggregation of lines of credit granted to individual customers. Scarcely any of these lines can be heavily reduced out of season without the infliction of serious damage

---

[1] Interest is paid on deposits payable on a fixed date, but not on demand deposits.

upon the business of the parties called upon to repay." [1] The Canadian banks kept their discount rates practically constant throughout the period under study.[2] They repeatedly claimed that no deserving request for an extension of credit was refused. There is no evidence that, at any time during the period under study, they used their power over the volume of loans to adjust their cash reserve ratios. There is abundant evidence, on the other hand, that the first consideration of the banks was the meeting of the credit needs of their customers, and that they neither contracted nor expanded their current loans primarily because of the state of their cash reserves. The Canadian banks also grant a relatively small amount of call loans in Canada. A reduction or increase in the amount of these loans would not necessarily make any change in the cash assets of the banks, but they would bring about a corresponding reduction or increase, respectively, in the total liabilities of the banks and thus would affect the reserve ratio. But, owing to the narrow market for securities in Canada, call loans in Canada are really not payable on demand, and the statistics of the amounts of call loans do not show sufficient variation in short periods to indicate that they are used to any extent as a means of regulating the cash reserve ratio.[3] Throughout the period under study the variation in the amount of call loans of the Canadian banking system from one month to another reached $5,000,000 on only one occasion. Assuming a 10 per cent cash reserve, a variation of $5,000,000 in the amount of deposits consequent upon a corresponding variation in the amount of call loans would be equivalent to a change of only $500,000 in the amount of the cash reserves, or of less than one tenth of 1 per cent in the cash reserve ratio.

It has been shown that the amount of the total demand liabilities of the banks is determined by the financial conditions and the banking needs of Canada, and that the banks are powerless to break the dependence of their total liabilities on conditions

[1] H. P. M. Eckardt, "A Comparison of Cash Reserves," *Journal of the Canadian Bankers' Association*, vol. xviii, No. 4 (July, 1911), p. 285.

[2] Cf. *Cost of Living Report*, vol. ii, pp. 736–738.

[3] Cf. J. F. Johnson, *The Canadian Banking System*, p. 73.

and circumstances over which they themselves have little control. The banks could therefore have succeeded as they did, in maintaining their cash reserve ratios constantly at the desired level through seasonal fluctuations in demand liabilities and cyclical fluctuations in business conditions, only by deliberately adjusting their cash reserves to their total demand liabilities, and not vice versa. Otherwise the constancy of the cash reserve ratio in the face of great Canadian borrowings abroad in sharply fluctuating amounts cannot be satisfactorily explained. Since the cash reserves of the banks closely represent the amount of monetary gold in Canada, it follows that gold movements into and out of Canada are directly dependent upon the amount of the total demand liabilities of the banks, and are not directly dependent upon the state of the international balance of payments. This is further confirmed by the fact that the variations in both cash reserves and total demand liabilities were much less marked than the variations in the rate of borrowings abroad.

"Outside Reserves" of the Canadian Banks and Gold Movements

What enables the Canadian banks to maintain their cash reserve ratios at so uniform a level is their use of a system of "secondary reserves" held outside of Canada, and often referred to as the "outside reserves," as distinguished from the "cash reserves" held in Canada. These outside reserves consist of funds loaned on call in New York and London, and net balances kept with New York and London banks. Of these items call loans in New York are by far the most important. The chart on page 165, which was used to demonstrate the constancy of the ratio of cash reserves to total liabilities, shows also the variations in the amounts and the ratios to total liabilities of the outside reserves. The outside reserve ratio, unlike the cash reserve ratio, shows frequent and substantial variations.

The outside reserves of the Canadian banks, although they are not cash, are regarded by the Canadian banks as a "call" on the gold supply of New York and London. To the banks, outside reserves have the advantage over cash reserves that even while they are carrying out the reserve function they are earning some income. By using the outside reserves as a fund to absorb temporary surpluses or to provide cash to meet foreign demands, the Canadian banks are able to extend credit in Canada in the volume demanded by the state of business and at the same time to keep the ratio of cash reserves to total liabilities close to what under the circumstances of the moment seems to them to be the lowest safe point. If total liabilities expand, or if disturbed business conditions make a higher cash reserve ratio seem expedient, the banks draw on their outside reserves. If total liabilities decline or if general business confidence and prosperity make a smaller cash reserve ratio appear safe to the banks, they transfer their surplus cash to the outside reserve.[1] There is no evidence that the banks use their outside call loans as an alternative to the extension of loans in Canada. In the first case, the prosperity of the Canadian banking system is so closely dependent on the prosperity of Canadian business that even from a selfish point of view it would be short-sighted policy for the banks to refuse to respond to legitimate demands for credit in Canada in order to loan their funds outside of Canada. Secondly, the rate of return on their outside loans is much lower than the earnings which the same amount of cash would yield in Canada if it could safely be used as a basis for Canadian loans.

The fluctuations in the outside reserves of the Canadian banks operate to adjust the Canadian balance of payments to capital borrowings in the manner attributed to gold movements in the generally accepted explanation of the mechanism of international trade. A Canadian railroad corporation, let us say, borrows $100,000,000 in London. To make the hypothesis as simple as possible, assume that it wants to use the entire proceeds of the loan in making purchases and paying wages in Canada. It will thereupon apply to the London branch of a Canadian bank to

---

[1] Cf. H. P. M. Eckardt: "The bank holdings of specie and Dominion notes do not fluctuate broadly with the accumulation or decrease of the temporary surpluses. It is the call loans and bank balances abroad that receive the surpluses and yield them up again. These items show wide fluctuations during the course of the year." *Journal of the Canadian Bankers' Association*, vol. xvi (October, 1908), p. 105.

transfer its London funds to Canada at the current rate of exchange. The Canadian bank will buy New York exchange with the sterling funds obtained from the railroad, and will establish a deposit for the corporation in Canada. So far the situation is as follows: the railroad has $100,000,000 on deposit in Canada; the bank has increased its deposit liabilities in Canada by $100,000,000, and has increased its funds in New York by $100,000,000. To maintain its normal cash reserve ratio, which we will assume to be 10 per cent, the bank will import from New York $10,000,000 of gold, using its New York funds to obtain the gold. The remaining $90,000,000 it will lend on call in New York.

The increase in Canadian bank deposits, unaccompanied by an increase in the quantity of goods in Canada, will cause a rise in the Canadian price level. Imports will be stimulated, exports checked. To pay for the excess of imports over exports, the Canadian importers will buy foreign exchange from their banks, giving checks upon their deposits in payment. If the excess of imports over exports exactly equals $100,000,000, the amount of the loan, the Canadian deposits will fall by $100,000,000, the banks will reëxport $10,000,000 gold from their cash reserves, and will use this $10,000,000 plus $90,000,000 of their funds on call in New York to meet the foreign bills of exchange which they had sold to their customers. Prices, deposits, cash reserves, outside reserves, will all be back to their levels prior to the flotation of the loan, and the borrowed capital will have moved into Canada in the form of commodities.

If the borrowing from abroad is not a single transaction but is continued indefinitely at a constant rate, deposits, cash reserves, prices, outside reserves, will be definitely maintained at their increased levels. Withdrawals from deposits and consequently from the cash reserves and outside reserves, to pay for the constant excess of imports over exports, will be simultaneously offset by new accretions resulting from the continued flow of loans. If the borrowing increases, but at an irregular rate with occasional declines in the rate of borrowing, as was the case during the period under study, there will be correspondingly irregular variations in the several items. Cash reserves, outside reserves, prices,

deposits, will all increase with every increase in the rate of borrowings, and will decrease with every decrease in the rate of
borrowings.

This is, of course, a highly simplified description of the process, and rests on several presuppositions which may not have
been true. It assumes, for instance, that the volume of deposits
would have remained constant if there had been no borrowings,
and that a uniform cash reserve ratio would be maintained as a
matter of policy. If a decline in business activity coincided with
a period of increased borrowings from abroad, the decrease in
bank deposits consequent upon business depression might more
than counterbalance the increase in deposits due to the borrowing. If the increased borrowing came at a time of general business optimism, the banks might feel that their cash reserve ratio
was unnecessarily high. If so, they would allow their deposits
to increase without bringing in any outside funds. These quali-
fications, though they render more difficult and uncertain the task
of inductive verification, do not invalidate this account of the
process as a description of tendencies which may of course be
counteracted by opposite tendencies arising from other causes.

There is still another qualification to be made, however, and one
of greater significance. It was assumed above that the rise in the
Canadian price level consequent upon the increase in deposits
would be just sufficient to bring about an excess of imports over
exports equal to the volume of borrowings. But the unfavorable
balance of trade might well be for some time either greater or less
than the volume of borrowings. Assume that the unfavorable balance is less than the volume of borrowings. The usual explanation
of the mechanism of adjustment would contend that this would
cause a steady inflow of gold until prices rose sufficiently to stimulate imports and check exports to the extent needed to adjust the
balance. In Canada, however, such a situation would simply
result in a piling-up of deposits in Canada and of outside reserves.
Until the unfavorable balance of trade equaled the amount of
borrowings, deposits would be steadily increasing, prices rising,
imports increasing, exports decreasing. To take now the opposite hypothesis, namely that the increase in deposits consequent

upon foreign borrowings has resulted in a rise in prices which stimulates imports, checks exports, to such a degree that the unfavorable balance is greatly in excess of the borrowings. Canadian importers, to pay for the excess, will draw heavily on their deposits, and buy foreign exchange therewith. The banks will provide the foreign funds from their outside reserves, if these are ample. Only if the outside reserves are not adequate to the task will they withdraw funds from their cash reserves. In any case, deposits will have fallen in Canada for, unlike withdrawals from deposits on domestic account, checking on deposits for foreign account means a reduction in the total of deposits, not merely a shifting of deposits from depositor to depositor and bank to bank. The reduction in deposits will cause a fall in Canadian prices; exports will increase, imports decrease; the unfavorable balance of trade will fall until it is in equilibrium with the borrowings. The Canadian process is as automatic as the process described in the generally accepted theory. It differs from the latter solely in that fluctuations in bank deposits and in outside reserves play the part in Canada which the classical theory attributes to gold movements.

It may be objected that the Canadian process is simply the process described by Mill, as modified everywhere by the development of deposit banking. The generally accepted theory, however, if presented in the form most nearly in keeping with Mill's exposition of the theory — and moreover in the form not yet shown by anyone to be untrue for other gold standard countries than Canada — would explain the variations in the Canadian bank deposits as the effect and not the cause of the gold movements; it would contend that an inflow of gold would stimulate deposits and an outflow of gold would bring about their contraction.

Through their use of outside reserves the Canadian banks can control and regulate the movement of gold into and out of Canada, largely irrespective of the state of the balance of payments. But if the outside reserves are regarded as equivalent to gold in Canada, then the Canadian process of adjustment of international balances approaches more closely that set forth *a priori* in the generally accepted theory. It is probable, however, that the Canadian variation from the typical method, by preventing sudden inflows and withdrawals of gold, operated to bring about a steadier and smoother adjustment of price levels and trade balances in the face of huge and irregular borrowings abroad than would have been possible if gold movements into and out of Canada were as automatic and free as they are elsewhere. The outside reserves, in other words, acted as a shock absorber in so far as Canadian economic and financial conditions were concerned. They appear, on the other hand, to have accentuated by their sudden contractions the financial difficulties of New York at critical moments.

Under certain circumstances the process of adjustment of the Canadian balance of indebtedness to borrowings has a slightly different phase from that described above. A Canadian corporation floating a large loan in London may have no immediate need in Canada for all or part of the proceeds, but may expect shortly to need foreign funds to meet payments on foreign purchases. The corporation may, therefore, leave the proceeds of the loan in London as a sterling deposit with the branch of a Canadian bank, checking upon it as it needs foreign funds. In this way the proceeds of the loan do not enter Canada until the foreign goods they pay for have been purchased, but the outside reserves and the outside deposits [1] of the Canadian banks expand temporarily until the proceeds of the loans are used by the borrower. One operation of this sort of sufficient magnitude to show in the bank returns took place in 1913. The Canadian Pacific Railway in that year sold to its shareholders, mainly in Great Britain, $105,000,000 of its stock, payable in the same year in five equal instalments at the Bank of Montreal in London. The payment of each instalment, if it came near a reporting-date for the bank, showed itself in the increase in the outside deposits and outside reserves of the bank. As the railway company drew on its London deposit to meet British obligations or for transfer to Canada, the outside deposits decreased. The funds "transferred" to Canada presumably appeared in the deposits in Canada, but the

[1] I. e., deposits with the branches of Canadian banks outside of Canada.

bank needed to transfer to Canada only sufficient gold to maintain its normal reserve ratio against demand liabilities, the remainder of the unexpended proceeds of the railway's loan remaining in the outside reserves.[1]

Some writers credit transfers of securities with being one of the important methods of adjusting balances of payments, the transfers being made profitable in one direction or the other as the exchange rates fluctuate above and below the mint pars. But the fluctuations in New York exchange in Canada are within too narrow a range appreciably to affect the profitability of security transactions, and the fluctuations in sterling exchange in Canada are governed by the state of the New York market for sterling exchange and not by the Canadian balance of payments with Great Britain. Moreover, security transactions in Canada are predominantly of an investment character, and the market for "floating securities" in Canada is too narrow to be much of a factor in settling trade balances.[2] In any case, transfers of securities cannot be important in the adjustment of the balance of payments to a continued debit balance of indebtedness, since this would be equivalent to saying that a borrowing country facilitates the process of receiving its borrowings in a form other than gold, by lending to the lending country.

While transfers of securities by private individuals are not, therefore, a significant factor in the settlement of Canadian balances, the Canadian banks hold substantial amounts of securities as a sort of tertiary reserve, and they may perhaps use these holdings as one of their means of meeting demands for foreign funds or of disposing of temporary surpluses of cash. The securities held by the Canadian banks increased at a fairly

[1] Cf. *Journal of the Canadian Bankers' Association*, vol. xxi (October, 1913), p. 10.

[2] "Those securities purchased or held abroad against the solid consideration of economic interest are *genuine investment securities*, while that mass of stocks and bonds which is ready to shift its ownership and residence at the call of a change of bank rates may be spoken of as *floating securities*. Speaking broadly the investment security goes to a country to stay, until a change in comparative rates of general economic interest or some great national event dislodges it." A. C. Whitaker, "The Ricardian Theory of Gold Movements," *Quarterly Journal of Economics*, vol. xviii (February, 1904), p. 225.

steady ratio from $36,195,000 in January, 1900, to $104,397,000 in December, 1913. Some of these securities were Canadian, but if the banks confined their securities purchases and sales to the New York and London markets, it would make no difference in the settlement of balances whether the securities were Canadian or foreign. But the holdings of securities, except for the general upward trend, varied slightly from month to month. It was the policy of the banks to keep a fairly constant percentage of their liabilities in liquid securities and to rely upon the outside reserves for flexibility. Nevertheless, the increase of over $68,000,000 in the amount of securities held by the banks during this period, to the extent that these securities were foreign or, if Canadian, were purchased abroad, operated to facilitate the adjustment of the Canadian balance, whether through deliberate policy or not. The increases in the holdings came mainly at periods of surplus outside funds and absorbed part of them.

The Method of Operation of the Outside Reserves

The reasoning of this chapter lends itself only to a limited extent to statistical verification. Increased borrowings result in increased deposits in Canada and in increased outside reserves only if the unfavorable balance of trade does not keep pace with the borrowings. Moreover, increased deposits in Canada may result from causes not connected with borrowings from abroad. It is possible, however, to obtain a rough measure of the variations in the amount of the demand liabilities in Canada due to the foreign borrowings by subtracting from the total demand liabilities the amount of loans. It is a well-established principle of commercial banking that loans give rise to note and deposit liabilities of closely corresponding proportions and that, in the ordinary course of commercial banking, total loans and total note and deposit liabilities of the system as a whole move in close harmony with each other. If the explanation which has here been offered, of the method whereby Canadians who borrow abroad obtain a transfer of their foreign funds into Canadian funds, is sound, this normal close relationship between loans and note and deposit liabilities should not hold during periods of greatly increased borrowings from abroad. At such periods there should be a substantial volume of bank deposits in Canada which are the result of borrowings abroad and not of loans made by Canadian banks. The variations in the excess of total note and deposit liabilities over total loans should provide an approximate measure of the variations in the amounts of such liabilities which arose out of borrowings abroad and not out of loans by Canadian banks.

Some obvious features of commercial banking operations make this only a rough and not an exact measure. The normal relationship between loans and note and deposit liabilities is not one of absolute equality: the "created deposit" is less than the loan which establishes it by the amount of the discount charged by the bank; some of the capital is commonly drawn out in the form of government cash and, while this cash ordinarily returns after a brief interval, an increasing volume of deposits will ordinarily be accompanied by an increasing volume of money in circulation; not all of the actual deposits are loaned out, as some portion thereof is retained for the cash reserves; purchases of securities by the banks operate alike with loans to increase bank deposits but do not operate to increase loans. The validity of the argument in the following pages is in some degree contingent upon the validity of the assumption that for the Canadian banking system during the period under investigation variations in the factors here mentioned were not sufficient of themselves to bring about *pronounced* variations in the quantitative relations of total note and deposit liabilities to total loans. This assumption is justified by the smallness of the total items, in Canadian banking and currency operations, which represent variations in the amounts deducted by the banks from deposits as discounts, in security investments of banks, in cash reserves, and in government paper currency in public circulation.

Chart III exhibits the amounts of capital borrowings, secondary or outside reserves, security holdings of the banks, and excess of deposit and note or "banking" liabilities over loans for each year of the period covered by this study. The amounts of excess of "banking" liabilities over loans are referred to as "foreign

CHART III

SECONDARY RESERVES, FOREIGN LOAN DEPOSITS, AND CAPITAL BORROWINGS,
1900 TO 1913

——— Capital borrowings, indirect estimate   — · — Secondary reserves of banks
— — — Capital borrowings, direct estimate   ········· Security holdings of banks
     — · · — "Foreign Loan" deposits of banks

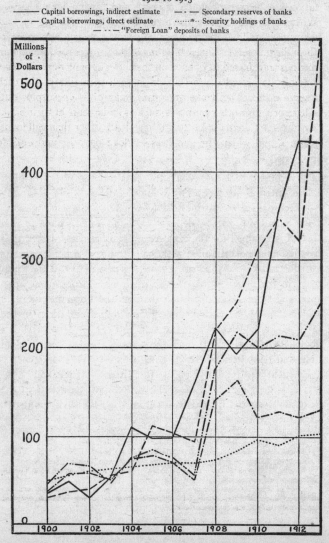

loan deposits," both for the sake of brevity and to distinguish them from the deposits "created" by the grant of loans by the Canadian banks themselves. The chart shows clearly the close relationship between outside reserves and foreign loan deposits. Without exception, they rise and fall together. The foreign loan deposits should be expected generally to be somewhat in excess of the outside reserves, since a fraction of the proceeds of foreign borrowings transferred to Canada on the books as bank deposits must actually be brought into Canada in cash to maintain the cash reserve ratio. The banks, moreover, may draw on surplus outside reserves for other purposes, such as an increase of their banking funds in Canada or of their foreign loans other than call loans, which would widen the gap between loan deposits and outside

DATA OF CHART III

SECONDARY RESERVES, FOREIGN LOAN DEPOSITS, AND CAPITAL BORROWINGS

In thousands of dollars

Year	Capital borrowings, indirect estimate [1]	Capital borrowings, direct estimate [2]	Secondary reserves of banks [3]	Security holdings of banks [4]	"Foreign Loan" deposits of banks [5]
1900	33,692	31,720	39,444	50,248	46,513
1901	49,964	37,169	58,796	56,290	70,989
1902	30,686	42,334	59,653	61,249	66,037
1903	52,499	54,671	52,238	63,590	46,783
1904	112,130	61,898	74,996	65,546	77,846
1905	98,749	112,551	77,995	68,994	85,703
1906	99,072	105,256	72,391	72,367	77,546
1907	160,985	95,088	50,819	71,088	55,068
1908	224,189	222,130	141,562	74,316	173,287
1909	193,448	253,400	164,345	85,795	218,176
1910	224,731	313,186	123,072	97,301	202,461
1911	358,202	348,410	128,699	94,904	213,660
1912	435,002	321,115	123,312	102,139	210,292
1913	433,085	546,699	129,820	104,397	251,773

[1] Capital Borrowings, indirect estimate: — Table XXVIII, p. 101, *supra.*

[2] Capital Borrowings, direct estimate: — Table XLIV, p. 139, *supra.*

[3] Secondary Reserves of Banks: — as of December 31 of each year, Chart II, p. 166, *supra.*

[4] Security Holdings of Banks: — as of December 31 of each year. Compiled from Monthly Bank Returns in *Canada Gazette.*

[5] "Foreign Loan" Deposits of Banks: — as of December 31 of each year; deposit and note liabilities in Canada, including government deposits, minus current and call loans in Canada, computed from Monthly Bank Returns in *Canada Gazette.*

reserves. The increase of the cash reserve ratio in the late years of the period[1] would also operate to widen the gap between loan deposits and outside reserves, especially if the outside reserves were drawn upon for the increase in cash reserves against both the ordinary demand liabilities and the foreign loan deposits. Also contributing to the widening of the gap between the loan deposits and the outside reserves after 1908 was the increase in the bank holdings of securities, an alternative use to which the banks could put the surplus outside funds resulting from foreign borrowings.

The decline in outside reserves in 1907, when borrowings, according to the indirect estimates, increased sharply, has been explained as due to (1) a forecast by the Canadian banks of impending financial trouble in New York and a desire to reduce their funds on call in New York, and (2) a desire to increase the cash reserves in Canada as a safeguard against possible financial difficulties.[2] This is not fully borne out by the facts. From January 1 to December 31, 1907, the cash reserves in Canada increased by only $8,900,000, whereas the outside reserves decreased by $21,600,000. At the same time the foreign loan deposits decreased by $22,500,000. It seems, therefore, that the decline in outside reserves was due chiefly to the existence of a debit balance of payments because of a more rapid increase in the debit balance of commodity and service transactions than in foreign borrowings, and was to only a slight extent the result of withdrawals from the outside reserves to strengthen the cash reserves.

The decline in outside reserves in 1907 can be readily explained in this way if it be granted that in those years when the direct estimate of capital borrowings shows smaller borrowings than the estimate derived indirectly from a calculation of the Canadian balance of indebtedness, the discrepancy is due to heavy Canadian imports made without previous provision for payment thereof or made in anticipation of their payment from the proceeds of loans still to be floated. The year 1907 was one of the

---

[1] See *supra*, p. 172.

[2] J. F. Johnson, *The Canadian Banking System*, pp. 81, 82.

years for which the two methods brought greatly divergent results. The direct estimate showed borrowings of $105,000,000 in
1906, $95,000,000 in 1907, $222,000,000 in 1908. The indirect
estimate showed borrowings of $99,000,000 in 1906, $161,000,000
in 1907, $224,000,000 in 1908.[1] This confirms the hypothesis
that in 1907 the outside reserves were heavily drawn upon to
meet obligations created by a greater excess of importation over
exportation of commodities and services than was warranted by
the amount of foreign borrowings actually floated.

The great increase in borrowings in 1908 and 1909 came in years
of hesitant business, and the borrowers did not make immediate
use of all of the proceeds of their loans for increased purchases
from abroad. The increase in borrowings was therefore accompanied by a great increase in loan deposits and outside
reserves. Confirmation of this reasoning is to be found in the
explanation of the increase in the outside reserves during these
years given by H. P. M. Eckardt, the foremost student of
Canadian banking:[2]

It is interesting to note the rapid manner in which the outside reserves
developed from the beginning of 1908, with the commencement of the extraordinary movement of British capital to Canada. . . . The total increase
in about a year and three quarters was $115,000,000. A considerable part
of this represented proceeds of new securities issued in London. In thus
finding temporary employment abroad for this large sum of new money,
the bankers undoubtedly followed a wise policy. The sudden injection of
so much new capital would have created disturbance in the Canadian financial system. So the funds were placed abroad at first and brought into use
in the Dominion gradually and carefully.

Although greatly increased borrowings occurred from 1911 to
1913, the banks failed to maintain the outside reserves and the
loan deposits at their previous level. These were years of great
industrial expansion in Canada and of imports of a magnitude
not justified even by the great amount of loans floated abroad.
Canadian concerns used in these years the surplus funds remaining from earlier borrowings, to finance their current imports. In
many instances they made foreign purchases in anticipation of

[1] See Table XLIV, p. 139.

[2] H. P. M. Eckardt, "The Immediately Available Reserve," *Journal of the
Canadian Bankers' Association*, vol. xx (July, 1913), pp. 252, 253.

loans still to be floated, and in consequence were hard pressed to meet their foreign obligations. This is confirmed not only by detailed items of information in the newspapers of the day, but, in a more general way, by the current comment in the Canadian financial journals, which in the same issues would publish statistics showing greatly increased borrowings from London and complaints that the London market had been closed to Canadian borrowers. No increase occurred in the outside reserves or loan deposits because the Canadian borrowers were using the proceeds of foreign loans as rapidly as they were available, and were even obtaining foreign funds from the Canadian banks, consisting largely of unused surpluses of earlier borrowings by other Canadians, to meet foreign obligations incurred in anticipation of the flotation of loans. There is also some evidence that the Canadian banks were drawing upon their outside reserves to meet the expanding demand for credit in Canada. Eckardt explains the decline in the outside reserves from the end of 1909 to the beginning of 1913 as follows: [1]

The steady decline in the combined cash and outside reserve ratio from the end of 1909 to the beginning of 1913 is impressive. That decline in reality constitutes the strongest point in favor of the contention that the Dominion must undergo a measure of compulsory liquidation. Various developments have combined to produce the declining ratio of reserve. The great activity of home trade and industry necessarily caused an increased demand for bank loans and advances. Speculation in town lots, city real estate and farm lands, and in stocks and commodities, too, always forces an expansion of credit.

Promotion of various companies or enterprises has played a part in absorbing the available floating capital. The inability of the London market to take new securities in volume has been potent in causing decline of the reserve ratio in Canada, for it forced the banks to draw heavily on their outside reserves in order to finance municipalities and corporations that had committed themselves to extensive expenditures in expectation of selling debentures and bonds.

Eckardt thus confirms the reasoning that the decline in the outside reserves from 1909 to 1913 was the result both of greater purchases abroad than were warranted by the volume of borrowings and of the withdrawal into Canada of part of the outside funds for use as a basis of credit expansion in Canada.

[1] *Journal of the Canadian Bankers' Association*, vol. xx (July, 1913), p. 250.

CHAPTER IX

CHANGES IN RELATIVE PRICE LEVELS AND THE ADJUSTMENT OF BALANCES OF INDEBTEDNESS

A. CONTROVERSIAL POINTS IN THE DEDUCTIVE THEORY

THE THEORIES OF THE EARLIER WRITERS

THE present discussion of the mechanism of adjustment of international balances of indebtedness has been related so far only to Mill's version of the theory. The major part of the credit for working out and formulating the theory is commonly attributed to Ricardo. The generally accepted theory of the mechanism of international trade, both in its broader phases and in its explanation of the particular problem under consideration here — the adjustment of balances of indebtedness to more or less permanent disturbing factors — is in fact often referred to in economic literature as the "Ricardian" theory. It will be demonstrated in the present chapter, mainly by citations from an earlier author, Henry Thornton, that the explanation offered by Mill of the method of adjustment of balances of indebtedness to disturbing factors, which is the explanation accepted most generally to-day, originated with a writer prior to Ricardo. It will also be shown, by citations from Ricardo, that he rejected this explanation and offered one in conflict with it.

Mill's explanation of the adjustment of the balance of indebtedness, it will be remembered, ran as follows: The extension of loans to foreign countries would result immediately in an export of gold, with a consequent fall in prices in the lending country and rise in prices in the borrowing country. This change in relative price levels would stimulate exports, check imports, in the lending country, and in this manner there would occur an excess of exports over imports equal to the loans abroad. A clear formulation of this theory was made, apparently for the first time, by Henry Thornton in 1802, eight years before Ricardo published his first work.

Thornton takes as his hypothetical situation, for the purpose of illustrating the mechanism of adjustment of trade balances to a disturbing factor, the failure of the harvest in a grain-exporting country. Although loans abroad constitute a different situation, both phenomena present closely similar problems in the adjustment of international balances. In the case of a harvest failure, the problem is: how are the exports of commodities other than grain increased, or the imports decreased, so as to maintain or reëstablish an even balance between exports and imports in the face of the cessation of grain exports and the appearance of grain imports? In the case of the extension of loans abroad, the problem is: how are the total exports increased and the total imports decreased, as compared with their volumes before the extension of the loans, so as to result in an even balance of payments, that is, in an excess of exports over imports equal to the amount of the loans? In both cases the basic problem for solution is the mechanism whereby the relative demands of the two countries for each other's products change in response to the new factor in the situation. Thornton's explanation is as follows: [1]

At the time of a very unfavourable balance (produced, for example, through a failure of the harvest), a country has occasion for large supplies of corn from abroad: but either it has not the means of supplying at the instant a sufficient quantity of goods in return, or, which is much the more probable case, . . . the goods which the country having the unfavourable balance is able to furnish as means of cancelling its debt, are not in such demand abroad as to afford the prospect of a tempting or even of a tolerable price. . . . The country, therefore, which has the favourable balance, being, to a certain degree, eager for payment, but not in immediate want of all that supply of goods which would be necessary to pay the balance, prefers gold as part, at least, of the payment; for gold can always be turned to a more beneficial use than a very great overplus of any other commodity. In order, then, to induce the country having the favourable balance to take all its payment in goods, and no part of it in gold, it would be requisite not only to prevent goods from being very dear, but even to render them excessively cheap. . . . For this reason, it may be the true policy and duty of the bank to permit, for a time, and to a certain extent, the continuance of that unfavourable exchange, which causes gold to leave the country, and to be drawn out of its own coffers. . . .

---

[1] Henry Thornton, *An Enquiry into the Nature and Effects of the Paper Credit of Great Britain*, London, 1802, in J. R. McCulloch's *Collection of Tracts on Paper Currency and Banking*, London, 1857, pp. 220, 221.

This, it will be noted, is essentially the explanation given by Mill, and given to-day by Taussig and most of the other economists who take up this problem. It was not, however, Ricardo's theory. In his first published work, "The High Price of Bullion," he criticized Thornton's explanation as follows:[1]

Mr. Thornton has not explained to us why any unwillingness should exist in the foreign country to receive our goods in exchange for their corn; and it would be necessary for him to show, that if such an unwillingness were to exist, we should agree to indulge it so far as to consent to part with our coin.

If we consent to give coin in exchange for goods, it must be from choice, not necessity. We should not import more goods than we export, unless we had a redundancy of currency, which it therefore suits us to make a part of our exports. The exportation of the coin is caused by its cheapness, and is not the effect, but the cause of an unfavourable balance: we should not export it, if we did not send it to a better market, or if we had any commodity which we could export more profitably. . . .

If, which is a much stronger case, we agreed to pay a subsidy to a foreign power, money would not be exported whilst there were any goods which could more cheaply discharge the payment. The interest of individuals would render the exportation of the money unnecessary.

Thus, then, specie will be sent abroad to discharge a debt only when it is superabundant; only when it is the cheapest exportable commodity. . . .

Thornton and Ricardo, therefore, were both agreed that gold would be exported only if it were redundant, but Ricardo denied, what Thornton affirmed, that redundancy of currency could be the *effect*, as well as the *cause*, of an unfavorable balance of trade.[2] Ricardo denied, moreover, that a crop failure or the grant of a subsidy would create either an unfavourable balance of trade, or, with a minor qualification made later, a redundancy of currency.

Malthus,[3] in a review of "The High Cost of Bullion," agreed

---

[1] (First edition, 1810), *Works*, McCulloch, editor, 1846, pp. 268, 269.

[2] Thornton, *op. cit.*, p. 220: "I conceive, therefore, that this excess [of currency], if it arises on the occasion of an unfavourable balance of trade, and at a time when there has been no extraordinary emission of notes, may fairly be considered as an excess created by that unfavourable balance, though it is one which a reduction in notes tends to cure."

Ricardo, *op. cit.*, p. 267: "The temptation to export money in exchange for goods, or what is termed an unfavourable balance of trade, never arises but from a redundant currency."

[3] *Edinburgh Review*, vol. xvii (February, 1811), pp. 342-345.

with Thornton as against Ricardo. He argued that Ricardo had not shown why the country to which a subsidy was granted should immediately demand at the same prices a greater quantity of the products of the country granting the subsidy than it had been in the habit of purchasing.[1] He agreed with Thornton, also, that the increase in the exports of the subsidy-paying country necessary to an adjustment of its balance of indebtedness could come about only through a preliminary export of gold which would lower prices and therefore increase the attractiveness of its products. But Malthus went even further. He denied that this export of gold would be the result of a redundancy of currency in the country granting the subsidy:

> But, as far as it is paid by the transmission of bullion, this transmission does not merely originate in redundancy of currency. It is not occasioned by its cheapness. . . . It is not merely a salutary remedy for a redundant currency: But it is owing precisely to the cause mentioned by Mr. Thornton — the unwillingness of the creditor nation to receive a great additional quantity of goods not wanted for immediate consumption, without being bribed to it by excessive cheapness; and its willingness to receive bullion — the currency of the commercial world — without any such bribe. . . . And, whatever variations between the quantity of currency and commodities, may be stated to take place subsequent to the commencement of these transactions, it cannot be for a moment doubted, that the cause of them is to be found in the wants and desires of one of the two nations, and not in any *original* redundancy or deficiency of currency in either of them.[2]

---

[1] Malthus admits that the fall in the price of bills on the country granting the subsidy will operate to increase the demand for the latter country's products, but he argues that if the subsidy is considerable, bills on the debtor country will fall to its gold export point: "We know indeed, that such a demand will to a certain degree exist, owing to the fall in the bills upon the debtor country, and the consequent opportunity of purchasing its commodities at a cheaper rate than usual. But if the debt for the corn or the subsidy be considerable, and require prompt payment, the bills on the debtor country will fall below the price of the transport of the precious metals. A part of the debt will be paid in these metals; and a part by the increased exports of commodities." (*Op. cit.*, pp. 344, 345.) This has bearing upon the theory of Professor Hollander, criticized in an earlier chapter, to the effect that variations in the exchanges would be adequate of themselves to adjust balances without the necessity of gold movements. (See p. 150, *supra*.) But Ricardo at first denied to either gold movements or variations in the exchanges any part in the mechanism of adjustment of the commodity balance of trade to the subsidy.

[2] *Op. cit.*, p. 345. As will be pointed out later, the word *original* (italics mine) begs the whole question.

Ricardo made a rejoinder to Malthus's criticism, but he added little to his earlier argument.[1] He claimed, indeed, that since the final result of all the importation and exportation of gold necessary, according to Malthus, to adjust international balances, would be the exchange of commodities for commodities, with gold in both countries at their "natural" levels, it was inconceivable that these results should not be foreseen, and the expense and trouble of these needless operations prevented.[2] He adhered to his original position that gold would be exported only if it were redundant, but he made the admission that a harvest failure might of itself create a redundancy of currency and therefore cause an export of gold:[3]

If the circulating medium of England consisted wholly of the precious metals, and were a fiftieth part of the value of the commodities which it circulated . . . [and if] England, in consequence of a bad harvest, would come under the case mentioned [in the original Essay] of a country having been deprived of a part of its commodities, and therefore requiring a diminished amount of circulating medium, [the] currency, which was before equal to her payments, would now become superabundant; and relatively cheap, in the proportion of one fiftieth part of her diminished production; the exportation of this sum, therefore, would restore the value of her currency to the value of the currencies of other countries.

This is not the sort of gold movement, however, which was posited by Thornton and Malthus. The function of the gold movement according to Ricardo is *to maintain unaltered* the original relation to each other of "the proportion between money and commodities," that is, the price levels, in the two countries. Because of the reduction in the quantity of commodities in the country which has suffered the failure of the harvest, a redistribution of currency is required to maintain this original relation. In the case of a subsidy, presumably, there would be according to Ricardo a similar gold movement *after* the subsidy had begun to move out in the form of commodities, and for the same reason. But according to Thornton and Malthus, over and above the gold export from the debtor country which was adequate to maintain the original relation of price levels, there must be an addi-

[1] Appendix to fourth edition of "The High Cost of Bullion," *Works*, pp. 291 seq.

[2] *Ibid.*, p. 292. (See also p. 198, *infra*.) [3] *Ibid.*, p. 293.

tional gold export which will lower prices in the debtor country and so stimulate exports. This Ricardo denied.

Ricardo's argument can be summarized in the three following propositions:

(1) Gold will be exported only if it is relatively redundant as compared to other countries.

(2) An export of gold is always the *cause*, never the *effect*, of an unfavorable balance of trade.

(3) A failure of the harvest, or the grant of a subsidy or loan to a foreign country, does not create a redundancy of currency, that is, does not make the existing level of prices in the country suffering the failure of the harvest, or granting the subsidy or loan, too high, and, therefore, does not result in the export of gold.[1]

Thornton would reject the last two of these propositions; Malthus would reject all three.

The first of these propositions is unquestionably sound. But it requires more careful definition than is given to it by Ricardo. Two countries [2] have the proper amounts of currency relative to each other if the relative price levels in the two countries are such that trade between the countries results in an even balance of international payments. Any cause which makes the price level of a country too high to bring about an even balance of international payments, whether it be an over-issue of paper currency, or a crop failure, or the grant of a foreign loan, or a sudden decline in the relative demand of foreign countries for its products as compared to its demand for foreign commodities, makes currency redundant in that country.

The second proposition turns upon a question of time: can the unfavorable balance of trade precede the export of gold, or is it always caused by a preceding export of gold? Ricardo, in supporting the position that the export of gold is never the result, but always the cause, of an adverse trade balance, in effect maintains that gold is never exported to settle old obligations but is always exported to supply funds for obligations still to be made. But to take the case of the grant of a loan, the moment the loan is made

---

[1] With the later qualification, however, which was discussed above.
[2] Assuming that only two countries are concerned.

there will be an unfavorable balance of payments, unless at the same moment the foreign demand for the lending country's products increases sufficiently to offset the debits created by the grant of the loan.[1] Ricardo argues that the grant of a loan will not create an unfavorable balance of payments, because: (1) the lending country will meet its loan obligations in goods and not in gold unless gold is cheaper than goods; and (2) there is nothing in the grant of a loan to make gold cheaper. But it is now necessary for the borrowing country to purchase a greater quantity of the lending country's goods than it purchased before the grant of the loan, if the even balance of international payments is to be maintained. Ricardo fails to see that if the foreign demand for the lending country's goods is not immediately, automatically, and proportionately increased by the grant of the loan, prices in the lending country, which were at their proper level before the flotation of the loan, are too high now; if the borrowing country before the loan took 1,000,000 pounds of wool at 20 cents a pound, this price is too high, that is, gold is too low, if it must now be induced to take 1,500,000 pounds. Ricardo fails to show why or how the borrowing country's demand for the lending country's products will increase because of the loan so that it will take more commodities at the *same* prices. He fails to meet Malthus's argument that the borrowing country will not be willing to accept more of the lending country's goods at the *same* prices because, although "it is unquestionably true, as stated by Mr. Ricardo, that no nation will pay a debt in the precious metals, if it can do it cheaper by commodities; . . . the prices of commodities are liable to great depressions from a glut in the market [to put it in more modern language, greatly increased quantities of commodities cannot be sold except at substantially lower prices] whereas the precious metals, on account of their having been constituted, by the universal consent of society, the general medium of exchange, and instrument of commerce, will pay a debt of the largest amount at its nominal estimation, according to the quan-

---

[1] It is necessary to shift the discussion at this point from "balance of trade" to "balance of payments" terms, because in the case of a lending country there will be an adverse balance of payments even in the presence of a favorable balance of trade if the excess of exports is not as great as the amount of the loan.

tity of bullion contained in the respective currencies of the countries in question." [1]   Malthus is undoubtedly right in claiming
that a debt payable in gold can be liquidated in gold without discount, whereas to pay it in commodities may require their sale
at reduced prices.   It follows, therefore, that the grant of a
loan to a foreign country may, and ordinarily will, immediately
create an unfavorable balance of payments and a redundancy in
currency.   Immediately thereafter the export of gold will begin —
the effect, as Thornton and Malthus claim, and not the cause, as
Ricardo claims, of an insufficient export of goods and a consequent
unfavorable balance of payments.

Similarly, in the case of the failure of the harvest, while prices
remain at their former levels, imports and exports with the exception of grain will remain at their former levels.   The cessation
of grain exports will prevent imports and exports from balancing
evenly.   There will be, therefore, unfavorable balances of trade
and of payments, which will be the cause and not the effect of an
export of gold from the country whose harvest has failed.

That the third proposition of Ricardo is also unsound has
already been demonstrated in the course of the analysis of the
first two propositions.   A failure of the harvest in a given country,
or its grant of a subsidy or a loan to a foreign country, makes the
existing prices too high in the given country to permit of a volume
of exports adequate to liquidate the claims of the other country:
that is, it makes the currency redundant.   There results an unfavorable balance of payments, which in turn results in an export
of gold.

Ricardo seems to have been led into his erroneous conclusions
in part by his exaggerated notion of the obstacles which exist to
the exportation of gold.   As has already been pointed out, Ricardo
denied that gold would be exported if it were soon to be reim-
ported: [2]

The ultimate result then of all this exportation and importation of money,
is that one country will have imported one commodity in exchange for another, and the coin and bullion will in both countries have regained their
natural level.   Is it to be contended that these results would not be foreseen,

---

[1] *Edinburgh Review*, February, 1811, p. 345.
[2] Appendix to fourth edition of "The High Cost of Bullion," *Works*, p. 292.

and the expense and trouble attending these needless operations effectually prevented, in a country where capital is abundant, where every possible economy in trade is practised, and where competition is pushed to its utmost limits? Is it conceivable that money should be sent abroad for the purpose merely of rendering it dear in this country and cheap in another, and by such means to insure its return to us?

But gold when exported does not always return. If the loans or subsidies continued indefinitely, the gold would not return. In any case, when gold is exported no one knows definitely whether the loss of gold will be permanent or not. Even if it were known that the gold, if exported, will return, say, after a year, Ricardo does not disclose the machinery by which the immediate claims of foreigners will be liquidated without gold shipments, or who will exert himself to stop the gold payments. It would be almost as reasonable to suppose that if in domestic trade an individual was to sell his products in January, knowing that in December next he will use the proceeds to buy the products of the purchaser, he would customarily be able to avoid the necessity of using money as a medium of exchange. Moreover, gold is not sent abroad "for the purpose merely of rendering it dear," but to settle obligations which cannot be as conveniently or cheaply settled in any other fashion. Nor is the change in the relative value of gold in the two countries the only result of the export of gold. By making the products of the gold-exporting country cheap and those of the gold-importing country dear, the export of gold affects the commodity balance of trade between the two countries.

Ricardo also gives an unrealistic description of the endeavors which an individual having foreign obligations to meet will undergo in order to make payment in the cheapest possible medium: [1]

If I owed a debt in Hamburgh of £100, I should endeavor to find out the cheapest mode of paying it. If I send money, the expense attending its transportation being, I will suppose, £5, to discharge my debt will cost me £105. If I purchase cloth here, which, with the expenses attending its exportation, will cost me £106, and which will in Hamburgh sell for £100, it is evidently more to my advantage to send the money. If the purchase and

---

[1] "The High Price of Bullion," *Works*, p. 269.

expenses of sending hardware to pay my debt will take £107, I should prefer sending cloth to hardware, but I would send neither in preference to money, because money would be the cheapest exportable commodity in the London market.

But, to quote Ricardo himself, "each transaction in international trade is an individual transaction." If a person has a monetary payment to make abroad, he will not ordinarily look about for a commodity which will serve the purpose of making payment, make the necessary purchase thereof, find a buyer in the country to which he must send his remittance, and in this roundabout way obtain the foreign funds he needs. Even though the situation is such that payments can theoretically be made more profitably in commodities than in gold, payments must in practice be made in gold until, through the mediation of merchants and of exchange brokers, commodity sales abroad are increased and foreign credits are thus made available to offset the foreign debits. An adjustment of this sort will take time. In the meanwhile, foreign payments will be made in gold. There is no reason to suppose, however, that Ricardo was unaware of the practical obstacles to the smooth and complete working out of a theoretically desirable mechanism. These obstacles were of the category of "facts," whereas he was interested only in "principles." [1]

In private correspondence with Malthus, Ricardo receded in some minor particulars from the position taken in his original essay. He conceded to Thornton that crop failures, changes in the foreign demand, the grant of a subsidy, as well as changes in

[1] *Letters of Ricardo to Malthus*, p. 18: "The first point to be considered is, what is the interest of countries in the case supposed? The second, what is their practice? Now it is obvious that I need not be greatly solicitous about this latter point; it is sufficient for my purpose if I can clearly demonstrate that the interest of the public is as I have stated it. It would be no answer to me that men were ignorant of the best and cheapest mode of conducting their business and paying their debts, because that is a question of fact, not of science, and might be urged against almost every proposition in Political Economy. . . . When you say that money will go abroad to pay a debt or a subsidy, or to buy corn, although it be not superabundant, but at the same time admit that it will speedily return and be exchanged for goods, you appear to me to concede all for which I contend, namely, that it will be the *interest* of both countries, when money is not superabundant in the one owing the debt, that the expense of exporting the money should be spared, because it will be followed by another useless expense, — sending it back again."

the supply of the currency, might create a redundancy of currency.[1] He gave a prominent place in the mechanism of adjustment of international balances to variations in the exchanges, and even maintained that an unfavorable rate of exchange resulting from the necessity of paying a subsidy would tend to persist long after the subsidy had been fully paid.[2] He admitted that the description he had given of the mechanism of adjustment of international balances was intended to apply only to a state of affairs in which all persons knew, actively sought, and were able to achieve, what was in the absence of "friction" their best interest, and that under actual conditions the adjustment might work out somewhat differently.[3] He still maintained, however, that a shift in relative prices in subsidy-granting and subsidy-receiving countries, respectively, was not a part of the mechanism of adjustment of the commodity balance to the subsidy. He claimed that, if the fall in the exchange of the subsidy-granting country was not of itself sufficient to result in an increase in exports sufficient to pay the subsidy, and gold was therefore exported, the amount of gold exported would necessarily be a smaller proportion of the total stock of gold in the country than the proportion of the commodity exports sent in payment of the subsidy to the total stock of commodities. Prices in the subsidy-granting country would not fall, therefore, during the payment of the subsidy, and would be higher after payment had been completed than they were before. The exchange for this reason would continue permanently unfavorable to this country.[4]

Ricardo does not state the grounds on which he rests his assertion that the export of gold would be in relatively smaller proportions than the export of commodities. There can be little likelihood, however, that commodity shipments in payment of a subsidy or a loan will affect the commodity side of the equation between commodities and money as much as the gold shipments will affect the money side. An increase in exports does not neces-

[1] *Letters of Ricardo to Malthus*, p. 13. Malthus denied this.

[2] *Ibid.*, p. 20.   [3] *Ibid.*, pp. 18, 19.

[4] *Ibid.*, pp. 20, 21. In a previous letter he had contended that after the payment of the subsidy "the exchange would again accurately express the value of the currency," *i. e.*, would return to the mint par. (*Ibid.*, p. 15.)

sarily reduce the flow of commodities (and services) requiring
mediation of their exchanges in the exporting country. In any
case, even a huge subsidy is likely to be a small proportion of the
total volume of commodities and services exchanged for money
in the course of the year, whereas a relatively small fraction of the
subsidy paid in gold may represent a large fraction of the total
supply of gold of the exporting country.[1]

MODERN CRITICISMS OF MILL'S THEORY

Later writers for some time almost invariably followed Thornton and Malthus, rather than Ricardo. Tooke[2] added further
strength to the case for the necessity of gold movements by
stressing the delays which must ensue before a change in conditions, even a sharp fall in prices, can lead to increased exports
and the payment therefor. The delays incident to the spreading
of information about price changes, the shipment of commodities
and the payment therefor, are not as important now as they were
then, but nevertheless it must still remain true that the full commercial response to changes in price levels cannot be expected to
take place immediately.[3] Mill, as we have seen, accepted Thornton's rather than Ricardo's explanation, as did Cairnes also.[4]
Francis Walker in 1883, after reviewing the controversy between
Thornton and Malthus on the one hand and Ricardo on the
other, but with special reference to its bearing on monetary
theory, sided also with Thornton and Malthus rather than with
Ricardo.[5]

---

[1] In recent discussions of the theory of international trade under inconvertible
paper some writers have in similar manner exaggerated the significance on prices
in the lending country of the export of the goods sent in payment of the loans.
Only if the loans were extraordinarily great in volume could they have an appreciable effect on the total volume of domestic exchanges of goods and services.

[2] Thomas Tooke, *The State of the Currency* (2d ed.), London, 1826, p. 106. William Blake, writing in 1810, also follows Thornton rather than Ricardo, when he
argues that gold movements will arise not only from changes in the volume of currency but also from harvest conditions, subsidies, foreign remittances, etc. (*The
Course of Exchange; and the Present Depreciated State of Currency*, pp. 4, 5.)

[3] See p. 214, *infra*.

[4] J. E. Cairnes, *Some Leading Principles of Political Economy*, 1874, Part III,
Ch. III, § 6.

[5] Francis A. Walker, *Money*, New York, 1883, pp. 48 seq., 150 seq., 519.

Bastable, in 1889, concerned mainly with the defense of Ricardo's theory that the terms of international exchange are identical under a money economy with what they would be under a barter economy, gave hesitating support to Ricardo's theory that gold would not move from a borrowing to a lending country and thus bring about a change in relative price levels: [1]

It is also doubtful whether Mill is correct in asserting that the quantity of money will be increased in the creditor [that is, the borrowing] and reduced in the debtor [that is, the lending] country. The sum of money incomes will no doubt be higher in the former; but that increased amount may be expended in purchasing imported articles obtained by means of the obligations held against the debtor nation. . . . Nor does it follow that the scale of prices will be higher in the creditor than in the debtor country. The inhabitants of the former, having larger money incomes, will purchase more *at the same price*, and thus bring about the necessary excess of imports over exports.

The old controversy has recently been reopened,[2] but without adequate reference to the original participants therein, and apparently without full realization of the extent to which Ricardo's conclusions had been rejected by other writers. Professor Taussig, in an article dealing more especially with some points of theory relating to international trade under depreciated currency, began his exposition with an explanation of the adjustment of balances to loans under the gold standard precisely identical with that offered by Mill, but apparently under the impression that it was the Ricardian theory. Professor Hollander replied in rebuttal by an appeal to the opposing theory of Ricardo, but apparently under the impression that Ricardo's theory was the generally accepted one.[3] Hollander added, what was not a part of Ricardo's

[1] C. F. Bastable, "On Some Applications of the Theory of International Trade," *Quarterly Journal of Economics*, vol. iv (October, 1889), p. 16. (Italics his.) For a discussion of Ricardo's theory that the terms of international trade are not altered by the introduction of money, see p. 295, *infra*.

[2] In the *Quarterly Journal of Economics*: F. W. Taussig, "International Trade Under Depreciated Paper," vol. xxxi (May, 1917); Knut Wicksell, "International Freights and Prices" (with a rejoinder by F. W. Taussig), vol. xxxii (February, 1918); J. H. Hollander, "International Trade Under Depreciated Paper: A Criticism"; F. W. Taussig, "A Rejoinder," vol. xxxii (August, 1918).

[3] J. H. Hollander: "From the day of Ricardo it has been agreed that 'specie will be sent abroad to discharge a debt only when it is superabundant; only when

original explanation and has already been disposed of above,[1] that the increase in the exports of the lending country would be the result of a preceding decline in the price of bills on the lending country. He makes the further point, however, that to prove the possibility of a gold movement, it is necessary to assume that the equation of international demand is disturbed.[2] But this is precisely what the flotation of a loan does. Moreover, if the equation of international demand were not disturbed, the parity of the exchanges would not be disturbed. The equation of international demand denotes not necessarily an even ratio between the relative demands of two countries for each other's commodities, but an even ratio between immediate obligations in both directions, arising from whatever cause, so that these immediate obligations will be liquidated without the use of gold. The grant of a loan to a foreign country, by increasing the demand in the lending country for bills on the borrowing country without proportionately increasing the supply thereof, disturbs the equation of demand, the balance of payments, and the parity of the exchanges. As Professor Hollander himself says: "What may be conceived as really taking place is that the loan transaction will entail an increase in the demand for New York exchange in London and an increase in the supply of sterling bills in New York."[3] This would not be true if the grant of the loan did not disturb the equation of international demand nor, to return to another phase of Hollander's argument, would it be true if gold had not become superabundant in the lending country because of the loan.[4]

Professor Wicksell also replied to Taussig's article, mainly along the lines of Bastable's argument, to the effect that the transfer

it is the cheapest exportable commodity.'" (*Quarterly Journal of Economics*, vol. xxxii, p. 677.)

F. W. Taussig: "Let it be borne in mind that both Professor Hollander and myself are discussing the accepted [Ricardian] theory, and that neither of us undertakes here to correct or to verify it." *Ibid.*, p. 690.

[1] See pp. 150 seq., *supra*.

[2] *Quarterly Journal of Economics*, vol. xxxii, p. 680.

[3] *Ibid.*, p. 678.

[4] Cf. Ricardo, "Principles" (*Works*, p. 84): "When each country has precisely the quantity of money which it ought to have, money will not indeed be of the same value in each, . . . but the exchange will be at par."

of purchasing power from the lending to the borrowing country would operate, without gold movements on a scale sufficient to result in price changes, to bring about the necessary excess of exports over imports in the lending country.[1] Taussig, in his original article, had argued that generally not all the proceeds of a foreign loan would be used by the borrowers immediately in making purchases of foreign goods, but that part of the proceeds would be brought to the borrowing country to be used in buying domestic commodities and hiring labor. Wicksell pointed out that even the domestic purchases would operate to adjust the international balance, since they would reduce the amount of commodities in the borrowing country available for export. Nevertheless, even with this correction, Taussig's argument still holds that without gold movements and changes in price levels there is no visible mechanism whereby increased purchases by the borrowers of foreign commodities, and of those domestic commodities which otherwise would be exported, will exactly equal the amount of the borrowings.[2] It is quite possible that none of the proceeds of a loan shall be used directly in making foreign purchases. In the absence of changes in prices consequent upon gold movements and of special circumstances, what should be theoretically expected is that the proceeds of foreign loans will on the average be used in the first instance by the borrowers in making purchases of foreign goods and of domestic goods which would otherwise be exported in the same proportions, respectively, as foreign purchases prior to the flotation of the loans were to total purchases, and as purchases of export commodities were to total purchases. Assume that a country annually imports $1,000,000 of foreign goods and that its domestic production of goods amounts annually to $10,000,000, of which $2,000,000 consists of commodities of a class of which $1,000,000 is exported, $1,000,000 consumed at home. Assume that the country borrows abroad, for general purposes, $1,000,000. The theoretical expectation would be that, in the year in which the loan was floated, in the absence of price changes, the commodity imports would increase by $100,000,

---

[1] *Quarterly Journal of Economics*, vol. xxxii, p. 405.
[2] F. W. Taussig, *ibid.*, vol. xxxi, pp. 393, 394.

the exports would decrease by $100,000, and $800,000 of the loan would be taken in gold.[1] In the absence of special circumstances such as the requirement that the proceeds of the loan be immediately used in making purchases in the lending country, and in the absence of price changes, there is no reason why borrowings abroad should disturb the proportions in which the total purchasing power in the borrowing country, including that derived from the loan, is used in buying domestic and foreign commodities. Without a disturbance in these proportions the loan cannot wholly enter in the form of commodities.[2]

SECTIONAL PRICE LEVELS

The theory maintained above, that changes in price levels resulting from gold movements play an important part in the mechanism of adjustment of international balances, has been attacked also by Professor Laughlin, but from an altogether different point of view. In his criticism of the theory, which is merely a phase of his general denial of the validity of the quantity theory of the value of money,[3] Laughlin contends that changes in price levels cannot play an important part in the mechanism of adjustment of international balances of trade, on the ground that the general price levels of two countries cannot move in opposite directions, and cannot move in the same direction in substantially different degrees, since "the action of the international markets, with telegraphic quotations from every part of the world, precludes the supposition that gold prices could in general remain on a higher level in one country than another (cost of carriage apart) even for

[1] In the above illustration the total domestic consumption in the absence of loans is $10,000,000, of which $1,000,000, or one tenth, consists of imported commodities and an equal amount consists of articles of a class which has an export market.

[2] J. S. Nicholson (*Principles of Political Economy*, London, 1897, vol. ii, pp. 287-291) attacks Mill's reasoning with regard to gold movements and price changes and provides an alternative solution similar to that of Wicksell discussed above. Although he finds Mill's reasoning absurd, he presents no argument not already considered here. Nothing is to be gained, therefore, from a detailed consideration of his explanation of the mechanism.

[3] J. L. Laughlin, *Principles of Money*, p. 369.

a brief time." It would be pertinent here to cite as complete rebuttal of this argument the statistical evidence afforded by various comparative studies of prices which reveal striking differences
in gold price levels in different countries, or the charts of the
comparative trend of prices in Canada and other countries given
in the next chapter, which demonstrate that price levels do move
differently in different countries. But the argument can be met
by deductive reasoning which adheres to the spirit while extending
and amplifying the details of the accepted theory. One attempt to
meet Professor Laughlin's criticism in this manner may here be
noted. Whitaker,[1] in an otherwise brilliant and conclusive reply
to Laughlin, argues that if the highly developed means of communication have brought about so great a uniformity of price
levels that disturbances of relative price levels have become almost imperceptible, it is only because the forces considered in
the orthodox theory operate more effectively now than in earlier
days in bringing about uniformity. He claims that the orthodox
theory does not at all assert that prices *maintain* different levels
in different countries, and he further claims that the "normal
situation" — by which he means apparently the situation char-
acterized by a stable balance of trade adjusted without further
gold movements to the balance of indebtedness — is uniformity
of price levels. He asks whether Laughlin would argue, because
Chicago and Liverpool prices are adjusted one to the other by
telegraph, that a difference in the price of wheat at these points
is not the cause of the movement of wheat between them.

It can be demonstrated from the writings of the classical school
that Whitaker misinterprets their theory and that they would not
agree that gold prices must find a uniform level throughout the
world.[2] On the other hand, such slight differences of prices, other

[1] A. C. Whitaker, "The Ricardian Theory of Gold Movements," *Quarterly Journal of Economics*, February, 1904, pp. 236 seq.

[2] David Ricardo, "Principles," Ch. VII, *Works*, p. 81: "The value of money
is never the same in any two countries, depending as it does on relative taxation,
on manufacturing skill, on the advantages of climate, natural productions, and
many other causes."

J. S. Mill, *Principles*, Bk. III, Ch. XIX, § 2: "The countries whose exportable
productions are most in demand abroad, and contain greatest value in smallest
bulk, which are nearest to the mines, and which have least demand for foreign pro-

than those accounted for by transportation costs, as can exist for more than a day or two between markets connected by telegraph and for commodities steadily moving in *one* direction in international trade, cannot explain such tremendous adjustments of balances of trade as are necessary when a country of the relatively minor economic importance of Canada increases the rate of its capital borrowings by $100,000,000 in one year.

The adjustment of balances of trade where the disturbing element to an existing equilibrium is important cannot be explained by those "scarcely perceptible" changes in relative prices which Whitaker considers the direct cause governing such adjustments. The possibility of important changes in relative price levels is demonstrated inductively in the following chapter. In view of Laughlin's statement with respect to the equalizing influence of rapid communication on price levels in international trade, how can such changes in relative price levels be explained deductively?

Laughlin's statement with regard to the necessary uniformity of prices between countries in telegraphic communication is true only of commodities which move in trade regularly and in large quantities between these countries, and is true even here only with important reservations. Laughlin acknowledges that relative prices of a given commodity in two countries may differ by

ductions, are those in which money will be of lowest value, or in other words, in which prices will habitually range the highest."

J. E. Cairnes, *Some Leading Principles*, Part III, Ch. v, § 1: "I ought here, perhaps, to refer to a maxim advanced by some writers on monetary questions which, if well founded, would seem to preclude the existence of the phenomenon, the character of which I propose to discuss. It is held by the writers to whom I refer that the value of gold is, and must ever be, 'the same all the world over.' Now if this be so, as the value of gold is merely another expression for the gold prices of commodities, it must follow that a high or a low scale of general prices existing in any country, and not shared by every other, is an impossible occurrence. As there is no local value of gold, so there can be no local scale of prices. I have no hesitation, however, in expressing my opinion that the doctrine in question, with whatever confidence advanced, is absolutely destitute of foundation." And in a footnote to the above: "It has certainly no support from any writer of authority."

Whitaker, in a recently published book (*Foreign Exchange*, 1920, pp. 618 seq.), not only attributes once more to Ricardo the theory that gold has uniform purchasing power throughout the world, but he also attributes to him Thornton's doctrine that "excessive imports of goods" are one of the usual causes of gold movements.

the cost of transportation. But if prices of a given commodity in two countries may differ by *exactly* the cost of transportation, it can easily be demonstrated that while the prices in one country remain constant, the prices in the other may vary within the limits of a fraction of the cost of transportation and twice the cost of transportation. Countries A and B both produce a given commodity. On a given date its price is X in A, and Y, a higher price, in B. The cost of transportation between the two countries is Z, which equals Y–X. This would be the normal situation while the commodity was moving from A to B. But it would be theoretically possible for the price of the commodity in A to settle at any point between X and X + 2Z and to remain at that point while the price in B remained unchanged. Stated in other terms, if the price of wheat in Liverpool is \$2 and remains at \$2, and the cost of transportation in either direction between Chicago and Liverpool is 40 cents, the Chicago price of wheat may settle at any point between \$1.60 and \$2.40. If the cost of transportation rises or falls, there is a corresponding change in the possible range of fluctuations of relative prices.

What has been said above with regard to the relation of transportation costs to relative price levels in different countries applies with equal force to import duties. If in the above illustration T is the specific import duty on a commodity in both country A and country B, the price may range in country A between X – T and X + 2Z + T, while remaining at Y in country B. The Canadian tariff, measured by usual standards, is a high tariff. Only for commodities, therefore, which are readily transportable at small cost and which are not subject to duty is the possible range of fluctuation in their relative prices in Canada and in other countries very closely limited.

But there are commodities which, because of their great bulk in proportion to their value or for other reasons, are costly to transport, and for such commodities the possible range of fluctuation in relative prices may be several times the price of the article in the low-price country. There are other commodities which, because they are perishable or because they meet a demand which is wholly local, never or rarely move in international trade, and the prices of such commodities are in all cases largely, in some cases wholly, independent of any direct influence of foreign prices. There are also commodities which are immovable, such as land and buildings, and there are services which cannot be detached from the person rendering them and therefore have limited mobility, and these also have prices which are not directly subject to competition from abroad. If the general price levels of any two countries be considered, including the prices of services, there is therefore a considerable range within which the price levels may diverge from each other in response to factors which are not common or identical in both countries.

Price levels of different countries, therefore, although in part interdependent, are also in part independent of each other. The direct interdependence is largely confined to the prices of those commodities which move freely and in substantial amounts in international trade, commodities which may be conveniently termed "international commodities." The prices of bulky commodities are subject also to direct external influence, but only in the sense that foreign prices set broad limits to their fluctuations — if these commodities fall to abnormally low prices exportation may be stimulated and the influence of foreign prices may become important, and similarly, if they rise to abnormally high prices competition may set in from imported commodities. The prices of services and of what may be termed "domestic commodities," commodities which are too perishable or too bulky to enter regularly and substantially into foreign trade, are wholly or largely independent of *direct* relationship with foreign prices. World price-factors influence them only through their influence on the prices of international commodities, with which the prices of domestic commodities, as part of a common price-system, must retain a somewhat flexible relationship.

An important improvement in the classical theory was made when the analysis of the part played by price changes in the adjustment of balances was extended beyond a general and unqualified discussion of changes in "general price levels" to an analysis of the trends of the sectional price levels. The application, to the general theory, of the fruits of this analysis has been made most completely and effectively by Professor Taussig. Cairnes, however, appears to have been the first writer clearly to perceive that it was important for the theory of international trade to distinguish between general price levels and what are here termed "domestic," "import," and "export" price levels, although he made use of the distinction only to prove his point that gold was not of the same value in all countries. Cairnes's description of the "sectional" price levels is worth quoting:[1]

. . . . Among countries commercially connected there is a large class of commodities — all those, namely, which constitute the great staples of commerce, such as corn, flour, tea, sugar, metals, and most raw materials of industry — of which the prices can not vary much in different localities. As a rule the difference of prices will not be greater than the cost of carriage between the countries of production and consumption, always, of course, excepting the case where such articles come under the operation of local fiscal laws. In the exchange for commodities of this description, the value of gold, though not the same all the world over, does not greatly vary within the range of general commerce. But besides the commodities which form the staples of commerce, there are those which, through unsuitableness for distant traffic, or owing to some other obstacle, do not enter into international trade. With regard to these, there is nothing to prevent the widest divergence in their gold prices, or, therefore, in the value of gold in relation to them, not merely in remote quarters of the world, but sometimes even in localities within the same country; and the class of goods to which this description applies — it will vary in extent with the situation of each country and the means of communication at its command — far from being insignificant, must under all circumstances include some of the most important articles of general consumption. To perceive this, it is only necessary to remember that the group includes the items of house accommodation, meat, and a large proportion of those things which fall under the head of "provisions" — a list which would have to be greatly enlarged if we had to deal with countries lying aside from the leading thoroughfares of commerce, or in which the means of communication have been imperfectly developed.

The part played by gold movements in the adjustment of the Canadian balance of trade to Canadian borrowings from abroad has already been submitted to an inductive examination, whose results showed that, if allowance was made for the controlling influence exercised on gold movements by the peculiar system of outside reserves of the Canadian banks, gold movements operated in the manner indicated by Thornton, Mill, and their followers.

---

[1] *Some Leading Principles*, Part III, Ch. v. § 1.

The next chapter is devoted to an inductive analysis of the part played by price changes in the mechanism of adjustment of the Canadian balance of trade. It should provide a further test of the validity of the deductive theory as expounded by Thornton and Mill, and it should, moreover, serve to verify the amplification of the theory made by Professor Taussig with reference to the operation of the sectional price levels.

CHAPTER X

CHANGES IN RELATIVE PRICE LEVELS AND THE MECHANISM OF ADJUSTMENT OF TRADE BALANCES

B. INDUCTIVE VERIFICATION

INTRODUCTORY

IN this chapter an attempt is made to verify inductively, by an analysis of price movements, the deductive theory with respect to the part played by changes in prices in the mechanism of adjustment of trade balances, which was presented in the preceding chapter. Before proceeding to the analysis of the relevant price statistics, it is essential, however, to establish deductively a further detail which has escaped the attention of writers on the theory of international trade.

If borrowings abroad continue after their inception at a constant rate, it is stated or implied by those writers who follow Mill that the initial relative rise in prices in the borrowing country must be maintained definitively and undiminished so that there may be an equally definitive and undiminished excess of imports over exports. Assume that we start in 1900 with an even balance between imports and exports and with no borrowings; that borrowings begin in 1901 at the rate of $50,000,000 annually and continue for an indefinite period thereafter at the same rate; that the Canadian price level rises 5 per cent in 1901 relatively to the world price level; and that this relative rise in prices is just sufficient to bring about an excess of imports over exports in 1901 equal to the borrowings in that year. The generally accepted theory would hold that this relative rise of 5 per cent in the Canadian price level must be maintained *undiminished* throughout the continuance of the borrowings if imports are to maintain their necessary excess over exports.

There is valid deductive ground, however, for believing that if an initial relative rise of 5 per cent in the Canadian price level is sufficient to bring about in the first year of its occurrence an excess of imports over exports amounting to $50,000,000, it will be more than sufficient to bring about an equivalent excess of imports over exports in subsequent years. Before a change in relative prices can exert its full influence on trade, information as to the price changes must first become widespread, old commitments must be liquidated, new merchandising and credit connections must be established, inertia must be overcome, habits and tastes must be trained to find new forms and styles of commodities acceptable, industry must be adapted to the exploitation of raw materials having perhaps slightly different chemical or physical properties or graded according to hitherto unfamiliar standards. How long it will be before price changes in one country will exert their full potential influence on the trade with other countries is not subject to exact determination, but under normal circumstances it will unquestionably take more than one year. The problem is one "of determining the effects of a new stimulus applied to trade. Working an analogy from applied psychology, the problem is to ascertain whether a stimulus of uniform strength continuously applied (1) produces a cumulative effect, or (2) gradually loses its stimulative potency. It seems to me that there is a clear presumption that for an initial period at least the effect of the trade stimulus will be to produce a steadily increasing result." [1]

If a given divergency in price levels will have a progressive effect on trade for several years and, after that, a constant effect at the peak, which has been shown to be a reasonable hypothesis, it should be expected, given a constant rate of borrowings, that the initial relative rise in prices in the borrowing country will later prove to be unnecessarily great and therefore will not be fully maintained. Moreover, even though a given divergency of prices should be expected to exert a constant *relative* influence on trade, it should exert an increasing *absolute* influence on trade as measured in money if the total monetary volume of trade is increasing, whether this increase reflects an increase in physical

---

[1] I am indebted to Professor Edmund E. Day, formerly of Harvard University, for this useful analogy. The quotation is from a letter to the writer.

volume, in prices, or in both. During the period under study, the rate of Canadian borrowings abroad and the total volume of Canadian trade both had a generally upward trend, but at an irregular rate of increase and with some temporary recessions. An analysis of price trends should be expected, therefore, to reveal not a steady and continuous rise in the Canadian price level relative to foreign price levels, but an irregular rise with some recessions, and with the general upward trend in prices less marked than the general upward trend in the rate of borrowing. Since the rate of borrowings was very much greater throughout the later part of the period than in the earlier years, it should be expected, however, that the Canadian price levels should be throughout the later part of the period higher in relation to foreign price levels than they were at the beginning of the period.

Since there is *a priori* ground for expecting that there will *not* be anything approaching exact mathematical correspondence between the variations in the divergencies of price levels and in the trade balances which these divergencies bring about, the use of subtle statistical methods for measuring the degree of correlation is not called for, and simple tabular comparisons or natural-scale charts will adequately serve the purpose of inductive verification.

PRICE LEVELS IN DIFFERENT COUNTRIES

The period under study was marked by a world-wide rise in prices. To verify the theory presented in the preceding chapter, it is therefore necessary to show, not only that there was a rise in the Canadian price level, but that Canadian prices rose more than did prices outside of Canada, and especially that Canadian prices rose more than did prices in the countries in which the Canadian loans were chiefly floated. No factor was operating during this period, other than the import of capital, which would adequately explain a substantially greater rise in prices in Canada than in the world at large. Foreign trade is relatively of much greater importance to Canada than to the United States, and both the per capita volume of foreign trade and the percentage of production for export to total production are unquestionably several times greater for Canada than for the United States. The tariff therefore has possibilities in Canada of interference with the natural course of industry, trade, and prices, to a degree not attributable to it in the United States. Fortunately for this study, the Canadian tariff remained substantially unaltered during the entire period under investigation. It must of course be conceded that the economic significance of an unaltered schedule of import duties will change as basic economic and trade conditions change; but a careful survey of the situation appears to justify the conclusion that the Canadian tariff did not operate

CHART IV

INDICES OF WHOLESALE PRICES FOR CANADA AND THE WORLD, 1900–1913

——— Canada (272 commodities) unweighted   — — — World—Coats's Index (145 commodities)
—·—· Canada (145 commodities)   ·········· World—Knibbs's Index

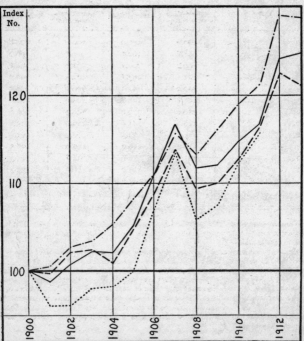

more strongly to create a relatively high price level in Canada in the later than in the earlier years of the period under study. The increase in manufacturing and the modernization of its technique in Canada have in fact operated in recent years to reduce the excess of the Canadian prices of protected manufactured commodities over foreign prices, and to make many of the import duties exert but a partial influence on Canadian prices. While the tariff may be partly responsible, therefore, for the actual level of Canadian prices, it cannot be charged for this period with responsibility for any marked variations in the Canadian price level from its customary relationship with the

DATA OF CHART IV

INDICES OF WHOLESALE PRICES FOR CANADA AND THE WORLD

Year	Canada — (272 commodities) unweighted [1]	Canada — (145 commodities) [2]	World—Coats's Index (145 commodities) [3]	World — Knibbs's Index [4]
1900	100.0	100.0	100.0	100.0
1901	98.8	100.5	99.8	96.2
1902	100.7	102.7	102.0	96.1
1903	102.1	103.3	102.3	98.0
1904	102.0	105.3	100.9	98.3
1905	105.1	108.1	104.6	100.0
1906	110.9	110.9	108.7	106.8
1907	116.6	115.6	113.8	113.2
1908	111.6	113.3	109.4	105.9
1909	112.0	116.0	110.0	107.5
1910	114.7	119.0	112.8	112.3
1911	116.8	121.3	116.3	115.7
1912	124.2	129.2	122.6	....
1913	124.8	128.7	121.2	....

[1] Canada: — 272 commodities, unweighted. (*Cost of Living Report*, vol. ii, p. 146.) This is the official Department of Labour index number of wholesale prices reconstructed from its details, by R. H. Coats, to 1900 as a base.

[2] Canada: — 145 commodities, unweighted. Prices in 1900 = 100. Constructed by Coats (*ibid.*, p. 240), from the price quotations for the identical commodities included in his world index.

[3] World, Coats's Index: — 145 commodities, unweighted. Prices in 1900 = 100. (*Ibid.*, p. 238.)

[4] World, Knibbs's Index:— This index, constructed by G. H. Knibbs, Commonwealth Statistician of Australia (*Prices, Prices Indexes and Cost of Living in Australia*, 1912, pp. 76 seq.) is based on the averages of the wholesale index numbers given in the best indices for the countries included, viz.: Great Britain, Belgium, Germany, Italy, France, the United States, New Zealand, Australia, Canada. Knibbs, in combining the indices, used weights representing relative populations. His index has not been carried beyond 1911.

world price level. In the absence of any other conspicuous factor which could be cited in explanation of an upward movement in Canadian prices more than proportionate to the general world movement, a substantial relative rise, if it occurred, must be explained as due to the import of capital and therefore must be accepted as confirmatory of the classical theory.

Chart IV compares two Canadian price indices with two world price indices, one constructed by R. H. Coats, the Dominion Statistician, from price quotations in various countries for specific commodities, and the other constructed by G. H. Knibbs, Statistician for Australia, from the price indices for various countries. Both world indices show a more moderate rise than either of the Canadian indices, and to this extent confirm the theory. The divergency between the two series is substantial, even though the methods of construction of the two world price indices, especially because they give too much weight to prices in the capital-borrowing countries, are such as to exaggerate the rise in world prices. The fairest comparison is probably between Coats's Canadian and world price indices for the same 145 commodities. Coats says of his index of world prices that it has a defect "in the fact that the averages for certain commodities represent a larger number of countries than those for others. For over forty articles in the . . . list, for example, the average is for Canada and the United States alone, where prices have been exceptionally buoyant. The . . . world numbers, therefore, might be presumed to err on the side of buoyancy." The countries whose price-quotations were used in the construction of this index, grouped in *ascending* order according to the degree of "buoyancy" which their prices showed, are as follows: (1) Great Britain, France, Italy, Belgium, Holland, and Norway; (2) Germany, Austria, Russia; (3) India, Australia, New Zealand; (4) Japan, Hungary, the United States, Canada. Although it is not to be contended that the international movement of capital is the sole factor determining the trend of price levels in different countries, it is significant that in general the capital-lending countries experienced the least rise in prices, and the capital-borrowing countries the greatest rise. It is to be noted also that not only was the

CHART V

WHOLESALE PRICES IN CANADA AND GREAT BRITAIN, 1900–1913

——— Canada, weighted
– – – Great Britain, Labor Dept. Board of
     Trade, weighted
·········· Great Britain, Sauerbeck
– · – Great Britain, *Economist*

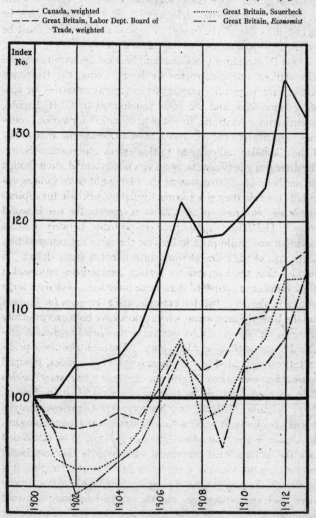

rise in the Canadian price level as compared with 1900 greater than in the world price level, but for most of the years of the period it was greater also than the rise in the price level of any other of the countries included in the index of world prices.[1] A comparison between the Canadian price level and the price level of the world exclusive of Canada would show, therefore, an even more marked relative rise in Canadian prices.

[1] *Cost of Living Report*, vol. ii, p. 243.

DATA OF CHART V

WHOLESALE PRICES IN CANADA AND GREAT BRITAIN

Year	Canada weighted [1]	Great Britain		
		Labor Dept. Board of Trade weighted [2]	Sauerbeck [3]	*Economist* [4]
1900..................	100.0	100.0	100.0	100.0
1901..................	100.2	96.7	93.4	96.4
1902..................	103.6	96.4	92.0	89.1
1903..................	103.7	96.9	92.0	90.5
1904..................	104.5	98.2	93.4	92.7
1905..................	107.6	97.6	96.0	94.5
1906..................	113.5	100.8	102.7	99.1
1907..................	122.1	106.0	106.7	104.5
1908..................	118.2	103.0	97.4	101.4
1909..................	119.4	104.1	98.7	94.5
1910..................	121.0	108.8	104.0	103.2
1911..................	123.9	109.4	106.6	103.6
1912..................	136.0	114.9	113.3	106.8
1913..................	131.9	116.5	113.3	113.6

[1] Canada: *Cost of Living Report*, vol. ii, p. 22. Official Canadian index number weighted by Coats on basis of system suggested by the British Association for the Advancement of Science (*Reports of Committee on Index Numbers*, 1887–1890). Of the 100 weight units, 55 are given to foodstuffs raw and manufactured, 10 to fuel, 2 to house furnishings, 11 to clothing, 22 to metals, lumber, etc. Converted by the writer from 1890–1899 to 1900 base. A statistical error is involved in this conversion to a different base, of an index constructed from relative instead of actual prices (see U. S. Dept. of Labor, Bureau of Labor Statistics, *Bulletin* No. 181, pp. 251 seq.) but it is unavoidable, and the great number of commodities covered by the Canadian index, plus the fact that the 1900 prices were not greatly different from the average prices 1890–1899, make the probable error a slight one.

[2] *Cost of Living Report*, vol. ii, pp. 148 seq. (Great Britain: Labour Dept., Board of Trade): weighted for 47 articles, chiefly raw materials and foodstuffs. Prices in 1900 = 100. Weighted average of relative prices for other years.

[3] *Ibid.*, Sauerbeck (London *Statist*): unweighted index for 32 commodities, chiefly raw materials and foodstuffs. Prices in 1900 = 100. Unweighted average of relative prices for other years.

[4] *Ibid.*, London *Economist*: unweighted index for 43 commodities, chiefly raw materials and foodstuffs. Prices in 1900 = 100. Unweighted average of relative prices for other years. Prices as of January 1 each year.

Canada's international economic relations are predominantly with Great Britain and the United States. Comparison of the trend of prices in Canada with the trend of prices in these two countries should therefore provide a better inductive test of the truth of the theory than comparison with the world at large.

Prices in Canada compared with Prices in Great Britain

Chart V compares the official Canadian price index, weighted, with the official British price index, weighted on substantially the same basis, and with two unofficial British price indices. Chart VI compares the trend of prices of fifty-two identical articles in Canada and in Great Britain. Both comparisons exhibit a clear and marked rise in Canadian prices relative to British prices. This is especially significant because, since the close commercial relationships of the two countries should tend to have an equalizing influence on their price levels, the divergency in prices can be more confidently attributed to the fact that Canada and Great Britain stand, in relation to each other and to the world at large, as borrowing and lending countries respectively.

All of the British price indices are constructed predominantly from quotations for raw materials and foodstuffs. These are largely import commodities in Great Britain.[1] In a lending country during a period of increasing loans abroad, such as this was for Great Britain,[2] import prices should rise relative to domestic and export prices. Moreover, the rise in prices throughout the world after 1900 was universally more marked in raw materials and in foodstuffs than in manufactured products.[3] The

---

[1] Of the 47 price series used in constructing the British Board of Trade Price Index, 35 are not only for import commodities but are the average import values. (Cf. A. W. Flux, "Measurement of Price Changes," *Journal of the Royal Statistical Society*, vol. lxxiv, p. 169.)

[2] Cf. C. K. Hobson, *The Export of Capital*, p. 219.

[3]

	WORLD RISE IN PRICES		
Year	Foods	Raw materials	Manufactured products
1900	100.0	100.0	100.0
1912	134.0	135.5	117.2
1913	125.8	130.4	118.3

(*Cost of Living Report*, vol. ii, p. 247.)

CHART VI

WHOLESALE PRICES IN CANADA AND GREAT BRITAIN, 1900–1913

(52 identical commodities)

——— Canada   — — — Great Britain

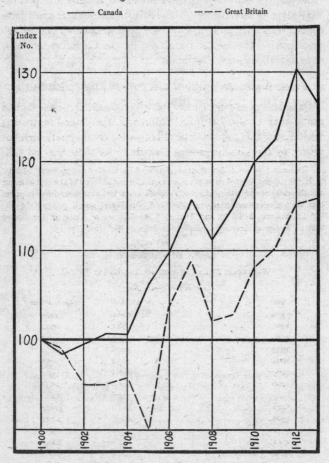

Canadian index number gives adequate representation to manufactured products, for over half of the quotations used are for manufactured articles. The British price indices on the other hand include very few articles advanced beyond the preliminary stage of manufacture. The British price indices must have tended, therefore, to exaggerate the upward trend of the British price level.[1] The greater rise shown by the Canadian indices is therefore all the more significant.

Prices in Canada compared with Prices in the United States

Canada is even more closely related economically to the United States than to Great Britain. Moreover, the United States was itself during this period a capital-borrowing country, although not nearly to the same degree as Canada.[2] As there was no sub-

---

[1] Two other indices of British prices, one by A. L. Bowley and the other by Mrs. G. H. Wood, constructed so as to reflect more clearly the trend of the cost of living and therefore of domestic prices, both show a much less pronounced rise in prices than the indices presented above. (*Cost of Living Report*, vol. ii, p. 157.)

[2] Cf. Bullock, Williams and Tucker, "The Balance of Trade of the United States," *Review of Economic Statistics*, Preliminary Vol. No. 3, p. 230.

DATA OF CHART VI

WHOLESALE PRICES IN CANADA AND GREAT BRITAIN

(*52 identical commodities*) [1]

Year	Canada	Great Britain
1900	100.0	100.0
1901	98.5	99.1
1902	99.5	95.1
1903	100.8	95.0
1904	100.6	95.7
1905	106.1	90.1
1906	109.7	103.6
1907	115.7	108.8
1908	111.2	102.0
1909	114.6	102.7
1910	120.0	108.1
1911	122.8	110.3
1912	130.4	115.2
1913	126.6	115.7

[1] *Cost of Living Report*, vol. ii, pp. 157 seq. Unweighted index for 52 identical commodities in Canada and Great Britain. Prices in 1900 = 100. Canadian prices from Dept. of Labour Reports. British prices, 42 from Dept. of Labour, Board of Trade, 8 from Sauerbeck, 2 from *Economist*.

stantial change in tariff relations or in freight rates between the two countries during the period under study, the price indices of the two countries should be expected to show closely similar trends. On *a priori* grounds, there should be expected a moderately greater rise in prices in Canada than in the United States, because of the relatively and absolutely greater capital borrowings by Canada than by the United States. On the other hand, the great degree of self-sufficiency possessed by the United States probably makes its price level more independent of and less responsive to external influence than that of Canada, and therefore more likely to move in response to purely domestic conditions.

Chart VII compares the official price indices of the two countries, weighted and unweighted. Both index numbers are constructed from quotations for a considerable number of commodities, many of which are common to both. Raw materials, foodstuffs, and manufactured products receive representation in about the same proportions in both indices. Different methods are used, however, in weighting the two indices. The American index is weighted with reference to relative importance in output, whereas the Canadian index is weighted more crudely and with reference to supposed relative importance in consumption.

The weighted index number of prices in Canada showed a much more pronounced rise than the unweighted, whereas for the United States index the weighting made little change in the final results. The unweighted index numbers for the two countries kept closely together from 1900 to 1911, with the American index number for each year generally higher than the Canadian. Only after 1911 does the Canadian unweighted index number show a distinctly more pronounced rise in prices, as compared to 1900, than does the American.

In general, statistical authority would support the use of weighted in preference to unweighted index numbers as measures of the general trend of prices, if the weights used were not wholly arbitrary, but were based even though very roughly on the relative importance of the commodities included in the index. The weighted index for Canada shows a decidedly more pronounced rise than the American weighted index in the years

CHART VII

WHOLESALE PRICES IN CANADA AND THE UNITED STATES, 1900-1913

Canada, unweighted   United States, unweighted
Canada, weighted   United States, weighted

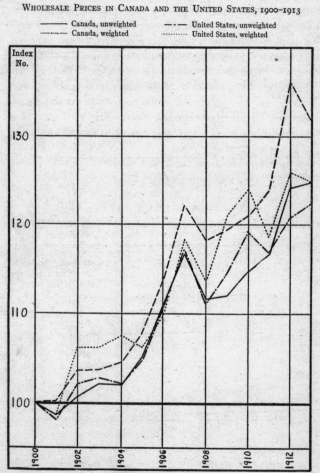

1911 to 1913, years in which the Canadian borrowings showed sharp increases over the preceding year.[1]

A further basis for comparison of price trends in the two countries is furnished by index numbers constructed by Coats from price quotations for 135 articles common to the official indices of both countries. These indices, presented in Table XLVIII, show that as compared with 1900, prices were higher in Canada than in the United States in most of the years in which there were substantial borrowings abroad by Canada, and that the greater buoyancy of Canadian prices was especially marked from 1911 to 1913, when the Canadian borrowings were in greatest volume.

All of the comparisons made above between prices in Canada and in the United States indicate that the trends of prices in the

[1] See Table XXXI, p. 106, *supra*.

DATA OF CHART VII

WHOLESALE PRICES IN CANADA AND THE UNITED STATES

Year	Canada		United States	
	Unweighted [1]	Weighted [2]	Unweighted [3]	Weighted [4]
1900	100.0	100.0	100.0	100.0
1901	98.8	100.2	98.2	98.8
1902	100.7	103.6	102.1	106.2
1903	102.1	103.7	102.8	106.2
1904	102.0	104.5	102.2	107.4
1905	105.1	107.6	104.9	106.2
1906	110.9	113.5	110.8	109.9
1907	116.6	122.1	117.2	117.3
1908	111.6	118.2	111.1	113.6
1909	112.0	119.4	114.5	121.0
1910	114.7	121.0	119.1	124.7
1911	116.8	123.9	116.9	118.5
1912	124.2	136.0	120.9	125.9
1913	124.8	131.9	122.3	124.7

[1] Canada, unweighted: — all commodities, 272 articles. Department of Labour index, reconstructed by Coats to 1900 base. (*Cost of Living Report*, vol. ii, p. 146.)

[2] Canada, weighted: — see note 1 to Chart V.

[3] United States, unweighted: — all commodities, 252 articles. United States Bureau of Labor Statistics unweighted index, reconstructed by Coats to 1900 base. (*Ibid.*, p. 166.)

[4] United States, weighted: — all commodities, 297 articles. United States Bureau of Labor Statistics weighted index (*Bulletin* No. 181 [1915], p. 16). Converted by writer from 1914 base. The method of construction of this index number permits of shifting of base without error.

two countries kept closely together throughout most of the period, but that Canadian prices rose much more sharply than American prices during the last few years of the period when Canadian borrowings were in greatest volume.[1]

SECTIONAL PRICE LEVELS

Much more light can be thrown on the method of operation of price changes in the adjustment of trade balances by comparing the different trends of the sectional price levels in Canada. That phase of the classical explanation of the mechanism of international trade which relates to the operation of price changes may be restated so as to make use of the considerations discussed above relating to sectional price levels,[2] and with special application to the Canadian situation, as follows:

Let us assume once more that we begin with an equal balance between imports and exports, and that Canada begins to borrow

[1] Cf. Table LI, *infra*, presenting a comparison of the trend of prices of domestic commodities in Canada and in the United States, which shows a substantially greater relative increase, throughout the period under study, in Canada than in the United States.   [2] See pp. 209 seq., *supra*.

TABLE XLVIII

WHOLESALE PRICES IN CANADA AND THE UNITED STATES [1]

(*135 identical articles*)

Year	Canada	United States
1900	100.0	100.0
1901	100.8	99.1
1902	101.9	103.9
1903	102.8	103.3
1904	103.6	102.8
1905	107.8	104.5
1906	110.8	110.8
1907	116.2	117.6
1908	112.7	110.0
1909	113.6	113.2
1910	117.5	118.0
1911	120.0	118.4
1912	128.0	122.6
1913	127.7	119.6

[1] *Cost of Living Report*, vol. ii, p. 168. Unweighted index for 135 identical commodities based on prices given in the official price statistics of the two countries. Prices in 1900 = 100. The commodities are well distributed.

capital from abroad. There results an increase in bank deposits in Canada accompanied by an increase in the cash reserves. The increase in deposits will cause a rise in the prices of commodities produced for the domestic market, and of services. The prices of import commodities will not be appreciably influenced by changes in Canadian conditions, since they are governed by conditions in the producing countries and perhaps also in the important consuming markets, of which Canada, because of its small population, generally is not a part. The relative rise in the prices of domestic commodities will not only make imported commodities which are different in kind from the domestic commodities more attractive to the purchaser, but may lead to a substitution, by consumers, of imported commodities for domestic commodities of the same kind, thus shifting these commodities from the domestic to the import class. A decrease in exports will result also. The increase in purchasing power in Canada unaccompanied by an immediate increase in production will of itself result in the consumption in Canada of a greater proportion of the supply of domestic commodities. Labor also will be withdrawn from industries producing for export, to the development of the enterprises for which the foreign capital was borrowed. The changes in sectional price levels will operate as a further check on exports. The prices of export commodities, except in the few cases where a great proportion of the world's supply is produced in Canada, are mainly determined, proximately by the "ruling market" in the consuming countries, ultimately by world-wide relations between supply and demand. The rise in the prices of domestic commodities and services raises the money cost of production of the export commodities. Where the producers succeed in raising their prices in sympathy with the rise in costs, it will lead to a diminution in exports, and even to the cessation of exports and the shift of the commodity from the export to the domestic class. Where the producers cannot raise their prices, they may after an interval of resistance to the price tendencies turn to other activities, and the commodity in extreme cases may even shift from the export to the import class.

Domestic, Import, and Export Commodity Prices

Chart **VIII** presents an inductive verification of the reasoning given above. This chart shows that the rise in the prices of domestic commodities was most marked, that the prices of import commodities, which are least subject to the influence of domestic conditions, rose least, and that the rise in the prices of export commodities, which are subject to both internal and ex-

CHART VIII

INDICES OF DOMESTIC, IMPORT, AND EXPORT, WHOLESALE COMMODITY PRICES
1900–1913

——— Domestic prices — — — Import prices ·········· Export prices

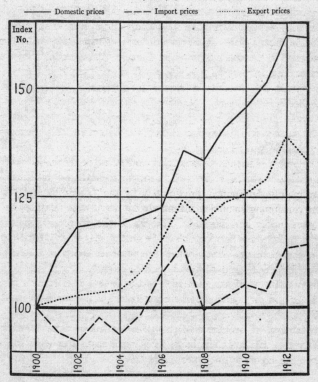

ternal influences, was intermediate between the rise in import prices and the rise in domestic prices. The differences in degree of rise between the three sectional price indices are great enough to make of the chart a clear and substantial verification of the deductive theory presented above.

DATA OF CHART VIII

INDICES OF DOMESTIC, IMPORT, AND EXPORT, WHOLESALE COMMODITY PRICES [1]

Year	Domestic [2]	Import [3]	Export [4]
1900	100.0	100.0	100.0
1901	111.5	94.8	101.7
1902	118.5	92.5	102.8
1903	119.1	97.7	103.3
1904	119.1	94.0	104.0
1905	120.9	98.3	107.9
1906	122.8	107.3	115.3
1907	135.6	114.2	124.4
1908	133.6	99.5	119.9
1909	141.0	102.2	123.6
1910	145.7	105.0	125.7
1911	151.4	103.8	129.0
1912	161.8	113.1	138.8
1913	161.7	114.1	133.9

[1] Constructed by the writer from price quotations in Dept. of Labour *Reports on Wholesale Prices* and in *Cost of Living Report*, vol ii, pp. 250 seq.

[2] Domestic Commodity Prices: —23 commodities, as follows: hay; straw; fresh beef; mess pork; fresh eggs; milk; salt mackerel; strawberries; beans; potatoes; bread; salt; denims; ticking; bituminous coal (Crow's Nest Pass); matches; common building bricks; putty; common kitchen chairs; draught ale; fowls; apples; tomatoes. The sharp rise in the first few years is due chiefly to the quotations for salt mackerel and potatoes, both of which increased 75 per cent or over in price between 1900 and 1903, and decreased in price thereafter.

[3] Import Commodity Prices: — 30 commodities, as follows: *Raw materials:* corn; cotton; silk; rubber; anthracite coal; American bituminous coal; Connellsville coke; tin; lead; spelter; crude petroleum; iron, pig; brass; copper. *Foodstuffs:* bananas; chocolate; coffee, Rio; cream of tartar; currants; lemons; molasses; oranges; pepper; prunes; raisins; rice; sugar, granulated; sugar, yellow; tapioca; tea. The raw materials group is given twice as much weight as the foodstuffs group in making up the total import commodity index. The official import statistics during this period indicate that the imports of raw materials are approximately twice as much in value as the imports of foodstuffs. This crude weighting does not substantially alter the index.

[4] Export Commodity Prices: — 41 commodities, as follows: wheat, Manitoba northern, No. 1; barley, Ontario, No. 2; oats, Canada western, No. 2; hay, No. 1; cattle, western butchers; bacon; hides, No. 1; calfskins; whiskey, Canadian Club; potatoes; ground woodpulp; flaxseed; newsprint; bran; binder twine; cheese, western; codfish, dry; canned salmon; canned lobster; apples, fresh; flour, Manitoba first; leather, No. 1 special sole; flour, straight rollers; aluminum; nickel; silver, bar; copper; coal, bituminous, Nova Scotia; pig iron, Nova Scotia; pig iron, Summerlee; spruce deals; laths; muskrat; skunk; gold; asbestos; rags; clover; pine lumber, all grades; barley, Canadian western, No. 3; wool, Ontario, unwashed; shingles; halibut, fresh. Over 90 per cent of the Canadian exports are represented in this index.

Export Prices

The export price index presented in Chart VIII was an unweighted index representing the great bulk of the exports in the later part of the period under study. With a view to finding out whether a study of export prices would reveal that restrictive influence on exports which, according to the deductive theory presented above, should result from a rise in domestic commodity prices relative to export commodity prices, there are presented in Chart IX for comparison with the unweighted export commodity price index two other indices of export commodity prices for the more important of the export commodities, one weighted according to the relative importance of the various commodities in the export trade at the beginning of the period under study, and the other similarly weighted according to the relative importance at the end of the period.

If there was any substantial shifting of commodities from the export class to the domestic or the import classes because of the relative rise in domestic prices, this should show itself in a more pronounced rise in the index weighted according to the relative importance of the export commodities at the beginning of the period than in the index weighted according to the relative importance of the commodities at the end of the period. In other words, the export trade should be expected to have maintained itself only through the substitution, for commodities whose prices rose in full sympathy with the rise in the domestic price level, of other commodities whose prices, either because of their more complete dependence on foreign markets or because of special circumstances moderating the rise in their cost of production such as the discovery of new low-cost resources, did not keep full pace with the rise in the domestic price level.

The evidence presented in the chart offers a clear and substantial verification of this reasoning. The index weighted according to the relative importance of the export commodities in 1900 to 1904 rises to a greater degree than the index weighted according to the relative importance of the commodities in 1913. Moreover, the divergency of the two curves is especially marked in

CHART IX

INDICES OF EXPORT PRICES, 1900–1913

——— Weighted according to importance in 1900–1904
– – – Weighted according to importance in 1913
· · · · · · Unweighted

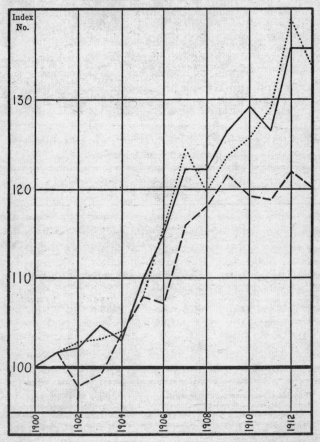

1906 and 1907, 1910–1913, years of marked accentuation in the rate of inflow of capital into Canada.

It may be objected that the data presented in Chart IX show only one thing, namely: that foreign countries relatively increased their purchases of those Canadian commodities which rose least in price and decreased their purchases of those which rose most in price, a result to be expected under any circumstances. If in all countries the prices of export commodities are governed wholly or even predominantly by internal conditions within those countries and especially by costs of production, this is a valid criticism. A rise in price, demand remaining the same, means a fall in sales. Whatever may be the normal situation,

DATA OF CHART IX

INDICES OF EXPORT PRICES [1]

Year	Weighted according to importance in 1900–1904 [2]	Weighted according to importance in 1913 [3]	Unweighted [4]
1900	100.0	100.0	100.0
1901	101.7	101.7	101.7
1902	102.1	97.9	102.8
1903	104.6	99.2	103.3
1904	103.0	103.6	104.0
1905	109.9	107.8	107.9
1906	114.7	107.1	115.3
1907	122.2	115.9	124.4
1908	122.2	118.1	119.9
1909	126.4	121.7	123.6
1910	129.2	119.3	125.7
1911	126.5	118.8	129.0
1912	135.7	121.7	138.8
1913	135.6	120.2	133.9

[1] These indices were constructed by the writer.

[2] Weighted according to importance in 1900–1904: — 21 most important commodities of export in 1900–1904 selected from list given in note 4 to Chart VIII, and roughly weighted according to their relative values in Canadian exports during these years by: (1) dividing them into 3 groups of 2, 4, and 15 commodities, so that each group represents an approximately equal value of exports, and (2) constructing an index for each group, and (3) taking an average of the three indices.

[3] Weighted according to importance in 1913: — 22 most important articles of export in 1913, roughly weighted according to their relative value in Canadian exports in that year. For general method of weighting, see note 2, above.

[4] As in note 4, Chart VIII.

however, these are not the conditions governing export prices in Canada.

The Canadian surpluses for export of the commodities that she produces are, with the exception only of two or three mineral products, but small fractions of the world's supply of these commodities. Their world prices, therefore, are not influenced appreciably by Canadian conditions. So long as Canadian producers wish to maintain their export thereof, they must passively accept the world prices. Those commodities which advance most in price *in the world markets* should become, other things being equal, the most profitable to produce for export, and should consequently become a larger instead of a smaller proportion of the total exports. But the reverse was true in so far as *Canadian prices* were concerned. It was the commodities whose prices rose least whose exportation increased most. This proves conclusively the proposition made above: the relative rise in prices of the commodities important in the export trade in the early part of the period was due predominantly to Canadian conditions, and was not simply a reflection of conditions in the world market. The factors incident to great capital borrowings operated to break the normal relationship between the trends of prices of export commodities in Canada and in the world markets, and thus tended to restrict export trade.[1]

Import Prices

It has already been shown that the price index for import commodities rose least of all as compared with the other sectional price levels and with the general price levels. Chart X and Tables XLIX and L throw further light on the trend of import commodity prices.

Chart X presents the price indices for imported foodstuffs and for imported raw materials from which the index for all imported commodities in Chart VIII was constructed. Although, as is to be expected, they show wider fluctuations in prices than did the total import price index, in general their trend is the same and they both appear to reflect the same price influences.

[1] See p. 261 seq., *infra*, for further discussion of exports and export prices.

A considerable part of the Canadian imports consists of manufactured products, especially iron and steel products from the
United States and textiles from Great Britain. The Canadian
official price statistics do not permit of the construction of indices
for such commodities with any degree of assurance that domestic
commodities are not being included. The United States Department of Labor index for manufactured commodities is included in
Chart X, as roughly representative of the trend of prices in such
imports from the United States. There is unfortunately no

CHART X

INDICES OF PRICES OF IMPORT COMMODITIES AND OF ALL COMMODITIES,
1900–1913

——— Imported foodstuffs   —·—·— United States manufactures
——— Imported raw materials   ·········· All commodities

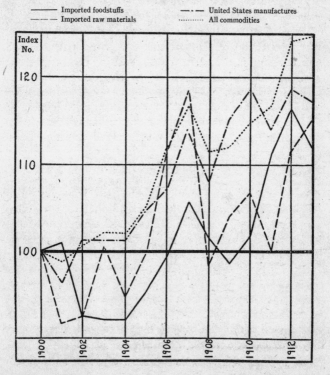

satisfactory British index for manufactured textile products. It is to be noted that all the import price indices presented in this chart show a less pronounced rise than does the Canadian un-weighted index for all commodities, thus further confirming the reasoning presented above.

Table XLIX compares an index of all foodstuffs for which Canadian official price statistics are published, with an index for imported foodstuffs. The index for all foodstuffs shows a much greater rise in price than the index for imported foodstuffs, in-dicating once more that the domestic commodity price level rose more than did the import commodity price level. Table L, which makes a similar comparison, but only for the years from 1907 to 1913, of the price trend of all raw materials in Canada with the price trend of imported raw materials, shows that there was a greater rise in domestic commodity prices than in import commodity prices.

DATA OF CHART X

INDICES OF PRICES OF IMPORT COMMODITIES AND OF ALL COMMODITIES

Year	Imported foodstuffs [1]	Imported raw materials [2]	United States manufactures [3]	All commod-ities [4]
1900	100.0	100.0	100.0	100.0
1901	100.9	91.7	96.5	98.8
1902	92.6	92.5	101.2	100.7
1903	92.2	100.4	101.2	102.1
1904	92.2	94.9	101.2	102.0
1905	95.4	99.8	104.7	105.1
1906	99.2	111.3	107.0	110.9
1907	105.7	118.5	114.0	116.6
1908	101.6	98.4	108.1	111.6
1909	98.6	104.0	115.1	112.0
1910	101.6	106.7	118.6	114.7
1911	111.4	100.0	114.0	116.8
1912	116.2	111.5	118.6	124.2
1913	112.0	115.1	117.4	124.8

[1] Constructed by the writer. Imported Foodstuffs: — 16 commodities. (Listed in note 3 to Chart VIII.)

[2] Constructed by the writer. Imported Raw Materials: — 14 commodities. (Listed in note 3 to Chart VIII.)

[3] United States Manufactured Commodities: — U. S. Dept. of Labor, Bureau of Labor Statistics, weighted. Converted to 1900 base from 1914 base by writer. (*Bulletin* No. 181, p. 25.) The method of construction of this chart permits shifting of base without error.

[4] All Commodities, unweighted: — see note 1 to Chart IV.

TABLE XLIX

INDICES OF WHOLESALE PRICES OF ALL FOODSTUFFS AND IMPORTED FOODSTUFFS

Year	All foodstuffs [1]	Imported foodstuffs [2]
1900	100.0	100.0
1901	106.9	100.9
1902	107.5	92.6
1903	106.3	92.2
1904	107.8	92.2
1905	110.4	95.4
1906	115.3	99.2
1907	125.7	105.7
1908	125.2	101.6
1909	130.8	· 98.6
1910	135.2	101.6
1911	134.6	111.4
1912	149.3	116.2
1913	145.2	112.0

TABLE L

INDICES OF WHOLESALE PRICES OF ALL RAW MATERIALS AND IMPORTED RAW MATERIALS

Year	All raw materials [3]	Imported raw materials [4]
1900	....	100.0
1901	....	95.8
1902	....	94.5
1903	....	102.5
1904	....	97.7
1905	....	102.1
1906	....	113.3
1907	117.0	117.0
1908	....	97.3
1909	....	103.0
1910	....	104.0
1911	122.7	98.1
1912	129.5	111.9
1913	127.1	113.4

[1] All Foodstuffs: — 100 commodities. Constructed by the writer from Dept. of Labour indices for 5 groups of foodstuffs by averaging the indices of the groups and then reconverting from 1890–1899 to 1900 base. That the statistical error arising from both (1) the weighting resulting from the use of group averages and (2) the conversion to a different base is not important is evidenced by the fact that an unweighted index constructed by Coats from quotations for the same 100 articles with 1897 as a base shows an increase in the 1913 index over the 1909 index of 9.3% as compared with 11.0% in the present index. (*Cost of Living Report*, vol. ii, p. 30.)

[2] Imported Foodstuffs: — see note 1 to Chart X.

[3] All Raw Materials: — 89 commodities. 1907 = 117.0. Converted by writer from Coats's Index based on average prices 1890–1899. Indices not available for years not given. (*Ibid.*, p. 31.)

[4] Imported Raw Materials: — see note 2 to Chart X.

Domestic Commodity Prices

There remains for special consideration, of the sectional commodity price levels, only the prices of domestic commodities, namely those which do not enter in significant amounts into either export or import trade. The domestic commodity price index presented in Chart VIII showed a much greater rise than the other commodity price indices, and the greater rise of domestic prices was reflected also by subsequent charts already discussed above. The price quotations available for use in the construction of the domestic commodity price index were unfortunately few in number and restricted in the range of commodities represented. Commodities which would be domestic commodities in most countries are in many cases export or import commodities or both in Canada, because the transportation costs to a market in the United States from a producing region in Canada or vice versa are often less than the transportation costs between Canadian producing region and Canadian market. In the absence of tariff restrictions, and to some extent in spite of these restrictions, there are phases of the Canadian commerce with the United States which exhibit more fully the characteristics of domestic trade than does the trade between different sections of Canada. Differences between Canada and the United States in fashion, habit, industrial methods, are not sufficient to result in national differentiation and localization of commodities. In many cases even highly perishable commodities such as fresh milk, fresh eggs, strawberries, cross the national boundary in substantial quantities. Three of the properties of domestic commodities, bulkiness, perishability, and adaptation to local modes and fashions,[1] are often not sufficient

---

[1] Cf. Professor Taussig: "What will be the range of prices for those commodities which do not enter into the sphere of international trade — those which are not exported or imported, but are bought and sold solely within the country? The quantity of such commodities is very great, and in all countries probably much exceeds that of commodities having a world range of prices. Many things are too bulky to be transported over any considerable distance — as stone, bricks, timber. Many are perishable, as milk, butter, eggs, fruits, vegetables. No doubt modern improvements in the transportation of bulky goods and in the preservation of those that are perishable tend to enlarge the sphere of foreign trade. But such

to prevent trade between the United States and Canada in commodities having such characteristics. It is probable that in Canada those commodities come nearest to being domestic in character, in the sense of the term used here, which are produced in Canada under the shelter of higher tariff protection than they need, even though these commodities are typically neither perishable nor especially bulky. The domestic commodity price index presented above must be supported, therefore, by further evidence before it can be accepted as a reliable index of the trend of that part of the Canadian price level which was not directly subject to the influence of foreign prices.

The prices of individual commodities cannot by themselves be accepted as important evidence of general price trends, because they may have been subject to particular factors more powerful for the commodities in question than the general forces operating on the general price levels. Nevertheless, the following details are presented for what they are worth as additions to the accumulation of evidence.

Bricks are one of the commodities listed by Professor Taussig in the class of domestic commodities, and common building-bricks are represented in the domestic commodity price index given in Chart VIII. The price index for bricks first found showed a very moderate rise from 1900 to 1913. Further examination showed that it was constructed from the price-quotations for

things are still sold mainly in their own region and at the prices of their own region. . . . Some of the articles used in building houses — boards and laths, doors and windows, locks and hinges — may indeed be sent to distant regions. But even these are much affected by the customs and fashions of the several countries, and are usually made and sold on the spot or near it. A multitude of articles which might conceivably be brought from foreign countries are in fact made chiefly at home, because of the persistent sway of habit and tradition. Such are clothing and boots, tools and machines, wagons and harness. The reader's imagination will easily enlarge the list. The prices of all these things are determined under domestic conditions. They do not enter into international trade, and have no world level of prices." (*Free Trade, the Tariff, and Reciprocity*, pp. 73, 74.)

Unfortunately for the ease of this study, the situation is not nearly so simple in so far as Canada is concerned. For Canada, the reader's imagination must be directed to reducing instead of enlarging the list given by Professor Taussig. The Canadian boundary line represents little obstruction to trade other than that arising from import duties, and little difference in habits and fashions.

both building-bricks, a domestic commodity, and fire-bricks, less bulky in proportion to their value and largely imported. From 1900 to 1913, common building-bricks *advanced* 57 per cent in price, fire-bricks *fell* 9 per cent in price.

There are no official price quotations for sand and gravel, which are probably the cheapest articles of commerce in proportion to their bulk. They must, therefore, be primarily domestic commodities. If they are exported from Canada, it can only be a frontier trade which reflects local and not national price conditions. The Canadian export statistics for quantities and values indicate a rise, from 1905 to 1913, in the price per ton from 48.5 cents to 71 cents, or 46 per cent.

Table LI presents a comparison of the index for domestic commodities in Canada, as presented in Chart VIII, with an index constructed from price quotations in the United States for the identical or closely similar articles.

TABLE LI

INDICES OF CANADIAN AND AMERICAN PRICES OF CANADIAN DOMESTIC COMMODITIES

Year	Canada [1]	United States [2]
1900	100.0	100.0
1901	111.5	101.5
1902	118.5	106.0
1903	119.1	105.8
1904	119.1	108.5
1905	120.9	102.7
1906	122.8	109.5
1907	135.6	112.1
1908	133.6	110.1
1909	141.0	115.8
1910	145.7	118.1
1911	151.4	122.3
1912	161.8	130.5
1913	161.7	123.0

[1] See note 2 to Chart VIII.

[2] Constructed by the writer from price quotations for the U. S. in *Cost of Living Report*, vol. ii, pp. 250 seq. Commodities included same as in Canadian index, but with the following omissions because of lack of quotations: straw, strawberries, draught ale, fowls, apples, tomatoes. Of these six commodities in the Canadian index, the rise in price from 1900 to 1913 was greater than the average rise for other domestic commodities for straw, fowls, and tomatoes, equal to the average rise for apples, less than the average rise for strawberries, while draught ale fell absolutely in price from 1900 to 1913. No appreciable change in the Canadian index would result from the omission therefrom of these commodities.

The divergence between the two indices in the above table is much more marked than in any of the previous comparisons of Canadian and American prices.[1] The great relative rise in domestic prices in Canada cannot be attributed, therefore, to world influences affecting particularly the class of commodities included in the domestic price index.

Prices of Services

Since in Canada almost any commodity which is movable may enter into foreign trade, the prices of *services*, which have no greater mobility than that of the persons rendering them, are especially important evidence as to the trend of domestic prices. In Chart XI, indices reflecting the trend of prices of four important classes of services, hospital services, house rents, business rents, and wages, are compared with the general commodity price index. The index for the average cost per hospital patient per day reflects a whole range of prices of commodities and services belonging to the domestic class which are not adequately represented in any commodity price indices.[2] House and business rents are not only important *per se*,[3] but they reflect the trend of prices of immovables, land and buildings, important commodities, wholly "domestic" in character, which do not enter into the ordinary commodity price index. The trend of rates of wages should reflect all of the price factors which are domestic in character, and especially retail prices, a separate analysis of which was not feasible because of the absence of comprehensive data.

[1] See *supra*, pp. 223 seq.

[2] "An obvious purpose of such an inquiry into costs of hospital services is to measure fluctuations in the prices of yet another 'necessary,' namely, skilled care during severe illness. A second object was to throw a sidelight on the field of personal and household expenditures, through an examination of the maintenance costs of public institutions. In the absence of family budgets, such costs offer perhaps the best evidence of how the advancing prices of the past few years have worked out in a practical way." (*Cost of Living Report*, vol. ii, p. 342.)

[3] "House-room and shelter, a most important article of consumption and purchase, cannot be transported at all, and so may vary widely in price in different countries." (F. W. Taussig, *Free Trade, the Tariff, and Reciprocity*, pp. 73, 74.)

CHART XI

INDICES OF SERVICES AND OF ALL COMMODITIES

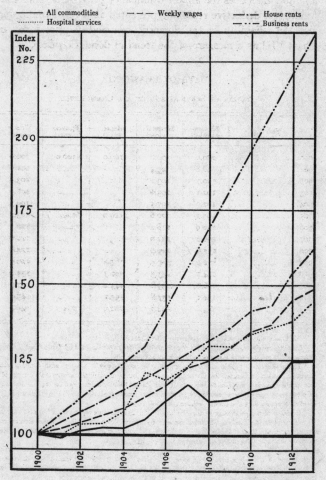

All of the services indices exhibited in Chart XI rise to a much greater degree than does the general commodity price index, and *a fortiori* than does the import commodity price index, thus confirming the deductive reasoning presented above and confirming also the reliability of the domestic commodity price index in Chart VIII as a measure of the trend of domestic prices.

DATA OF CHART XI

INDICES OF SERVICES AND OF ALL COMMODITIES

Year	All commodities [1]	Hospital services [2]	House rents [3]	Business rents [4]	Weekly wages [5]
1900	100.0	100.0	100.0	100.0	100.0
1901	98.8	99.5	....	....	101.6
1902	100.7	103.2	....	....	103.8
1903	102.1	103.6	....	....	106.5
1904	102.0	107.5	....	....	109.3
1905	105.1	120.8	119.0	129.4	113.1
1906	110.9	118.4	....	....	116.5
1907	116.6	122.6	....	....	122.6
1908	111.6	129.9	....	....	124.8
1909	112.0	129.5	135.4	....	129.0
1910	114.7	133.3	140.7	....	134.0
1911	116.8	135.8	143.2	....	137.9
1912	124.2	137.8	153.7	....	145.0
1913	124.8	144.7	162.0	234.5	148.9

[1] All Commodities, unweighted: — see note 1 to Chart IV.

[2] Hospital Services: — average cost per patient daily. Index constructed by Coats (*Cost of Living Report*, vol. ii, pp. 342 seq.) based on returns from 131 hospitals.

[3] House Rents: — typical six-roomed dwelling in workingmen's quarter, with sanitary conveniences. Index constructed by Coats (*ibid.*, p. 379), based on original statistics from correspondents of the *Canada Labor Gazette* throughout Canada. A similar index based on original statistics collected from real estate agents shows an even more pronounced rise (*ibid.*). A weighted index based on the same data also shows a greater rise (*ibid.*, p. 377).

[4] Business Rents: — average of three indices for (a) typical store in first-class business section; (b) typical store in second-class business section; (c) typical down-town office. Three indices constructed by Coats (*Cost of Living Report*, vol. ii, p. 378) and averaged by writer. Weighted indices based on the same data show much greater increases (*ibid.*, p. 376).

[5] Weekly Wages: — constructed "on a weekly basis so as to make allowance for current change in hours and thus to reflect net earning capacity." (*Ibid.*, p. 427.) As there was a steady downward trend during this period in the length of the working day (*ibid.*, p. 431), this index minimizes the extent of the increase in rates of wages per hour. It is an index not of actual earnings but of weekly *rates* of wages. It is based "on a series of over 1000 continuous and reliable records back to 1900, picked over the available field with the sole purpose of rendering the final result as representative as possible" (*ibid.*, p. 431). The index is weighted according to the relative importance of the occupations for which wage quotations were used. (See p. 248, *infra*.)

In Chart XII, on the other hand, are presented five indices for the prices of as many important classes of services; these indices not only show in every case a relative decline as compared to the general commodity price index, but they show in every case but one, the index for passenger fares, an absolute decline. The rise shown by the index for passenger rates is much more moderate than the rise in the general commodity price index. The

CHART XII

PUBLIC UTILITY CHARGES, 1900–1913

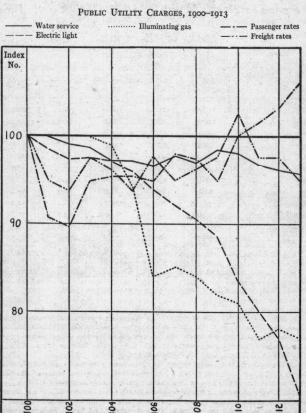

failure of the prices of these services to move in sympathy with the general upward trend of prices is due to the special circumstances governing both the costs of rendering the services and the determination of their prices. All of these indices are for services which are rendered either by municipal plants, or by public utilities whose charges are regulated by their franchises, by statute, or by public commissions. Improvements in methods of production and operation and the increase in population have lowered the cost per unit of service in many cases. In some cases the services have been sold with little regard to their cost. These

DATA OF CHART XII

PUBLIC UTILITY CHARGES

Year	Water service [1]	Electric light [2]	Illuminating gas [3]	Passenger rates [4]	Freight rates [5]
1900	100.0	100.0	100.0	100.0	100.0
1901	100.0	98.5	100.0	90.7	94.9
1902	99.3	97.4	100.0	89.6	93.7
1903	98.6	97.5	100.0	94.8	97.5
1904	97.2	97.2	99.0	95.3	96.2
1905	97.1	95.9	94.0	95.3	93.7
1906	96.5	93.9	84.0	94.8	97.5
1907	97.7	92.1	85.0	97.9	94.9
1908	96.9	90.5	84.0	97.4	96.2
1909	98.4	88.6	82.0	94.8	97.5
1910	98.0	83.5	81.0	100.0	102.5
1911	96.7	80.2	77.0	101.6	97.5
1912	96.2	77.1	78.0	103.1	97.5
1913	95.6	70.7	77.0	106.2	94.9

[1] Coats's Index: — *Cost of Living Report*, vol. ii, pp. 307 seq.

[2] *Ibid.*, pp. 317 seq.

[3] *Ibid.*, pp. 327 seq.

[4] Canadian Pacific Railway, *Annual Reports:* C. P. R. average gross earnings per passenger per mile, fiscal years beginning July 1. The official railway statistics for all railways in Canada, available since 1907, show an increase in average earnings per passenger per mile from 1907 to 1913 of 3.2 per cent, as compared with 12 per cent according to the C. P. R. data for the same period. (Canada: Dept. of Railways and Canals, *Railway Statistics*, 1907–1913.)

[5] Canadian Pacific Railway, *Annual Reports:* C. P. R. average gross earnings per ton mile, fiscal years beginning July 1. Coats from a study of the freight tariffs of 1900–1904 and 1914 found a decrease in rates of from 5 to 6 per cent from 1900 to 1914. (*Cost of Living Report*, vol. ii, p. 337.) The official railway statistics for all railways in Canada available since 1907 show a decrease in average earnings per ton mile from 1907 to 1913 of 8.2 per cent, as compared with no change according to the C. P. R. data for the same years. (Canada: Dept. of Railways and Canals, *Railway Statistics*, 1907–1913.)

CHART XIII

INDICES OF WEEKLY WAGES IN CANADA, GREAT BRITAIN, AND THE
UNITED STATES, 1900–1913

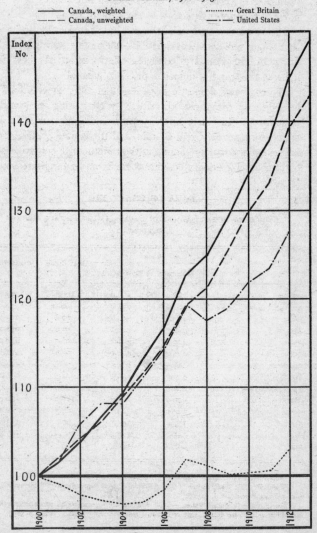

indices do not, therefore, discredit the results of the preceding price-studies. They reflect special conditions which have made the prices of certain kinds of services, if not always their costs, move in a counter direction to the general trend.

The trend of wages, if allowance be made for the probability that wages will show considerable inflexibility during periods of fluctuation in general price levels, offers perhaps the best single index of the trend of domestic prices in general.

The course of domestic price levels in different countries can be indirectly compared, therefore, by comparing the trends of wage levels. In Chart XIII a comparison is presented of wage indices for Canada, Great Britain, and the United States. These indices are not similar enough in their methods of construction to be altogether comparable, but there is no apparent reason for

DATA OF CHART XIII

INDICES OF WEEKLY WAGES IN CANADA, GREAT BRITAIN, AND THE
UNITED STATES

Year	Canada		Great Britain [2]	United States [3]
	Weighted [1]	Unweighted [1]		
1900	100.0	100.0	100.0	100.0
1901	101.6	102.0	99.1	101.7
1902	103.8	104.3	97.8	105.7
1903	106.5	106.1	97.2	108.2
1904	109.3	108.8	96.7	108.1
1905	113.1	111.6	97.0	111.2
1906	116.5	114.5	98.4	114.2
1907	122.6	119.2	101.8	119.2
1908	124.8	121.1	101.2	117.6
1909	129.0	125.4	100.0	118.8
1910	134.0	129.7	100.3	121.8
1911	137.9	133.1	100.5	123.3
1912	145.0	139.3	103.0	127.5
1913	148.9	142.9	....	....

[1] Weekly Wages in Canada: — see note 5 to Chart XI, and p. 248, *infra*.

[2] Weekly Wages in Great Britain: — Great Britain: Labour Dept., Board of Trade, unweighted. (*Cost of Living Report*, vol. ii, p. 558.)

[3] Weekly Wages in United States: — I. M. Rubinow's index computed from statistics collected and published by United States, Dept. of Labor, Bureau of Labor Statistics. (*Ibid.*, p. 565.)

doubting that they reflect closely enough for the present purpose the actual course of wages and of domestic prices in general in the three countries. For Canada a weighted and an unweighted index, both constructed by Coats, are presented. The weighting was crudely done, but the great differences in the relative importance of the occupational groups for which wage quotations were used in constructing the index make it the preferable one to use even for comparison with the unweighted indices for wages in Great Britain and the United States.[1]

The chart shows a much more pronounced rise in wages in Canada than in Great Britain. Wages in Canada and in the United States ran closely together until 1907, after which they increased to a much greater degree in Canada than in the United States. It will be remembered that the great flow of capital into Canada began in 1907. This chart supplies further confirmation, therefore, of the explanation offered in this and the preceding chapter, of the operation of variations in price levels in the adjustment of the Canadian trade balance to borrowings from abroad.

COATS'S EXPLANATION OF THE RELATIVE RISE IN CANADIAN PRICES

Mr. R. H. Coats, the Dominion Statistician, has offered an explanation of the relatively greater rise in Canadian than in world prices, which differs from and is somewhat inimical to that offered here.[2] He claims that an investigation of price trends in different countries shows that the rise from 1900 to 1913 was greatest in those countries in which industrial expansion was taking place at the most rapid rate, and especially in those countries in which this expansion took the form of the increase of primary plant and equipment, such as (1) the opening-up of new territory to settlement, with its attendant railway construction,

---

[1] Coats weighted his index on the basis of census returns of wage-earners by occupations. The necessity for weighting is indicated by the fact that the weights used ranged from 20 for agricultural workers and 20 for domestic servants to $\frac{1}{2}$ for municipal employees and $\frac{1}{2}$ for brewery and distillery workers. (*Cost of Living Report*, vol. ii, p. 431.)

[2] *Cost of Living Report: Synopsis of Exhibit by the Statistical Branch, Department of Labour*, pp. 15 seq.

road-making and town building, and (2) "industrialization," or the process of transformation of an "agrarstaat" into an "industriestaat." He explains the greater rise in prices in these countries by the fact that a period of considerable duration elapses before expansion of this sort results in increased production. During this interval the supply of commodities and of labor does not keep pace with the demand, and prices therefore rise.

If expansion of this sort in a given country was financed from domestic savings, it would simply mean, however, that those having purchasing power were voluntarily shifting their demand from consumers' goods to producers' goods and from labor engaged in producing consumers' goods to labor engaged in industrial development. What might be expected to happen would be that producers' goods would rise and consumers' goods would fall in price. The general price level should not be affected by this change in the character of the demand. On the other hand, if the expansion was financed by borrowings from abroad, there would still be available the normal supply of consumers' goods, the extra supply of goods and labor necessary for the industrial development being provided directly or indirectly by the lending country. In so far as the industrial expansion *per se* was concerned, there would again be no obvious reason why prices should rise more rapidly in this than in other countries, and there would even be some reason for expecting a relative fall in prices.

It unquestionably was true that in general the countries in which industrial expansion was taking place at the most rapid rate were also the countries in which prices were rising at the most rapid rate. But these were also the countries which were borrowing capital from abroad in the greatest volume, notably Canada, the Argentine, Australia, New Zealand, Japan, the United States. It is not proved, therefore, that it was the industrial expansion *per se* rather than the borrowings from abroad which made prices rise more in these countries than in the older European countries. Capital borrowings and industrial expansion are not unconnected. Capital is usually borrowed for purposes of industrial expansion. There is no reason to suppose that prices would have been less buoyant in the borrowing countries if the loans made to them had been "spendthrift loans."

Coats supports his theory with further evidence. He argues that the process of industrialization involves, at least during its earlier stages, the diversion of labor from the production of food to the production of plant and equipment. He then claims, on the basis of price statistics: that the rise in the prices of materials has been much the same the world over; that the rise in the prices of foods has shown much greater divergence in different countries; and that the relative rise in prices in the countries with the most buoyant prices has been essentially a rise in food prices. Since the countries with the most buoyant prices were also the countries in which industrialization was proceeding at the most rapid rate, he again claims to demonstrate the existence of a causal relationship between industrialization and relative rises in price levels.

The greater rise in the prices of foods than in the prices of materials in the capital-borrowing countries can be adequately explained, however, in accordance with the theory presented here, and without reference to industrialization. As Coats himself points out: "Materials are obtained as a rule over wider areas than foods; they lend themselves more readily to transportation, and their prices tend to move together as between country and country to an extent that is not true of foods, many of which are necessarily drawn from nearby sources." [1]

In the language of this study, materials are typically international commodities, foods are typically domestic commodities. The trend of prices of materials should not differ greatly from country to country. In capital-borrowing countries the prices of foods should rise more rapidly than the prices of materials. If some factor not directly connected with capital borrowings was operating in any case to make the prices of foods rise throughout the world relatively to materials, the relative rise in foods should be further accentuated in capital-borrowing countries. On the other hand, in capital-lending countries, if no other important factor were operating, foods should not rise as rapidly as mate-

[1] Cost of Living Report: Synopsis of Exhibit by the Statistical Branch, Department of Labour, pp. 20, 21.

CHART XIV

Capital Borrowings and Divergency between Domestic and Import Price Levels, 1900–1913

——————— Ratio of domestic to import price level
.... Capital borrowings, indirect estimate
— — — Capital borrowings, direct estimate

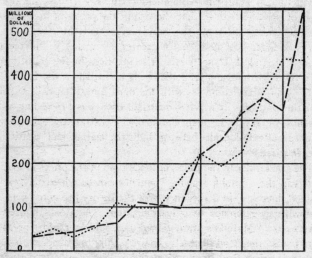

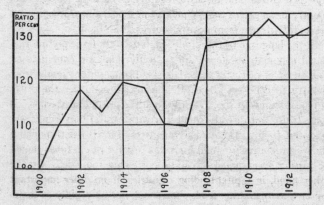

rials; if industrialization was causing a world-wide rise in foods relative to materials, this factor should be wholly or partly off-set by the counter-influence on the prices of domestic commod-ities of the export of capital.

The statistical evidence which Coats himself presents con-firms the present reasoning more closely than his own. In Canada, a capital-borrowing country, the increase in prices from 1900 to 1913 was 39 per cent for foods, 21 per cent for materials.[1] In Great Britain, a capital-lending country, the increase in prices from 1900 to 1913 was 12 per cent for foods, 14 per cent for mate-rials.[2] In the United States, which was borrowing capital from abroad but in relatively much smaller volume than Canada, the

[1] *Cost of Living Report: Synopsis of Exhibit*, p. 21.   [2] *Ibid.*, p. 22.

DATA OF CHART XIV

CAPITAL BORROWINGS AND DIVERGENCY BETWEEN DOMESTIC AND
IMPORT PRICE LEVELS

Year	Ratio of domestic to import price level [1]	Capital borrowings	
		Indirect estimate [2]	Direct estimate [3]
	Per cent	*Millions of dollars*	*Millions of dollars*
1900	100.0	34	32
1901	110.2	50	37
1902	117.4	31	42
1903	112.9	52	55
1904	119.4	112	62
1905	118.5	99	112
1906	110.1	99	105
1907	109.7	161	95
1908	127.6	224	222
1909	128.3	193	253
1910	129.0	225	313
1911	133.9	358	348
1912	129.4	435	321
1913	131.9	433	547

[1] Ratio of Domestic to Import Price Level: — domestic price level index constructed from indices for domestic prices used in this chapter with following weights: domestic commodity prices, 4; wages, 3; hospital services, 2; public utility services, 1; house rents, 2. Import price level as in Chart VIII. A series of link relatives was then computed in which the import price index for each year was made the base for that year, and the domestic price index the variable relative.

[2] Capital Borrowings, indirect estimate: — Table XXVIII, p. 101, *supra*.

[3] Capital Borrowings, direct estimate: — Table XLIV, p. 139, *supra*.

increase in prices from 1900 to 1913 was 34 per cent for foods, 17 per cent for materials,[1] the rise in each case being intermediate between the rises occurring in Great Britain and Canada respectively. A relative rise in the prices of foods, typically domestic commodities, in Canada and the United States, capital-borrowing countries, contrasted with a relative fall in the prices of foods in Great Britain, a capital-lending country.

SUMMARY

As a final inductive test of the reasoning presented in this and the preceding chapter, total indices of the course of domestic prices were computed from the partial indices already presented in this chapter, and the divergencies of the domestic from the import prices were measured by the use of link relatives. The results are presented in Chart XIV.

The stimulus to an excess of imports over exports resulting from variations in price levels should be roughly measurable by the divergency between the domestic and import price levels. With some qualification to be made for the progressive effect on trade for some time, of a given divergence in price levels, and also for the greater absolute effect on trade of a given divergency in prices when the volume of trade in general has increased, the divergency between domestic and import price levels should increase with every increase, and decrease with every decrease, in the rate of borrowings.[2]

If allowance is made for probable error in the estimates of the volume of capital borrowings and for the incompletely representative character of the price indices available, Chart XIV adequately substantiates the reasoning presented here. As the rate of borrowings increased, the divergency between domestic and import price levels widened. For the first four years, marked variations in the prices of the particular commodities entering into the indices, and a rate of borrowing too small to exert a distinguishable influence on the trend of prices, make inductive inference of questionable value. Marked relative increases in

---

[1] *Cost of Living Report: Synopsis of Exhibit*, p. 23.   [2] See p. 213, *supra*.

the rate of borrowing as compared to preceding years occurred in the years 1904, 1907, 1908, and 1911, according to the indirect estimates. In each of these years except 1907 there was a substantial widening of the divergency between domestic and import prices. According to the direct estimates, the rate of borrowings decreased in 1907, and the greatest relative increase in borrowings occurred in 1908, when there was also the greatest relative increase in the divergency between domestic and import prices. In 1912 and 1913, borrowings at the peak were accompanied by a divergency in prices very near, but not quite at, the peak, possibly because of the progressive effect of the divergency which made its appearance in the preceding years. Excluding the first four years, there was not a single case in which a substantial widening of the divergency in prices was not contemporaneous with a substantial increase in the rate of borrowings. In general, however, the curve of divergencies in price levels shows a closer correlation with the direct than with the indirect estimates of capital borrowings.

In so far as the inductive method permits of definitive results, it has been shown in this chapter that the increasing flow of capital into Canada was accompanied by a relatively increasing price level in Canada as compared with other countries; the rise was most pronounced in the prices of domestic commodities and services, least pronounced in the prices of import commodities, intermediate between these two in the prices of export commodities, thus operating to stimulate imports and to check exports, and so to adjust the Canadian commodity balance of trade to the capital borrowings. These results have been shown to be consistent with the classical theory, and even to be demanded by the classical theory, if it is completed so as to take into consideration sectional as well as general price levels. The inductive results of this chapter confirm the general proposition which has been laid down on deductive grounds, that the adjustment of the balance of trade to a newly introduced or increased disturbing factor is brought about through the influence of diverging price levels on the quantitative ratio of exports to imports.

It may be noted parenthetically here that this proposition has bearing not only on the theory of international trade but on the problem of how a new influence on prices arising in one country, such as the discovery of a gold mine, spreads its effects throughout the world. The connecting link between the price levels of various countries is to be found in the essential uniformity throughout the commercial world, and within the limits of transportation costs and tariff duties, in the prices of "international commodities." The "domestic commodity" and the service price levels of the individual countries can be influenced by foreign forces only through their relationship, within the national boundaries, to the prices of the "international commodities."

CHAPTER XI

THE COMMODITY BALANCE OF TRADE AND THE ADJUSTMENT OF THE BALANCE OF INDEBTEDNESS

The Commodity Balance of Trade

THE commodity balance of trade is by far the most important single factor in the final adjustment of international balances of indebtedness to more or less permanent disturbing factors. Gold imports and exports, as items in the commodity balance of trade, are a preliminary phase in the adjustment of balances. They exert their main influence, not through the effect on the balance of payments of their own values as debits and credits, but by their influence on price levels and through them on the remaining items in the commodity balance of trade.

Prices exert little direct influence on the volume of international transactions in services. Tourists' expenditures and insurance transactions will not be appreciably affected by changes in either direction in rates and prices. The amount of freight charges payable abroad or receivable from abroad by a given country is directly dependent on the volume of its foreign trade, on the proportions in which this trade is handled by foreign and domestic transportation companies, and on the amount of carrying business done for other countries, as well as on freight rates. A disturbing factor to a country's international balance of indebtedness, such as continued borrowings from abroad, will affect its balance of freight payments mainly through its influence through prices on the volume of commodity imports and exports, although it may conceivably affect the extent to which that country's capital and labor is engaged in the carrying trade. Interest payments are dependent simply on the amounts of capital borrowings, the rates of interest originally agreed upon, and the extent to which the debtors fulfill their contractual obligations.

Non-commercial transactions, such as immigrants' remittances, gifts, and the movements in and out of a country of migrants' personal effects, because they are non-commercial in character, are wholly free from direct influence of capital borrowings or changes in price levels, and in the main are not appreciably affected by them even indirectly. A possible exception is in the case of capital brought in by immigrants, for an increase in capital borrowings abroad tends to create in the borrowing country a situation favorable to labor, and thus stimulates immigration.

It follows that when a disturbing factor of substantial proportions and long-continued duration, such as the Canadian borrowings abroad during the period under study, breaks the even balance of debit and credit international obligations, an even balance of payments is reëstablished, and is maintained in spite of the debit balance of indebtedness, mainly through compensatory variations in the commodity balance of trade exclusive of gold.[1] Gold movements and transfers of securities and bank deposits are significant factors in the definitive adjustments of the balance only for casual and temporary disturbances in the balance of payments. Transfers of securities and bank deposits cannot be significant factors in the adjustment of the balance of payments to a continued debit or credit balance of indebtedness since they are themselves merely representative of some of the items in the balance of indebtedness to which adjustment must be made.

Chart XV presents a comparison of the variations in the total Canadian balance of international indebtedness with the varia-

[1] Cf. A. C. Whitaker, "The Ricardian Theory of Gold Movements," *Quarterly Journal of Economics*, vol. xviii (February, 1904), p. 231: "The investment of capital abroad, the travel of tourists, and all the other factors outside of the balance of trade itself are the comparatively independent variables, the balance of trade in goods is the compensatory variable in the balance sheet of total indebtedness." Where the carriage of a country's foreign trade is largely in foreign hands, the balance of freight payments will be a variable closely dependent on the volume of its commodity imports and therefore will also exert a compensatory influence on the total balance of payments. But if the imports are valued c. i. f., as, *e. g.*, in Great Britain, the freight charges payable on account of imports will already be accounted for in the debit side of the commodity balance of trade.

CHART XV

The Canadian Total Balance of International Indebtedness and the Partial Balances, 1900–1913

— — — Debit commodity balance of trade, gold coin excluded
.... Debit balance of gold coin imports and exports
— · — Debit balance of service transactions
— · · — Debit balance of non-commercial transactions
——— Total debit balance of international indebtedness

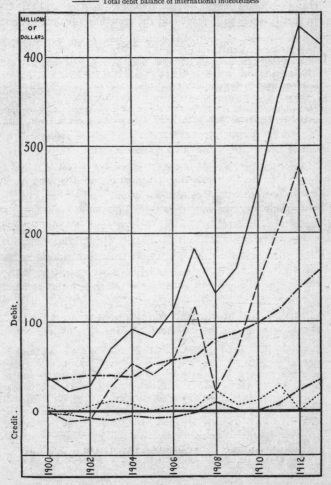

tions in the partial balances. In confirmation of the reasoning presented above, the commodity balance of trade shows the greatest degree of correlation of the partial balances with the total balance of indebtedness.[1] The balance of service transactions also shows a substantial correlation. In large part this is due to the fact that the balance of payments on account of freight charges is dependent upon the volume of imports and exports. In part it is due to the fact that the growth in the debit balance

[1] The coefficients of correlation of the partial balances with the total balance (Karl Pearson's formula) are as follows:

Commodity balance of trade, excluding gold coin: $r = + .98 \pm .007$.

Gold coin balance: $r = + .41 \pm .150$.

Balance of service transactions: $r = + .96 \pm .014$.

Balance of non-commercial transactions: $r = + .79 \pm .068$.

The numbers of pairs are so few that the probable errors are almost worthless, and the coefficients add little to the value of the graphical presentation.

DATA OF CHART XV

THE CANADIAN TOTAL BALANCE OF INTERNATIONAL INDEBTEDNESS AND THE PARTIAL BALANCES [1]

In millions of dollars

Year	Debit commodity balance of trade, gold coin excluded[2]	Debit balance of gold coin imports and exports [2]	Debit balance of service transactions [3]	Debit balance of non-commercial transactions [4]	Total debit balance of international indebtedness[5]
1900	0	4	35	3	37
1901	*12*	1	37	3	21
1902	*9*	5	40	9	27
1903	27	11	40	10	69
1904	51	8	37	5	91
1905	40	0	51	8	83
1906	56	5	56	7	112
1907	117	4	62	1	183
1908	23	22	80	8	132
1909	67	7	87	0	160
1910	142	12	97	0	251
1911	206	27	114	8	355
1912	276	0	136	23	435
1913	205	18	157	34	414

[1] Credit balances in italics.　　[2] Computed from Tables II and III, pp. 30, 32, *supra.*
[3] Table XXIX, p. 103, *supra.*　　[4] Table X, p. 61, *supra.*　　[5] Table XXX, p. 106, *supra.*

of interest payments followed closely the growth in net foreign capital investments in Canada, that is, in the total balance of international indebtedness. But Canada has always had a debit balance of service transactions, and the parallel growth in this period of this debit balance and the debit balance of international indebtedness shows not so much a true causal correlation as a false correlation arising out of the common pecuniary growth in all phases of Canadian economic activity during a period of general expansion and of rising prices. Only to a slight extent, therefore, was the correlation due to direct compensatory adjustments to the balance of international indebtedness.

In order that an even balance of payments should be substantially maintained after the first appearance and during the continuance of the debit balance of indebtedness — that is, in order that the capital borrowings should enter Canada in the form of goods instead of in the form of money—there was necessary a change in the quantitative relationship of commodity imports to exports such that there would be an excess of imports over exports to absorb the surplus foreign credits created by the borrowings abroad. As is shown in Chart XV, a small "favorable" commodity balance of trade in the first few years of the period shifted in 1903 to an "unfavorable" balance of trade increasing as the rate of borrowings abroad increased. Until 1903 the borrowings abroad were barely sufficient, or were less than sufficient, to meet the interest payments on earlier investments of foreign capital in Canada. From 1903 on, the new borrowings abroad exceeded the interest charges on the old borrowings,[1] and the surplus came into Canada mainly in the form of an excess of commodity imports plus freight charges thereon over commodity exports.

The shift from a favorable to an unfavorable commodity balance of trade which accompanied the increasing flow of capital borrowings could have resulted from either a decrease in exports below or an increase in imports above what they would have been respectively in the absence of capital borrowings, or from both combined. The method by which this result would be brought

---

[1] Cf. Table XXV, p. 94. *supra*, Table XXVIII, p. 101, *supra*, and Chart XV.

about, according to the deductive theory, has already been explained, and in the case of exports has been given some measure of inductive verification: a relative rise in prices in the borrowing country, due in Canada immediately to increased bank deposits, in other countries under similar circumstances due probably to a preliminary flow of gold, both stimulates imports and checks exports. The theoretical expectation would be, therefore, that the adjustment should be brought about by both an increase in imports and a decrease in exports.

The general expansion of industry and trade in Canada during the period under study operated independently of the influence of the capital borrowings, to increase both imports and exports. Moreover, the general rise in prices of itself operated to increase the money value of constant quantities of both imports and exports. It is impossible to determine with mathematical precision what the volumes of imports and exports would have been in the absence of capital borrowings. It is possible, however, from an analysis of the trade in individual commodities and of other related data, to ascertain with some degree of certainty whether the restrictive influence on exports and the stimulative influence on imports were both operating in the manner described in the deductive theory.

RESTRICTIVE EFFECT OF CAPITAL BORROWINGS ON EXPORTS

There follows an attempt to discover whether the capital borrowings operated to restrict the volume of exports. In Table LII estimates of the total volume of Canadian commodity production at the beginning and the end of the period under study are compared with the total exports from Canada for corresponding years. The data presented in this table show a marked decrease in the later part of the period under study, as compared to 1901, in the proportion of the total Canadian production of commodities which was sent abroad. Although the statistics for production are of uncertain accuracy, they probably serve well enough the present purpose. It should be noted, moreover, that much of the production in Canada during this period, and especially dur-

ing the later part of the period, was in the form of town, road and
railroad construction, and farm, building and plant development,
and that the production estimates given, which are for commodity
production only, are therefore probably a considerable underestimate of the actual increase in production.

It is difficult to explain the decline in the percentage of exports
to total commodity production, without reference to the capital
borrowings from abroad. Some of the relative decline in exports
was undoubtedly due to the increasing extent to which Canadian
raw materials were being manufactured in Canada for Canadian
consumption, instead of being exported in their crude form in
exchange for imported manufactured goods. But this increase
in manufactures would not have been possible in nearly the same
degree had it not been for the foreign investments of capital in
Canadian manufacturing enterprises. The expansion of manufacturing not only absorbed an increased proportion of the Canadian production of raw materials, but it withdrew labor, from the
production of raw materials which otherwise would have been
exported, to the construction of plant and equipment and the
fabrication, from imported raw materials, of manufactured com-

TABLE LII

TOTAL COMMODITY PRODUCTION IN CANADA AND TOTAL EXPORTS FROM
CANADA, 1901, 1911, 1912, AND 1913

In millions of dollars

Year	Total commodity production in Canada [1]	Total exports from Canada [2]	
	Value	Value	Per cent of total production
1901......................	943	205	21.7
1911......................	2,039	302	14.8
1912......................	2,761	376	13.6
1913......................	2,859	471	16.5

[1] For 1901 and 1911, *Cost of Living Report*, vol. ii, pp. 962–972; for 1912 and 1913, *Financial Post of Canada* (Toronto), January 3, 1914.

[2] Table III, p. 33, *supra*. Includes small amounts of reëxports of foreign products.

modities for domestic consumption. The development of roads, towns, and railroads, made possible by the borrowings abroad, absorbed a large part of the immigration of labor, and these consumed considerable quantities of Canadian commodities which would otherwise have been available for export. Changes in relative price levels resulting from the capital borrowings were also an important factor in restricting exports, operating coördinately with the factors explained above.

The influence of these factors on exports can best be traced by an analysis of the export trade by important groups of commodities. The export commodities were grouped as nearly as was practicable in accordance with the following rules: all the important export commodities were first divided into two groups, according to whether their export increased or decreased relatively to total exports during the period under study; second, each of these major groups was again divided into minor groups, according to whether its prices rose by more or less than 30 per cent during the period under study; third, each of these minor groups was divided into still smaller groups, on the basis of some important common characteristic relating to their production or consumption, where the second grouping had not already accomplished this. In all, the commodities grouped comprised 88 per cent of the total exports in 1900 and 86 per cent of the total exports in 1913, so that they are fully representative of the export trade as a whole. The items not included consisted in the main of commodities inadequately classified in the official export statistics, or for which price quotations were not available, or entering only irregularly and in insignificant amounts into the export trade. In two or three instances, notably oats and barley, commodities showing most prominently the influence of seasonal conditions and not reflecting a decided trend in any direction were omitted because they did not lend themselves to unambiguous grouping. It is indicative of the extent to which the export trade was influenced throughout by common factors that this elaborate system of grouping led finally to only five groups, of which only two groups represented a substantial volume of exports, and one of these two groups alone included one third of the total exports

during the period under study. In connection with the interpretation of the data about to be presented, it is important to
bear in mind: (1) that in most cases all of the commodities in
each group have in common the quantitative trend of their export, their price trend, and some characteristic relating to their
production or consumption; and (2) that the results shown for
each group reflect, therefore, not merely the aggregate trends for
the groups as a whole, but also the trends for each individual
commodity included therein.

Table LIII presents the results of the analysis for commodities
whose exports increased relatively to total exports. Group I
consists of commodities whose price rose less than 30 per cent
from 1900 to 1913 and which were produced during this period
largely from newly-discovered or newly-developed natural resources. They thus have in common the probability that a special
factor was at work tending to make their costs of production
resist the general upward trend characteristic of the period, and
thus tending to exempt them from the restrictive influence on
exports of the relative rise in the Canadian price level. Without
any exception, they also have in common the fact that they were
commodities produced in Canada in excess of the amount of
domestic consumption to such an extent that they were dependent very largely upon foreign markets for their sale. The commodities included are: wheat, wheat-flour, and flaxseed; copper,
nickel, silver, and aluminum; asbestos; pulp wood, wood pulp,
and paper.

The production of wheat for export did not develop to large
proportions until the virgin lands of the Canadian prairies, with
their high yields at low cost in the first years of cultivation, were
opened up to settlement, largely during the period under study
and with the aid of capital borrowed from abroad. In 1899, only
10,000,000 bushels of wheat were exported; by 1913, the exports
had increased to 120,000,000 bushels. The price of wheat clearly
was determined not in Canada but in the world market. Although the price of wheat did not rise as much as did domestic
prices in general, the development of wheat-growing was profitable,
nevertheless, because the virgin lands made cost of production

unusually low. Wheat-milling was dependent upon the production of wheat, and developed with its development.[1] Toward the end of the period under study, it became generally known that flaxseed was a profitable crop with which to bring virgin land into cultivation, and its production increased at a rapid rate. Flaxseed in Canada may be regarded, therefore, as essentially a by-product of the breaking-up, for cultivation, of virgin wheat

[1] The Canadian exports of wheat flour consist mainly of the lower grades, and are frequently sold at "dumping" prices. The Canadian consumer demands a higher grade of flour than the important export grades. Export flour is therefore a by-product of the production of flour for the domestic market, although the prices of the different grades must move in close harmony. (Cf. *Cost of Living Report*, vol. i, pp. 750 seq.)

TABLE LIII

TOTAL EXPORTS, AND EXPORTS WHICH INCREASED RELATIVELY TO TOTAL EXPORTS, 1900 TO 1913 [1]

| Fiscal years [2] | Total exports | | Exports which increased relatively to total exports | | | | |
| | | | Group I | | | Group II | |
	Value in millions of dollars	Per cent increase over 1900	Value in millions of dollars	Per cent of total exports	Weighted price index	Value in millions of dollars	Per cent of total exports
1900........	163.5	...	21.8	13.3	100.0	5.5	3.4
1901........	177.4	8.5	21.3	12.0	99.3	7.1	4.0
1902........	196.0	19.9	33.4	17.4	91.1	9.0	4.6
1903........	214.4	31.1	42.0	19.6	91.6	8.6	4.0
1904........	198.4	21.3	34.0	17.1	102.1	9.7	4.9
1905........	190.9	16.8	36.1	18.9	104.9	10.2	5.3
1906........	233.5	42.8	63.8	26.9	95.8	11.9	5.1
1907 [3]	180.5	...	45.5	25.2	...	9.2	5.1
1907........	246.7	50.9	84.3	34.2	108.3	13.7	5.6
1908........	242.6	48.4	92.9	38.3	115.6	13.7	5.6
1909........	279.2	70.8	113.0	40.5	118.6	18.1	6.5
1910........	274.3	67.8	110.9	40.4	114.7	20.6	7.5
1911........	290.2	77.5	124.8	43.0	111.5	20.4	7.0
1912........	355.8	111.5	172.8	48.6	114.5	25.5	7.2
1913........	431.6	164.0	230.3	53.4	104.9	32.0	7.4

[1] Data from Canada: Department of Trade and Commerce, *Annual Reports*. Merchandise Exports, Canadian Produce.

[2] *Ending* June 30 until 1906; *beginning* April 1 from 1907 on.

[3] Intercalary 9-month period from July 1, 1906, to March 31, 1907.

lands. The market for flaxseed was mainly in foreign countries. Its price was lower in 1913 than in 1900, but it rose from 1909, the first year in which there was a substantial Canadian production, to 1912. In 1899 there was practically no export of flaxseed. In 1913 the export amounted to 21,000,000 bushels, with a value of $25,000,000. The increase in the exports of flaxseed in spite of the failure of its price to rise in full sympathy with the general rise in Canadian prices is to be explained, therefore, by the special circumstances surrounding its production in Canada, namely, its low cost of production on virgin lands and its desirability as a means of preparing virgin land for wheat cultivation.

The production in Canada of copper, nickel, and silver in substantial quantities began practically with the opening of the twentieth century, when the discovery and development of rich low-cost bodies of ore led to a rapid expansion of the mining industry,[1] which was highly profitable under these circumstances even though the prices of these minerals remained almost constant during a period of marked upward movement in the general price level. Canada provided a market for only a small fraction of these products. In the case of nickel, Canada was the chief source of the world supply. Aluminum ore is not mined in Canada, but during the period under study a single plant was established in Canada to make aluminum from imported bauxite, using the cheap and newly-developed water power at Shawinigan Falls in the process. The products of this plant are almost wholly exported.

The main source of the world's supply of asbestos is the Eastern Townships region of the Province of Quebec, where asbestos has been mined for many years. The price of asbestos fell during the period under study. The increase in the export of asbestos, which, however, never reached $3,000,000 in value in any one

[1] "Previously to the opening of the present century the development of the mining industry of Canada had been comparatively small. The mineral resources of the Dominion were little known. The nickel fields of Sudbury [which also yield copper in large quantities] had been discovered but the commercial value of the deposits was not realized. Neither Cobalt [silver] nor Porcupine [gold: not developed until 1909] had been discovered. Since 1900 the industry has grown by giant strides." R. Goldwin Smith, *Monetary Times*, January 21, 1921.

year, may perhaps be accounted for by the working of new and richer resources, or by improved technological processes, or by the necessity of operating the mines because of the fixed investment of capital therein. The great proportion of the product was necessarily exported. It was generally known that the industry was not flourishing financially in the later years of the period under study.[1]

The prices of paper and its raw materials fell during the period under study, but the application to the industry in Canada, of American methods of large-scale production, and the building of railroads into the extensive northern timber regions situated near rivers providing both cheap power and a cheap means of transporting the logs to the mills, made production profitable even at the lower prices. The gradual exhaustion of the American timber resources, the great increase in the consumption of paper in the United States, and the provincial restrictions on the export of pulp wood, combined to create a market in the United States for greatly increased quantities of both paper and wood pulp.

The great increase shown in Table LIII in the export of the commodities in Group I in spite of the failure of their prices to keep pace with the general upward trend is to be explained in every instance, therefore, by the discovery or new development of low-cost resources or methods of production which prevented cost of production also from keeping pace with the general upward trend. Of the total increase in exports of all commodities, amounting to $268,000,000 from 1900 to 1913, $208,000,000, or almost 80 per cent, is accounted for by the increase in the exports of the commodities in Group I. If it be remembered that there was little increase in the prices of the commodities in Group I, and that much of the increase in the value of total exports reflected an increase of prices rather than of quantities, it becomes apparent, even without further analysis, that very nearly all of the increase in Canadian exports during a period of rapidly increasing population and production in general can be accounted for by special circumstances which caused the cost of production

[1] Cf. R. Pothier Doucet, "The Canadian Asbestos Industry," in *Canada's Future* (E. Victor, editor), Toronto, 1916, pp. 212 seq.

of a few important export products to resist the general upward trend.

Group II includes without further classification all the other commodities whose export increased substantially relatively to total exports. It was not feasible to carry out the general plan of classification explained above for the commodities in this group, either because the official commerce statistics were inadequately classified or because price quotations were not available. Nevertheless, the commodities included in this group have certain characteristics in common. The commodities included are as follows: rags, bran, and hides and skins; settlers' effects; fertilizers; "ores not elsewhere specified, including chromic iron"; clover seeds; agricultural implements, carriages and automobiles, and liquors. Rags, bran, and hides and skins are by-products of important industries. The amount of their production will not be determined to an important degree by either their own prices or their separate costs of production. If increased production in the industries of which they are by-products results in an excess in the supply of these commodities over the domestic demand, their export will increase largely regardless of general price trends. Settlers' effects are a non-commercial item, the volume of whose exports is independent of prices and costs of production. The export of miscellaneous ores may well have been governed by the same conditions which have been shown to have applied to the mineral products in Group I. No data are available which throw any light on the factors explaining the increased exports of clover seeds. The remaining items are manufactured products, largely specialties. The item, carriages and automobiles, consisted in the later years predominantly of automobiles. Their production in Canada began only toward the end of the period under study, and it is a matter of common knowledge that their export from Canada was confined wholly, or almost wholly, to exports to the other portions of the British Empire, to some extent with the advantage of preferential tariffs, from the Canadian plant of the Ford Company. The export of agricultural implements and of liquors was in each instance also confined largely to a few large concerns who had developed foreign markets for their specialized products. Not much significance attaches, therefore, to the increase in the exports of this group of commodities in the face of the general tendency of Canadian costs of production to rise more rapidly than prices outside of Canada. These commodities were by-products, or, like the commodities in Group I, were produced under special circumstances making costs of production unusually low, or were manufactured specialties not subject to keen price competition, or enjoyed special tariff privileges in export markets.

Of the total increase in exports from 1900 to 1913, amounting to $268,000,000, the commodities in Groups I and II account for $263,000,000 or approximately 98 per cent. If allowance is made for the general rise in prices, the aggregate exports of all other commodities not only decreased relatively to total exports, but decreased absolutely and to a substantial degree in terms of quantities. With the possible exception of some of the items in Group II for which no price quotations were available, not a single important instance was found of a commodity which rose in price as much as 30 per cent and which nevertheless maintained its relative proportion to the total exports. Since the rise in domestic prices was on the average substantially greater than 30 per cent, and since the general expansion of population and production in Canada during this period should have tended of itself to increase the volume of exports, this is a convincing inductive demonstration that the relative rise in Canadian as compared to foreign prices checked the export of all commodities except by-products and those which were favored by special factors operating, counter to the general trend, to check the rise in costs of production. In the large, the maintenance of the volume of Canadian exports in the face of rising costs of production was made possible only by the discovery and exploitation of new low-cost natural resources. There was not even a single conspicuous instance of what would have been altogether in keeping with theoretical expectations, namely, of a commodity whose relative importance in the total export trade was maintained even though its price rose in full sympathy with the rise in Canadian prices generally, because the world rise in the price of that commodity was greater than the general rise in world prices. This is a convincing inductive demonstration, therefore, that part of the mechanism of the adjustment of the Canadian balance of indebtedness to the capital borrowings was the restrictive influence exercised on exports by the increase in Canadian purchasing power and by the relative rise in the Canadian price level resulting from the capital borrowings abroad.

This is further confirmed by Table LIV, which presents a grouping of those commodities whose export declined relatively to total exports. Groups III and IV both include commodities whose prices rose in full sympathy with the general rise in domestic prices. These commodities were divided into two groups for

TABLE LIV

EXPORTS WHICH DECREASED RELATIVELY TO TOTAL EXPORTS, 1900 TO 1913[1]

Fiscal year[2]	Group III			Group IV			Group V		
	Value in millions of dollars	Per cent of total exports	Weighted price index	Value in millions of dollars	Per cent of total exports	Weighted price index	Value in millions of dollars	Per cent of total exports	Weighted price index
1900	43.7	26.7	100.0	33.6	20.6	100.0	39.3	24.0	100.0
1901	43.2	24.4	105.0	31.2	17.6	109.3	52.9	29.8	93.8
1902	52.0	26.5	107.8	36.0	18.4	114.1	45.2	23.1	98.7
1903	54.2	25.3	112.7	39.2	18.3	108.8	47.0	21.9	103.2
1904	50.9	25.7	113.5	34.1	17.2	103.8	47.5	23.9	91.8
1905	47.8	24.7	115.9	36.3	19.0	110.9	40.6	21.3	100.3
1906	59.9	25.7	127.8	34.9	14.9	120.5	42.7	18.3	106.9
1907[3]	47.0	26.0	. . .	27.2	15.1	. . .	33.1	18.3	. . .
1907	60.4	24.5	139.7	24.2	9.8	122.9	37.6	15.2	106.6
1908	54.7	22.5	136.5	23.0	9.5	121.5	32.6	13.4	108.5
1909	66.5	23.8	137.9	20.4	7.3	126.5	33.1	11.9	105.8
1910	63.1	23.0	141.2	18.9	6.9	145.3	32.1	11.7	109.8
1911	66.8	23.0	148.9	14.9	5.1	133.5	32.4	11.2	108.0
1912	65.0	18.3	154.5	8.6	2.4	149.2	37.5	10.6	115.0
1913	69.0	16.0	161.0	13.3	3.1	163.2	35.9	8.3	109.5

[1] Data from Canada: Department of Trade and Commerce, *Annual Reports.* Merchandise Exports, Canadian Produce.

[2] *Ending* June 30 until 1906; *beginning* April 1 from 1907 on.

[3] Intercalary 9-month period from July 1, 1906, to March 31, 1907.

separate analysis, according to the degree in which their export declined relatively to total exports. Group V includes commodities whose prices failed to keep pace with the general rise in prices.

Group III includes the following commodities: fisheries products, lumber, furs,[1] leather, hay, apples, and potatoes.[1] Their export in terms of dollars increased in spite of their rise in price, but it did not increase sufficiently to maintain their original proportion to total exports.

The increase in the value of the exports of commodities in this group was not as great as the increase in their prices both for the group as a whole and for most of the commodities in the group. In terms of quantities, therefore, there was an absolute decrease in export, which is reasonably to be attributed to the restrictive influence on exports of the relative rise in their prices as compared to world prices.

Group IV includes the following commodities: cattle, sheep, horses, bacon, eggs, butter, canned meats, and pease. All of these except pease are animal products or their derivatives. All were primarily domestic commodities even at the beginning of the period under study. Their prices consequently rose in full sympathy with the rise in domestic prices generally. The rise in prices, combined with an increased domestic market, operated almost wholly to eliminate their export. In the fiscal year beginning April 1, 1913, it is true, there was a revival of export, but this is to be attributed to the artificial and somewhat temporary stimulus arising out of the remissions and reductions of duties on these products in the United States Tariff Act of October 3, 1913, which was in force during half of this year. Chart XVI shows that these commodities were gradually moving during this period from an export to an import basis.

Group V includes only four commodities: bituminous coal, lead, gold (in quartz, nuggets, dust, etc.), and cheese, of which only the

---

[1] The exports of furs and potatoes increased in value slightly more than did the total exports. They were nevertheless included in Group III, perhaps illogically so, because their rise in price was so great that in terms of quantities they would have shown a very slight absolute increase in export and a substantial decline in relation to total quantity exports. The amounts of both items are small.

two last-named were important in the export trade. All of these commodities except coal were throughout the period primarily export commodities, finding their principal markets abroad. Even with respect to coal, exports were confined largely to the Nova Scotia product, which, during the winter months when water transportation to the important Canadian markets was impossible, was chiefly marketed abroad, especially in New England. The dependence of these commodities on foreign markets is re-

CHART XVI

IMPORTS AND EXPORTS OF COMMODITIES IN GROUP IV, 1900–1913

——— Imports   --- Exports

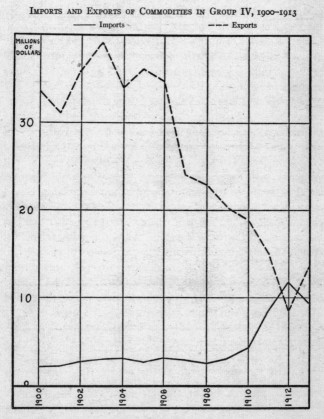

flected in the failure of their prices to rise in full sympathy with
the rise in the Canadian price level. With the stationary price for
crude gold, its production, which is almost wholly for export,
would have declined even more than it did had it not been for
the discovery of new and low-cost ore beds in the Porcupine dis-
trict in 1909.[1] Unlike other dairy products, the Canadian production of cheese has always been predominantly for export. Its
price, therefore, was determined largely in England, its most important market. Its price trend contrasts sharply with the price
trends of butter, milk, and eggs, domestic commodities. Compared in each case with 1900 prices, the increase in price in 1913
was: 32 per cent for butter; 29 per cent for milk; 85 per cent for
eggs; 14 per cent for cheese. The failure of the price of cheese
to rise as rapidly as the price of other products competing for the
same factors of production caused producers to turn from its

[1] It is assumed here that the price of gold always remains stationary in terms
of gold standard currency. As a matter of fact, during a period of rising prices
the price of gold ore tends to fall because of the greater money cost of smelting,
refining, and transportation to market.

DATA OF CHART XVI

IMPORTS AND EXPORTS OF COMMODITIES IN GROUP IV[1]

In millions of dollars

Fiscal year	Imports	Exports
1900	2.2	33.6
1901	2.3	31.2
1902	2.7	36.0
1903	3.0	39.2
1904	3.1	34.1
1905	2.6	36.3
1906	3.2	34.9
1907 [2]	3.2	27.2
1907	2.9	24.2
1908	2.6	23.0
1909	3.0	20.4
1910	4.3	18.9
1911	8.6	14.9
1912	11.6	8.6
1913	9.3	13.3

[1] Data from Department of Trade and Commerce, *Annual Reports:* animals, bacon, eggs, butter,
canned meats, and pease. Fiscal years *ending* June 30 until 1906; *beginning* April 1 from 1907 on.
[2] Not charted. Intercalary 9-month period ending March 31, 1907.

production to the production of more profitable commodities.[1] The decline in the exports of the commodities in this group, not only relatively to total exports but absolutely in terms of both values and quantities, is to be attributed to a decline in their production for export rather than to an increase in the domestic consumption. This is in turn to be attributed to their failure, owing to their dependence on foreign markets, to rise in price in proportion to the rise in their costs of production.

The foregoing analysis of the Canadian export trade has shown that the increase in the value of the total exports was due almost wholly to the entrance into the export trade of the products of newly-exploited natural resources, where special factors kept down the costs of production. Although production in general was undergoing great expansion during this period, the exports of all but a few commodities actually decreased in terms of quantities. In some cases exports declined because their prices rose in full sympathy with the general rise in Canadian prices and therefore became too high for foreign markets. In other cases exports declined because their prices did not rise in full sympathy with the general rise in Canadian prices, so that their production became less profitable. Prices rose most and exports declined most for those commodities which found a large part of their market in Canada. Throughout the range of the export commodities of which there was substantial consumption in Canada, there was convincing evidence of the restrictive influence on exports arising out of both the increased purchasing power acquired by a borrowing country and its relative rise in prices as compared to other countries.

COMMODITY IMPORTS AND THE BALANCE OF INTERNATIONAL INDEBTEDNESS

Variations in commodity imports are unquestionably, under usual circumstances, a more important factor than variations in commodity exports in the adjustment of international balances of indebtedness to capital borrowings. Countries which bor-

[1] Cf. Statement of R. M. Ballantyne, before Board of Inquiry on the Cost of Living, January, 1914. (*Cost of Living Report*, vol. i, p. 47.)

row capital on a large scale are typically possessed of abundant undeveloped natural resources for whose exploitation their own capital does not suffice. Under these circumstances their comparative advantage in foreign trade is generally largely confined to the export of the primary products of these natural resources, limited in their range but representing a large part of their total commodity production. Marked variations in the export of these few commodities therefore mean marked variations in their production. Continued production, however, is essential to the continued employment of labor and the payment of fixed charges on the capital investment. Production, and therefore export, will respond only slowly and incompletely to changes in prices. Except for commodities for which there is no important domestic demand, the volume of export will probably respond more conspicuously to changes in domestic demand, either for the products themselves or for labor, arising out of the capital borrowings, than to changes in relative prices. Imports, on the other hand, are for such countries more varied in their range, have less influence on the volume of domestic production, and are therefore more flexible in their volume. Marked and rapid fluctuations in imports cause less disturbance to industry in such countries, and necessitate less internal readjustment, than do correspondingly marked variations in exports. If capital borrowings require sharp adjustments in the commodity balance of trade of the borrowing country, these are effected more easily through variations in the rate of import than in the rate of export. Professor Williams, in his study of Argentine trade during a period of capital borrowings, clearly demonstrates the greater importance of variations in imports than in exports, in the adjustment of the commodity trade balance of that country to the capital borrowings.[1] In many respects the Argentine situation resembled the Canadian one. There is less specialization of production, that is, there is a greater variety of production and relatively more production for the domestic market, in Canada than in the Argentine, however, so that in Canada exports are more flexible than in the Argentine.

[1] J. H. Williams, *Argentine International Trade under Depreciated Paper*, Ch. xv.

Table LV compares the variations in the volume of imports into Canada with the variations in the volume of Canadian net borrowings from abroad. It demonstrates clearly that the borrowed capital was transferred to Canada mainly in the form of increased commodity imports. Some of the increase in the value of the imports was undoubtedly due to the rise in the prices of the import commodities and to the increase in population. Even if generous allowance is made for these two factors, there still remains an increase of imports sufficient to account for a large share of the capital borrowings. In spite of the operation of other factors in the adjustment of the balance of indebtedness, there is apparent a substantial measure of correlation between the variations in imports and the variations in net capital borrowings.

TABLE LV

COMMODITY IMPORTS AND THE BALANCE OF INTERNATIONAL INDEBTEDNESS

In millions of dollars

Calendar years	Commodity imports [1]		Debit balance of international indebtedness [2]	
	Amount	Increase over preceding year [3]	Amount	Increase over preceding year [3]
1900........................	189.3	....	36.6	....
1901........................	192.6	3.3	21.3	*15.3*
1902........................	212.8	20.2	27.4	6.1
1903........................	265.3	52.5	69.2	41.8
1904........................	256.8	*8.5*	91.0	21.8
1905........................	269.2	12.4	83.0	*8.0*
1906........................	329.6	60.4	111.6	28.6
1907........................	392.5	62.9	182.8	71.2
1908........................	312.6	79.9	131.7	*51.1*
1909........................	361.9	49.3	159.8	28.1
1910........................	450.4	88.5	250.6	90.8
1911........................	534.2	83.8	354.8	104.2
1912........................	651.2	117.0	435.2	80.4
1913........................	694.2	43.0	414.3	*20.9*
Total increase over 1900 rate....	....	2,462.4	....	1,858.9

[1] See Table III, p. 32, *supra.*   [2] See Table XXX, p. 105, *supra.*   [3] Decreases in italics.

Capital Borrowings and Imports of Capital Goods

It is often taken for granted that capital borrowings must result in corresponding imports of capital goods.[1] It is impossible to determine even with approximate accuracy what proportion of the imports is properly to be classed as capital goods. The classification of commodities in the Canadian import statistics is often inadequate for this purpose. In other cases the same commodities may be both consumers' goods and capital goods, depending upon the uses to which they are put by the owner. Coal, for instance, may be used in the heating of residences or in the production of railroad equipment. In order to discover whether the capital borrowings affected the proportions in which the imports consisted of capital goods and consumers' goods, respectively, the total imports were compared with the imports (1) of selected items chosen as being most nearly representative of capital goods and (2) of foods and a group of miscellaneous commodities selected as being typically consumers' goods. The results of the comparison are given in Table LVI.

Table LVI shows that during the period of increasing capital borrowings an increasing proportion of the total imports consisted of capital goods and a decreasing proportion consisted of consumers' goods, but the change in relative proportions was only moderate. C. K. Hobson has shown that British investments in railroad enterprises in the Argentine, India, and Australia were generally accompanied by increased imports into these countries of railroad equipment and materials.[2] Canada, however, unlike these countries, is itself an important producer of heavy machinery, railroad rolling stock, rails and other capital goods. Less correlation is to be expected, therefore, for Canada than for these other countries, between borrowings abroad for specific enterprises and imports of equipment and material for

[1] Cf. J. H. Williams, "Germany's Reparation Payments," *American Economic Review*, Supplement, March, 1920, p. 52: "The borrowings will take the form of goods, — construction materials, machinery, manufactures of various sorts; and past experience has shown that these goods, the direct product of loans, are most likely to be purchased in the country making the loans."

[2] C. K. Hobson, *The Export of Capital*, pp. 8 seq.

these enterprises. Moreover, in the interpretation of statistics of imports of capital goods, it should be remembered that a large part of these imports is unquestionably made for purposes of maintenance and replacement of already existent plant and equipment, and therefore does not reflect new investments. For most forms of capital investment a large part of the expenditure

TABLE LVI

TOTAL IMPORTS, IMPORTS OF SELECTED CAPITAL GOODS, AND IMPORTS OF SELECTED CONSUMERS' GOODS, 1900 TO 1913 [1]

In millions of dollars

Fiscal year [5]	Total imports	Imports of selected capital goods [2]		Imports of selected consumers' goods			
				Foods [3]		Selected miscellaneous commodities [4]	
	Value	Value	Per cent of total imports	Value	Per cent of total imports	Value	Per cent of total imports
1900	172.5	49.7	28.8	33.6	19.5	43.7	25.3
1901	177.7	48.4	27.2	34.0	19.1	45.2	25.4
1902	196.5	58.4	29.7	31.7	16.1	50.7	25.8
1903	224.8	72.7	32.3	33.2	14.8	60.0	26.7
1904	243.6	77.8	31.9	36.7	15.1	61.9	25.4
1905	251.6	78.2	31.1	37.9	15.1	64.5	25.6
1906	283.3	86.4	30.5	45.0	15.9	72.5	25.6
1907 [6]	249.7	79.7	31.9	38.8	15.5	63.4	25.4
1907	351.9	116.8	33.2	54.1	15.4	86.7	24.6
1908	288.2	84.3	29.3	51.1	17.7	71.4	24.6
1909	369.8	113.2	30.6	55.7	15.1	97.6	26.4
1910	451.7	151.6	33.6	66.9	14.8	110.2	24.4
1911	521.4	183.7	35.2	82.2	15.8	113.8	21.8
1912	670.1	255.7	38.2	92.2	13.8	142.6	21.3
1913	618.5	232.7	37.6	87.4	14.1	129.5	20.9

[1] Data from Canada: Department of Trade and Commerce, *Annual Reports.* Merchandise Imports Entered for Consumption.

[2] Bricks, clays, and tiles; cement; coal, bituminous; railroad cars; electric apparatus; ships; mineral oils; gunpowder and explosives; stone and manufactures thereof; wood and manufactures thereof; copper, iron, lead, tin, zinc, and miscellaneous metals other than gold, silver, and brass, and manufactures thereof.

[3] All foods, foodstuffs, and feedstuffs.

[4] Thirty items and groups, all typically consumers' goods.

[5] *Ending* June 30 until 1906; *beginning* April 1 from 1907 on.

[6] Intercalary 9-month period from July 1, 1906, to March 31, 1907.

is for wages and transportation services and not for material and equipment, and much of the material required is often necessarily of a local character. The data in Table LVI suggest that, while the capital borrowings entered Canada to some extent in the form of direct purchases by the borrowers of foreign capital goods, they entered more largely in the form of consumers' goods. Laborers directly engaged in the developments financed by borrowings from abroad, and laborers in other domestic industries engaged in producing capital goods to be used in these developments, received their real wages in part in the form of these imported consumers' goods. Payment for these imported consumers' goods was made indirectly out of the proceeds of the borrowings abroad.

CHAPTER XII

TRIANGULAR ADJUSTMENT OF THE BALANCE
OF INDEBTEDNESS

THE Canadian balance of international indebtedness was in extraordinarily large measure adjusted to the borrowings in Great Britain through triangular transactions with the United States. British funds made available to Canadians through the flotations of loans were used to buy New York exchange, which was in turn used to pay for increased imports from the United States. The adjustment of the British balance of international indebtedness to the capital investments in Canada was similarly effected through increased British exports to the United States, or even in a more circuitous fashion, through increased British exports to Latin America and the Orient, which were in turn paid for by increased exports from these regions to the United States and from the United States to Canada.[1]

Chart XVII, which compares by countries the Canadian commodity balances with the capital borrowings, demonstrates to how great an extent such triangular adjustment was carried in connection with the Canadian borrowings from Great Britain. In spite of the great amount of Canadian borrowings in London, Canada maintained throughout the period a "favorable" commodity balance of trade with Great Britain. On the other hand, in the trade with the United States and to a lesser degree in the trade with all other countries, the excess of imports over exports

---

[1] "Canada is borrowing money in London to finance her farmers, and with the capital borrowed in London Canadian farmers are purchasing American machinery, and the capital actually passes into Canada in this form. This means that we have to remit to the United States the capital we have lent to the Canadian farmer. But the United States do not require to import much English produce. They need silk, however, and this they purchase. And we have now to settle with Japan. Japan takes payment for the silk sold to America in raw cotton from India, and India receives payment for her raw cotton in cotton piece goods from Lancashire. Thus we export capital to Canada by exporting Manchester goods to Bombay." (*Statist*, London, October 21, 1905.)

CHART XVII

CANADIAN COMMODITY BALANCES AND CAPITAL BORROWINGS, 1900–1913

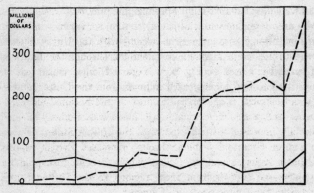

British capital investments in Canada
Excess of Canadian exports to, over imports from, Great Britain

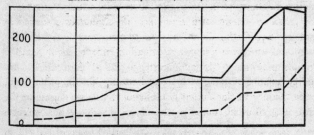

American capital investments in Canada
Excess of Canadian imports from, over exports to, United States

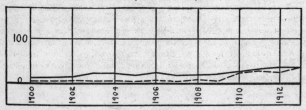

Other countries' capital investments in Canada
Excess of Canadian imports from, over exports to, other countries

substantially exceeded the volume of Canadian borrowings from these countries. The capital borrowed by Canada in Great Britain entered Canada largely in the form of American commodities.

Even when account is taken of the "invisible" items in the balance of indebtedness, it still appears that there was a great measure of triangular adjustment. In Table LVII a comparison is made, for the entire period under study and for both Great Britain and the United States, of the total balances of indebtedness with the net capital borrowings. The calculation of the balances of indebtedness with individual countries is beset with many difficulties, and the results presented in Table LVII are

DATA OF CHART XVII

CANADIAN COMMODITY BALANCES AND CAPITAL BORROWINGS

Year	Great Britain		United States		Other countries	
	Excess of Canadian exports to, over imports from [1]	Capital investments in Canada [2]	Excess of Canadian imports from, over exports to [1]	Capital investments in Canada [2]	Excess of Canadian imports from, over exports to [1]	Capital investments in Canada [2]
1900..........	51.9	10.1	47.2	17.9	11.5	3.7
1901..........	55.9	15.1	40.3	18.3	11.5	3.7
1902..........	63.6	11.9	55.6	33.4	13.7	7.1
1903..........	51.4	28.8	62.0	22.1	21.6	3.7
1904..........	43.1	29.5	83.5	25.8	21.3	6.6
1905..........	46.6	76.4	78.8	32.4	17.8	3.7
1906..........	52.6	68.5	100.5	29.5	21.4	7.3
1907..........	37.0	65.3	115.5	26.0	15.9	3.8
1908..........	51.8	181.4	109.6	32.7	18.0	8.0
1909..........	48.4	212.7	107.8	36.2	20.2	4.5
1910..........	29.8	218.5	161.5	72.7	26.9	22.1
1911..........	32.3	244.4	232.9	76.1	32.0	27.8
1912..........	33.3	214.8	268.8	81.7	35.3	24.6
1913..........	72.3	375.8	258.8	135.0	35.0	36.0
Totals.......	670.0	1,753.1	1,722.8	629.8	302.1	162.7

[1] Data from Canada: Department of Trade and Commerce, *Annual Reports.* Merchandise and Coin and Bullion, total imports and exports. Settlers' effects deducted. Adjusted to calendar year basis from fiscal year statistics on hypothesis of equal monthly distribution in each fiscal year.

[2] Direct estimates, Table XLIV, p. 139, *supra.*

offered only as rough and somewhat incomplete estimates, based mainly on the data used in Part I of this study.

The data presented in Table LVII show so great a divergency between Great Britain and the United States in the relation of the balances of indebtedness to the balances of borrowings, that they demonstrate conclusively, even with the most generous allowance for error in the estimates, that adjustment

TABLE LVII

TOTAL CANADIAN BALANCES OF INDEBTEDNESS AND CAPITAL BORROWINGS, 1900 TO 1913

	Great Britain		United States	
	Debit balances	Credit balances	Debit balances	Credit balances
Migrants' Capital.............	....	63.8	....	171.5
Non-Commercial Remittances ...	10.0	....	45.0	....
Freights.....................	8.0	....	131.0	....
Insurance Payments............	23.0	....	17.0	....
Tourist Expenditures...........	30.0	....	....	87.0
Interest Payments.............	815.0	....	50.0	....
Total — Invisible Items.......	886.0	63.8	243.0	258.5
Commodities..................	....	670.0	1,722.8	....
Debit Balance of Indebtedness...	....	152.2	....	1,707.3
	886.0	886.0	1,965.8	1,965.8
Capital Borrowings [1]..........	1,753.1	....	629.8	....
Capital Loans	7.0	....	133.0	....
Net Capital Borrowings........	1,746.1	....	496.8	....
Debit Balance of Indebtedness...	152.2	....	1,707.3	....
Adjusted Indirectly — Excess of Net Capital Borrowings over Debit Balance of Indebtedness	1,593.9	....	....	....
Adjusted Indirectly — Excess of Debit Balance of Indebtedness over Net Capital Borrowings ..	....	....	1,210.5	....

[1] Table XLIV, p. 139, *supra*.

of the balance of indebtedness was mainly triangular instead of direct. The table shows an excess, in the debit balance of indebtedness with the United States over the net borrowings from the United States, amounting to over $1,200,000,000, and yet falling short by almost $400,000,000 of the excess of the net borrowings from Great Britain over the debit balance of indebtedness with Great Britain. The remainder of the British excess of borrowings over indebtedness, not accounted for in this table, is to be explained partly by shortcomings in the present calculation, but mainly by additional triangular adjustment, through Canadian debit balances of indebtedness, with countries other than Great Britain and the United States.

Triangular Adjustment through Imports

Many factors were operating to bring about a triangular instead of a direct adjustment of imports to borrowings. In Canada the import of goods has always been governed by the circumstances connected with the goods themselves and the Canadian demand for them, without interference by the lenders of capital. In no case has any trace been found of loans to Canadians being made conditional upon the use of any part of the proceeds in making purchases of a specified kind or in a specified country. Nevertheless, there were differences in the typical relations to their investments of British and American investors such that the American investments were more likely to stimulate imports from the United States than the British investments were likely to stimulate imports from Great Britain.

Approximately 90 per cent of the British investments in Canada consisted of purchases of Canadian securities,[1] of which the greater proportion consisted of government securities and industrial and financial bonds and debenture stocks without voting rights. Most of the remaining 10 per cent of British investments in Canada went into the purchase for speculative purposes of town and agricultural land, or consisted of investments of British insurance companies in mortgages, loans and securities. In most of the comparatively few instances where British investors held

[1] Cf. Table XXXVIII, p. 126, *supra.*

a majority of the common stock of a Canadian enterprise, control of the enterprise, by tacit consent of the British shareholders, remained with the Canadian minority shareholders. In the case of the Canadian Pacific Railway, although Canadians owned less than 15 per cent of the common stock and almost none of the bonds and debenture stocks, the ownership being mainly British, almost all the directors were Canadians. There were only a few instances of British investments in Canada which were directly managed by the British investors or agents appointed by them, notably the Grand Trunk Railway and the Hudson's Bay Company. In many cases, most of the actual capital invested in American enterprises in Canada came from England through subscriptions to bond issues, the Americans retaining control through their ownership of the common stock, often representing nothing but the goodwill, the production technique, and the promoting ability of the American interest in the enterprise.

This divorce of capital ownership and control is not characteristic of British investments in other countries. Proximity to the situs of the investment and familiarity with local conditions are undoubtedly important factors in bringing about Canadian and American control of British investments in North America. They are not the sole factors, however, for in continental Europe, Latin America, and the Orient, where these factors must also be operative, the British direct their own investments. But the British investments outside of North America are made principally in countries where business enterprise and managerial ability, as well as capital, are scarce. To such countries the British export not only their capital but their business men and technicians, so that control of the investments, including purchases and technology, is retained by them. In Canada, as also in the United States, capital is relatively scarce and high interest rates are offered for its use, but business enterprise and technological ability are abundant and, moreover, are probably more efficient, especially for North American conditions, than the British supply thereof. As between the British on the one hand, and the Canadians and Americans on the other hand, there is a considerable degree of specialization of function with respect to Canadian investments: the British supply the capital, the Canadians and Americans supply the managerial and technical ability.

American investors, on the other hand, commonly retain directive control of their Canadian investments. Less than 40 per cent of the American investments in Canada during the period under study consisted of purchases of securities, and these were mainly in the last few years.[1] The remainder consisted principally of investments in branch plants of American industries, and in mining and lumbering enterprises controlled by the investors. In many instances the capital utilized in these American-controlled enterprises greatly exceeded the amount of American capital actually invested therein, the remainder being obtained by bond issues in Great Britain or in Canada and by loans from the Canadian banks. The American investors generally made their Canadian investments in enterprises closely resembling those with which they were familiar at home, and operated them under similar financial, sales, and technological methods.

It would be difficult to explain the substantial volume of American capital investments in Canada at the same time that the United States continued to be a debtor nation in so far as Europe was concerned, except on the basis of some degree of national specialization in investments. European capital was available for investment in gilt-edge securities of well-established American railroad and industrial concerns. American capital was available, although in limited amounts, for investment in mining and manufacturing enterprises to which American technical methods could be applied. The American investments in Canada typically had three outstanding characteristics in common: they were not made in routine enterprises, but demanded for their success capable and venturesome business direction and modern industrial technique; they were not conservative investments, in the narrow sense of the term, but required the assumption of considerable economic risk; they offered a chance of unusually high profits as well as of losses.[2]

---

[1] Cf. Table XLI, p. 134, *supra*, and pp. 127 seq. generally.

[2] Similar national specialization in investments is illustrated by the investments of Canadian financiers in light, power, and tramway enterprises in the United

The establishment in Canada of branch plants of American industries was promoted by the fact that Canada offered a market already trained to demand American-type commodities, but in many cases shut off from direct exploitation by a protective tariff. The compulsory working provision in the Canadian patent law further stimulated the establishment of branches in Canada in such cases where the commodity was sold by the patentees in the United States at a monopoly price which could be met by Canadian producers, either with or without the aid of tariff protection, if they had access to the basic patents. In the later years of the period under study, the rapid exhaustion of the timber and pulp-wood resources of the United States and the provincial restrictions on the export of pulp wood from Canada led to heavy investments of American capital in Canadian lumber and paper enterprises producing for the American market. The gradual extension of the system of preferential tariffs within the British Empire, and perhaps also the goodwill value of the "Made in Canada" trademark in trade with the British Empire, operated to promote the establishment in Canada of branch plants of American exporting industries to handle not only their Canadian trade but also their trade with other portions of the British Empire.

The greater degree of control over their Canadian investments exercised by American as compared to British investors, and the differences generally in the character of the investments made by Americans and British, operated to promote greater imports from the United States than from Great Britain. Sentimental preferences were probably of little or no significance, especially when it is considered that the enterprises in Canada in which outside capital is invested buy on a wholesale scale and with the profit and loss account constantly in mind. But the familiarity on the part of the American managers of Canadian industries with American styles, standards, specifications, ma-

States, Latin America, and Spain at the same time that Canada was very much a debtor country. By virtue of these investments, representing only a small fraction of the actual capital put into these enterprises, a group of Canadian financiers acquired the opportunity to apply their specialized promoting and operating ability in other countries when they had exhausted the Canadian field.

chinery, and production technique, led inevitably to purchases in the United States when similar Canadian articles were not available at satisfactory prices. Preference over British goods rested very little on sentimental considerations, not very much, perhaps, on price differentials, but principally on style, specification and type factors, and on old business connections. In many cases the branches in Canada of American industries are little more than assembling or finishing and distributing plants, and the parts or incompletely fabricated articles are shipped from the head plant in the United States. In the course of a few years the establishment of a branch plant in Canada may give rise to imports from the United States of equipment, machinery, materials, amounting to many times the amount of American capital invested in the plant.

More fundamental factors in Canadian commerce and industry than the differences in the character of the American and British investments were chiefly responsible, however, for the entrance of British capital into Canada preponderantly in the form of imports from the United States. As has already been shown, the proceeds of foreign borrowings are used in the purchase of the whole range of commodities, not only of producers' goods. The preponderance of imports from the United States over imports from Great Britain, shown in Table LVIII on page 289, was due primarily to the character of the domestic production, the exports, and the imports of these three countries.

In spite of the much greater flow of capital into Canada from Great Britain than from the United States, the proportions in which the Canadian merchandise imports came from Great Britain and the United States changed only slightly during the period under study, and what change did occur was in favor of the United States. Moreover, imports of coin and bullion, which are not included in this table, and which came almost wholly from the United States, increased greatly during the period under study.

Canada, since its adoption in 1879 of the policy of high protection for manufactures, and especially during the period under study, with the assistance of the capital secured abroad, had been steadily expanding its manufacturing industries. There resulted a gradual shift in the character of its imports from finished manufactured commodities to raw materials, machinery and equipment, and partly-manufactured goods. Great Britain was itself an importer of raw materials, whereas the United States had a surplus for export of coal, coke, mineral oils, cotton, certain types of lumber, and metals in their primary form and in preliminary stages of manufacture. Moreover, Canadian manufactures were developing typically along lines in which Great Britain was an important source of Canadian imports of the finished products, notably cotton and woolen textiles and iron and steel and tin products. As Canadian manufactures of these products increased,

TABLE LVIII

MERCHANDISE IMPORTS INTO CANADA ENTERED FOR CONSUMPTION, 1900 TO 1913 [1]

Fiscal year [2]	Total Imports	Imports from Great Britain		Imports from the U.S.	
		Value in millions of dollars	Per cent of total imports	Value in millions of dollars	Per cent of total imports
1900	172.5	44.3	25.7	102.1	59.2
1901	177.7	42.8	24.1	107.1	60.3
1902	196.5	49.0	25.0	114.7	58.4
1903	224.8	58.8	26.2	128.8	57.3
1904	243.6	61.7	25.3	143.0	58.7
1905	251.6	60.3	24.0	152.4	60.6
1906	283.3	69.2	24.4	168.8	59.6
1907 [3]	249.7	64.4	25.8	148.6	59.5
1907	351.9	94.4	26.8	204.6	58.2
1908	288.2	70.7	24.5	170.1	59.0
1909	369.8	95.3	25.8	217.5	58.8
1910	451.7	109.9	24.3	274.8	60.8
1911	521.4	116.9	22.4	330.4	63.4
1912	670.1	138.7	20.7	435.8	65.0
1913	618.5	132.1	21.4	395.6	64.0

[1] Settlers' effects included. All data, including percentages, from Canada: Department of Trade and Commerce, *Annual Report*, 1914, vol. i, pp. 20, 21.

[2] *Ending* June 30 until 1906; *beginning* April 1 from 1907 on.

[3] Intercalary 9-month period from July 1, 1906, to March 31, 1907.

it was chiefly the imports from Great Britain which were adversely affected thereby. Canadian manufacturing, building, and transportation methods almost invariably were modelled on American lines, so that the United States and not Great Britain was the main source of machinery, equipment, and materials not available in Canada. Semi-tropical and early season fruits and foodstuffs and raw tobacco, necessarily import commodities in Canada, could be obtained in the United States but were not produced in Great Britain. The styles demanded by the Canadian consumer, the brands and trademarks to which he had been accustomed by persistent advertising, by similarity of economic conditions and of standards of living, were American rather than British. American sales methods were more effective than the more conservative and old-fashioned British methods. The settlement of the Canadian prairie provinces, with their proximity to the important producing regions of the American Middle West, gave American exporters a decided advantage over their British competitors, in freights and in rapidity of communication and delivery, in a rapidly growing portion of the Canadian market. The shift in the character of the imports from relatively light highly-fabricated commodities to bulky raw materials, partially-manufactured products, and machinery and equipment, further handicapped the more distant British exporters, especially in their trade with the interior provinces to which direct water shipment without trans-shipment was either impossible throughout the year or was possible only during the seven months of the year when the St. Lawrence River was open to navigation.

Dating from 1897, many British products received a tariff preference over similar American products, and in those commodities where the British were able to offer serious competition, the preference aided them in retaining and in many instances in increasing somewhat their share of the Canadian market. The changing character of the Canadian imports and the many handicaps under which British exporters were operating were too powerful, however, to be offset by the tariff preference in so far as the import trade as a whole was concerned. The British loans to Canada, by furthering the growth of manufactures in Canada, operated indirectly to strengthen instead of to weaken the predominance of the United States as a source of Canadian imports.[1] All of these factors combined to prevent the adjustment of the Canadian trade balance to the capital borrowings from Great Britain, in so far as the import side of the balance was concerned, from being direct.

In the foregoing pages the preponderance of imports from the United States over imports from Great Britain, in spite of the preponderance of British over American capital investments in Canada, has been explained as due to fundamental economic factors which make the United States a more advantageous source than Great Britain for commodities of the sort wanted in Canada. No weight has been attached to the possibility that the closer connection between loans and trade in the case of the United States may have been due to deliberate control of their loans by American bankers and investors with a view to fostering the export trade of the United States. In evidence given before the Dominions Royal Commission in 1916, F. W. Field, formerly the editor of the *Monetary Times* of Canada and at this time British Trade Commissioner for Canada, presented a contrary view:[2]

Generally speaking, it may be stated that no great effort seems to have been made by British manufacturers and bankers to further Canadian trade specifically through the medium of British investments in Canada, although there have been exceptions. The matters of trade and loans apparently have been allowed to take their natural courses without an attempt being made to obtain new business as a result of new loans. The British investor hitherto has been largely content to invest in Canadian securities which bring him a fair income, give him little risk, but do not secure for him control of the enterprise in which his funds have been placed. The case of the United States is different. The bankers and manufacturers of that country have in many instances combined their efforts so that when the banker has arranged a loan to a Canadian borrower and the funds are to be used, say, for the installation of plant or machinery, there is an excellent prospect, or even a definite arrangement, that the plant or machinery in question shall be purchased in the United States and probably from a certain manufacturing firm. This practice has been in evidence even when the share of Canadian securities purchased by United States banking houses has been small compared with the share purchased by British houses.

---

[1] This is, of course, directly contrary to the common generalization about the relation between foreign investments and trade.

[2] F. W. Field, "Memorandum Regarding the Investment of British and Foreign Capital in Canada," Dominions Royal Commission, *Minutes of Evidence taken in the Central and Western Provinces of Canada in 1916*, Part I (Cd. 8548), p. 416.

The Commission commented on this evidence to the effect that it "was confirmed by their personal enquiries and by conversations with leading business men in the Dominion." [1] But the evidence printed in the reports of the Commission, which goes into great detail on this and other matters, contains no supporting data. If anything is meant by these statements other than that American manufacturers who invest their capital in branch plants in Canada often find it profitable to equip them with machinery and appliances manufactured by themselves, or to ship partly-manufactured products from their own American establishments to these branches for further manufacture, they are undoubtedly without substantial foundation in fact. There is certainly not a trace of evidence to support the charge that American bankers commonly attach limitations as to the country in which the borrowed funds are to be disbursed when they handle issues of Canadian securities. The same reasons explain the greater extent to which Canadian expenditures of borrowed capital are made in the United States than in Great Britain, which explain the greater extent to which Canadian expenditures of other kinds not even distantly connected with capital borrowings are made in the former than in the latter country.

Triangular Adjustment through Exports

Table LIX, which presents a comparison of the exports to Great Britain and to the United States, shows that in so far as exports were concerned the situation was the reverse of that found to be the case for imports. Great Britain was a much more important market than the United States for Canadian products. For both imports and exports, therefore, the situation was the reverse of what it would have been if adjustment of the commodity balance of trade to capital borrowings had been direct instead of triangular. Canada was predominantly an exporter of foodstuffs and raw materials, and for these Great Britain was a much more important importing market than the United States.

[1] Dominions Royal Commission, *Fifth Interim Report*, 1917 (Cd. 8457), p. 9.

In the years immediately preceding the war, the great increase of population in the United States, the relative increase in urban population as compared to rural and in manufacturing as compared to the primary industries, and the rapid exhaustion of her timber resources, were operating to increase the relative importance of the United States as a market for Canadian products. A continuance, for another decade, of the relative trend of exports to the United States and to Great Britain promised to make the United States the most important outside market for Canadian products as well as the most important source of Canadian imports. As a consequence of the abnormal wartime conditions, this result came about much sooner and in much more pronounced

TABLE LIX

MERCHANDISE EXPORTS, CANADIAN PRODUCE, 1900 TO 1913 [1]

In millions of dollars

Fiscal years [2]	Total exports	Exports to Great Britain		Exports to the United States	
		Value	Per cent of total exports	Value	Per cent of total exports
1900................	163.5	96.6	59.1	52.5	32.1
1901................	177.4	92.9	52.3	68.0	38.3
1902................	196.0	109.3	55.8	66.6	34.0
1903................	214.4	125.2	58.4	67.8	31.6
1904................	198.4	110.1	55.5	66.9	33.7
1905................	190.9	97.1	50.1	70.4	36.9
1906................	235.5	127.5	54.1	83.5	35.5
1907 [3]............	180.5	98.7	54.7	62.2	34.4
1907................	247.0	126.2	51.1	90.8	36.8
1908................	242.6	126.4	52.1	85.3	35.2
1909................	279.2	139.5	50.0	104.2	37.3
1910................	274.3	132.2	48.2	104.1	38.0
1911................	290.2	147.2	50.7	102.0	35.2
1912................	355.8	170.2	47.8	139.7	39.3
1913................	431.6	215.3	50.0	163.4	37.9

[1] All data, including percentages, from Canada: Dept. of Trade and Commerce, *Annual Report*, 1914, vol. i, pp. 22, 23.

[2] *Ending* June 30 until 1906; *beginning* April 1 from 1907 on.

[3] Intercalary 9-month period from July 1, 1906, to March 31, 1907.

fashion than was to be expected from the conditions existent during the period 1900–1913.

For both imports and exports, therefore, Canada's relations with Great Britain and the United States were such that the adjustment of Canada's trade balance to her borrowings from Great Britain was effected largely through triangular transactions with the United States. The trend in exports shown both before the outbreak of the war and since the close of the war suggests that, if when the time comes for repayment of the British loans it will be effected mainly through increased exports, the adjustment of the trade balance to repayments of capital borrowings will also be triangular; the Canadian obligations to Great Britain will be met in large part by exports to the United States. This tendency may be largely counteracted, however, if Great Britain extends her tariff preferences to a greater range of commodities produced in Canada and if the United States maintains high import duties on the chief articles of Canadian production and export.

CHAPTER XIII

SOME ECONOMIC CONSEQUENCES OF THE CAPITAL BORROWINGS

In this chapter there will be discussed briefly some phases of the influence on Canadian economic conditions of the great inflow of borrowed capital which are of interest to theory.

INFLUENCE OF CAPITAL BORROWINGS ON THE TERMS OF INTERNATIONAL EXCHANGE

It has already been shown that, according to those economists who follow Thornton and Mill rather than Ricardo in their explanation of the mechanism of adjustment of international balances, prices during a period of capital borrowings rise in the borrowing country, fall in the lending country. This theory has been verified inductively for Canada during the period 1900 to 1913, and it has also been shown that domestic and export prices rose relatively to import prices. It is a corollary of this reasoning that during a period of international borrowings the terms of international exchange shift in favor of the borrowing country and against the lending country — in other words, that the borrowing country obtains more foreign produce in exchange for each unit of its exports than it did prior to the period of borrowing. Adequate inductive verification of this proposition is supplied by the demonstration already made that export prices rose relatively to import prices.

There would be no such shift in the terms of international trade if the adjustment of the trade balance to capital borrowings were brought about, as Ricardo claimed, through automatic shifts in the relative demand of the two countries for each other's products, without preliminary gold movements and without changes in relative price levels. Moreover, another and more generally accepted phase of the Ricardian theory appears at first glance to be opposed to this reasoning that capital borrowings bring about a change in the terms of international exchange. Ricardo lays down the following "law": [1]

Gold and silver having been chosen for the general medium of circulation, they are, by the competition of commerce, distributed in such proportions amongst the different countries of the world as to accommodate themselves to the natural traffic which would take place if no such metals existed, and the trade between countries were purely a trade of barter.

Under a state of barter a loan would necessarily be made in terms of specific goods, would be transferred to the borrower in the form of these goods, and would not require for its adjustment a relative shift in the demand of the borrowing and lending countries for each other's goods and consequently in the terms of international exchange. The fact that the borrowing country was willing to accept a loan of these specific goods would *ipso facto* demonstrate that it already had a demand for them at the current rates of exchange with other goods, in excess of what it could satisfy without recourse to borrowings. Apparently, therefore, either Ricardo's law of the identity of the conditions of international trade under barter and under money exchange either does not hold true when the even balance of trade is disturbed by international borrowings, or else Ricardo is right when he denies the necessity of gold movements in the adjustment of trade balances to disturbing factors. It is this apparent inconsistency between Ricardo's law and Mill's theory of the function of gold movements in the adjustment of balances which led Bastable to doubt the validity of Mill's theory.[2]

Further examination, however, discloses the possibility of reconciling Mill's theory of gold movements with Ricardo's law. A shift in the reciprocal demand of borrowing and lending countries for each other's products and consequently in the terms of international exchange is essential to the adjustment of the trade balance to capital borrowings under either barter or money exchange. A loan of goods under barter will, it is true, move into

[1] "Principles," Ch. VII (*Works*, pp. 77, 78). Bastable terms this "Ricardo's greatest contribution to the theory of international trade." (C. F. Bastable, *Theory of International Trade*, 4th ed., London, 1903, p. 55.)

[2] See p. 203, *supra*.

the borrowing country directly and without need of preliminary changes in the rates of exchange of these goods with the goods of the borrowing country. The inflow of the borrowed goods, however, will disturb the even equilibrium between the *remaining* items in the balance of trade. The increase in the borrowing country in the supply of the lending country's goods will lower the rates of exchange of these goods with other goods both domestic and imported in the borrowing country. The borrowing country will therefore be unwilling to continue its purchases from the lending country in the volume and at the rates of exchange current prior to the beginning of the inflow of the borrowed goods. On the other hand, there will have been no reason why the lending country's demand for the borrowing country's goods should have fallen, or at least why it should have fallen to an extent which would exactly offset the fall in the demand of the borrowing country for its own goods. In other words, the loan of goods under barter will have caused a shift in favor of the borrowing country in the reciprocal demand of the two countries for each other's goods. The necessary equilibrium between exports and imports other than those representing the transfer of borrowed goods from lender to borrower will be reëstablished only if the lending country accepts smaller quantities of the borrowing country's goods in exchange for each unit of its own exports.[1]

There remains some difference between the function of the shift in the terms of international exchange under barter and under money exchange. Under barter, the transfer of the loan to the borrowing country in the form of goods comes first and is the cause, and not the effect, of the shift in the terms of international exchange; the shift serves to reëstablish equilibrium in the portion of the trade in commodities which is not directly connected with the borrowings. Under money exchange, the shift in the terms of international exchange is a necessary preliminary to the coming in of the loan in the form of goods.

[1] This is essentially Mill's reasoning — Mill, in fact, first demonstrates that a shift in the terms of international exchange is a necessary consequence of borrowings, subsidies, etc., for a hypothetical state of barter, and then applies his argument to similar conditions in a money economy. (J. S. Mill, *Principles*, Bk. III, Ch. XXI, § 4.)

The shift in favor of Canada in the terms of international exchange gave her the advantage, not only of obtaining a greater quantity of foreign goods in exchange for the money proceeds of her borrowings abroad, but also of exchanging her exports for foreign commodities on more favorable terms. There were operative, however, some factors which tended to restrict the extent to which Canada could profit through exchanging exports for imports on more favorable terms. If the foreign demand for Canadian products had a high degree of elasticity, there would be either a marked relative rise in Canadian prices, which would lead to a sharp reduction in the amounts which could be exported at the higher prices, and thus would make a reduction in Canadian exports an important factor in adjusting the Canadian balance to the borrowings from abroad, or else the rise in the price of Canadian export commodities would not be substantial. In all cases where Canada was not necessarily a predominant source of supply either for the world at large or for the particular country affected, the foreign demand for the Canadian product would be highly elastic, regardless of the character of the foreign demand for the product in general. A substantial rise in the Canadian price relative to the price in other producing regions would shift the demand to these other regions. Canada was the predominant source of world supply for only two or three mineral products. The elasticity of the foreign demand for Canadian products was operative, therefore, as an important check on the possibility of Canada's exchanging her exports for foreign commodities on more favorable terms because of her borrowings abroad.

The relative degree of rise in the domestic price level as compared to import prices measured the degree to which the shift in the terms of international exchange *temporarily* lowered to Canada the cost of the goods purchased abroad with the proceeds of the borrowings. But the degree of profit accruing to Canada from the exchange of her exports for foreign products on more favorable terms was not nearly so great. This reasoning is verified by the evidence presented in an earlier chapter to the effect that the prices of export commodities did not rise in nearly the same degree as did domestic prices.[1] It is further verified by the evidence presented in the preceding chapter to the effect that Canada's export trade would have been seriously checked, had it not been for the operation of special circumstances which made possible the profitable export of a few important products at prices relatively little higher than the import prices.[2]

CAPITAL BORROWINGS AND THE DISTRIBUTION OF INCOME IN CANADA

The great amount of foreign capital invested in Canada during the period 1900–1913, together with the normal increase in the domestic supply of capital from new savings, resulted in a much greater relative increase in the total stock of capital than in the supply of labor. The population of Canada increased by 30 per cent from 1900 to 1910 and by 45.8 per cent from 1900 to 1913.[3] According to the estimates made in Part I of this study, the amount of outside capital in Canada increased from $1,200,-000,000 in 1900 to $2,480,000,000 in 1910, an increase of 107 per cent, and to $3,700,000,000 in 1913, an increase of 208 per cent.[4] In further confirmation, there are presented in Table LX partial estimates of the increase in the total stock of capital in Canada from 1900 to 1910 and to 1913.

The data presented in Table LX, even after generous allowance for the inevitable shortcomings of the estimates and also for the influence of rising prices, clearly demonstrate that the increase in Canada of the supply of capital was relatively much greater than the increase in population, and, therefore, in the supply of labor. The available supply of land for town purposes also increased during this period owing to the extensive town-building, but the supply of building-sites of a given character and location presumably remained constant.

The generally accepted theory maintains that a change in the relative proportions of the factors of production tends to change their relative rates of return to the advantage of the relatively constant factors. Applied to the conditions present in Canada

[1] Chart VIII, p. 229, *supra*.
[2] Pp. 261 seq., *supra*.
[3] *Canada Year Book*, 1913, p. 519.
[4] See Table XXVIII, p. 101, *supra*.

during the period 1900–1913, there should be expected, in conformity with the theory, a rise in town rents relatively to wages and a rise in wages relatively to interest. With the purpose of testing the theory inductively, there is presented in Chart XVIII a comparison of the trends of rents, wages, and interest during the period under study. Unfortunately, the material available does not completely answer the requirements of inductive verification. The index for rents is based on house-rents for typical workingmen's dwellings, and reflects, therefore, variations in the rate of return to the capital invested therein as well as in land-rents proper. The indices for wages and rents, but not the index for interest, require downward correction if the influence thereon of the fall in the value of money is to be eliminated. In order that the index for interest may fully reflect variations in the rate of interest, it has been so constructed as to reflect not the actual per cent of return to invested capital in each year, but the rates

TABLE LX

PARTIAL ESTIMATES OF THE INCREASE IN THE STOCK OF CAPITAL IN
CANADA, 1900 TO 1913 [1]

	1900	1910		1913	
	Amount in millions of dollars	Amount in millions of dollars	Per cent increase over 1900	Amount in millions of dollars	Per cent increase over 1900
Savings Deposits in Government Banks....................	53	58	9.4	68	26.2
Agricultural Capital............	1,787	4,224	136.4	....	....
Capital in Fisheries............	11	19	72.7	24	118.2
Mining Capital.................	43	109	153.5	....	....
Manufacturing Capital.........	447	1,248	179.2	....	....
Private Railway Capital........	784	....	....	1,709	117.9
Electric Railway Capital........	39	141	261.5	....	....
Bank Premises.................	6	23	283.3	46	666.6
Building Values (1904 base year) .			232.0	....	316.8
Real Property Valuation in Towns (1900 base year).............			141.1	....	448.7

[1] Based on data in *Cost of Living Report*, vol. ii, pp. 916–934.

at which new loans could be made each year. The index for wages is a weighted index based on weekly rates in a wide range of occupations; as the average number of hours in the working-week was declining during this period, it minimizes the actual increase in money wage rates per hour.

The data in the chart confirm the theory only to a moderate extent. House rents, it is true, show a more marked rise than wages, and wages, in turn, show a greater rise than interest. But

CHART XVIII

INDICES OF HOUSE RENTS, INTEREST, AND WAGES, 1900–1913

—·— House rents   ·········· Interest   ——— Wages

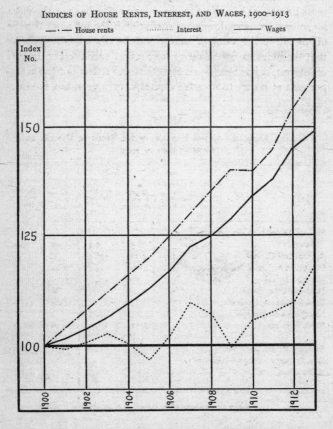

if it were feasible to reduce the data relating to rents and wages
to terms of "real" income, so as to discount the effect of the rise
in prices, it would probably appear that wages did not rise more
than did interest, whose index, being on a per cent basis, does
not reflect the rise in prices. The operation of other factors, including, perhaps, the well-known tendency of changes in wages
to lag behind changes in prices, may explain the lack of closer
agreement between the factual data and the theoretical expectations.

CAPITAL BORROWINGS AND PROSPERITY

There was every evidence of general prosperity in Canada during the period under study. The index of wages does not adequately indicate the economic situation of the working classes

DATA OF CHART XVIII

INDICES OF HOUSE RENTS, INTEREST, AND WAGES

Year	House rents [1]	Interest [2]	Wages [3]
1900	100.0	100.0	100.0
1901	....	99.2	101.6
1902	....	100.6	103.8
1903	....	102.6	106.5
1904	....	100.1	109.3
1905	119.7	96.9	113.1
1906	....	101.7	116.5
1907	....	109.5	122.6
1908	....	107.1	124.8
1909	140.0	99.6	129.0
1910	139.7	105.3	134.0
1911	144.5	107.3	137.9
1912	154.2	109.3	145.0
1913	161.2	117.6	148.9

[1] House Rents: — simple average of Labour Department's indices for typical six-roomed dwellings in workingmen's section, (a) with sanitary conveniences, and (b) without sanitary conveniences.
Data from *Cost of Living Report*, vol. ii, p. 379.

[2] Interest: — simple averages of Coats's indices of (a) the rates at which city mortgages could be
obtained, weighted by population of cities, (b) the rate at which farm mortgages could be obtained,
weighted by population of provinces, (c) the rates of return on provincial bonds at the current market
prices, and (d) call money rates in Montreal. (a), (b), and (d) from *Cost of Living Report*, vol. ii, pp.
723, 724, 739; (c) from C. H. Burgess, "Review of the Municipal Bond Market, 1896-1913," *Monetary Times Annual*, January, 1914, pp. 80, 81.

[3] Wages: — Coats's Index, weighted by occupations. See note 5 to Chart XI, p. 243, *supra*.

during this period, since it takes no account of the fact that there was generally full employment throughout the period. Rents were buoyant, business profits were unusually high and regular, and there was the gain already mentioned from the low prices, measured by relative Canadian levels, at which imports were obtained from abroad. To what extent this prosperity was

TABLE LXI

Total Investments in Canada by Classes of Investments, 1900 to 1913

In millions of dollars

	Great Britain	United States	Other countries	All countries
Dominion and Provincial Governments.....................	175	4	..	179
Municipal Governments........	200	60	..	260
Railroads.....................	670	50	47	767
Industrial Investments.........	420	180	30	630
Land and Timber..............	80	145	80	305
Mining......................	65	60	..	125
Insurance Companies...........	32	50	..	82
Miscellaneous.................	111	81	6	198
	1,753	630	163	2,546

sound and was not based on over-optimistic speculative anticipations of future income depends upon a good many factors concerning which no definite conclusions are possible. But this much is indisputable: whether the eventual period of repayment of the capital borrowings from abroad will be passed without economic distress in Canada depends to a large degree on whether these borrowings were used wisely or were squandered in unwise investments or in extravagant living.

An analysis of the uses to which the borrowed capital was put can offer some clues as to the probabilities. In Table LXI there is presented such an analysis, based in large part on the data used in Chapter VI in reaching the direct estimates of capital borrowings, but based also on a great variety of other data. The miscellaneous item in this table presents both investments which did not lend themselves to the method of classification followed in the table, and also security investments which could not be classified because of lack of information.

The foreign investments in Canadian lands were made largely in years of speculative land-booms in Canada, when prices were extravagantly high. Much of this capital has already been lost to the investors, and much of the remainder will never pay an adequate return. The losses, however, will be on the part of the foreign investors, since the overvalued land was generally their only security.

Other questionable items are the loans to the Dominion and local governments and the railroad borrowings. These involve little chance for loss to the investors, since even the railroad bonds in most cases were issued under government guarantees. Much of the capital borrowed by the Dominion and Provincial governments was for purposes of railroad construction or for the grant of subsidies to private railroad companies. The capital expenditures of the Dominion government on account of railroad construction amounted during this period to $178,000,000. In addition, the Dominion and local governments granted subsidies to private railroads amounting to $78,000,000, and some railroad construction was carried on by the Provinces themselves.[1] There is now general agreement that much of this railroad construction was unwise. Of the five great railroad systems in Canada in 1913, three, namely, the Canadian Northern, the Grand Trunk, and the Grand Trunk Pacific, have since been saved from bankruptcy only by the intervention of the government.[2] The Intercolonial Railway, as always, did not earn its fixed charges. Only the Canadian Pacific Railway was financially successful. The Federal Government is faced now with an annual deficit below operating charges amounting to millions of dollars on the railroads for which it is financially responsible. No one claims that the war was solely or even mainly responsible for the financial difficulties of the railroads, and no one now denies that

[1] *Cost of Living Report*, vol. ii, pp. 920, 921.

[2] With a loss to the common stock holders in the Grand Trunk systems of their total investments.

there was extravagant overconstruction of roads during the period 1900 to 1913. This overconstruction was due in large part to the moral and financial encouragement given by the government to new railroad enterprises and to its own ventures in railroad building. One motive was undoubtedly the desire of the Liberal Government to placate the western provinces for its failure to redeem its pledges to lower the tariff, by giving them additional transportation facilities for their grain.

The municipal borrowings were also in large part unhealthy. In the optimism of a period of rapid expansion and excessive growth of urban population, town-building was overdone. Many western municipalities are now in financial difficulties, and for the western towns in general, which were responsible for the bulk of the municipal borrowings, the immediate future presents a prospect of heavy taxation to meet the obligations incurred in constructing public works, pavements, and roads sufficient for a population much greater than they are likely to have for many years.

The investments in industrial and mining enterprises have more favorable prospects of success. The former, however, to the extent that they consist of investments in manufacturing enterprises, are very largely dependent for their prosperity upon the continuance of tariff protection. The heavy burden imposed on the farming community by the high prices of the things they buy, resulting from the tariff, and by the high freight rates made necessary by the overconstruction of railroads, has made the farmers determined to gain political control in Canada. If they should succeed and should make drastic reductions in the tariff, there would undoubtedly be revealed a considerable overinvestment of capital in Canadian manufacturing enterprises.

It is not an unduly pessimistic conclusion, therefore, that the borrowings during the period under study, if not too great in volume, were in large part invested in economically unsound ventures. The prosperity of the borrowing period was due in large measure to the borrowings. When borrowings cease, but interest payments must continue, and especially when the time arrives for repayment of principal, Canada will have to face a reversal of all the price trends present during the period of capital borrowings. Canadian prices and wages will move down instead of up relatively to other countries. It will be necessary for Canada to sell her products at lower prices in order to induce her creditors to accept increased quantities thereof in payment of their claims to interest and principal. Canada will thus be able to liquidate her indebtedness and to obtain her necessary imports only on less advantageous terms. The great additional foreign indebtedness incurred since 1914, much of it resulting from economically unproductive military expenditures, from the completion of an extravagant program of railroad and town building, from the construction of an unprofitable merchant marine, and from the further extension of manufacturing industries of which few would have any expectation of survival if their tariff subsidy were withdrawn, will intensify the seriousness of the problem which will face Canada when the borrowings cease and the difficult burden of repayment must be assumed.

The further discovery and exploitation of rich natural resources, a generous increase in population, an increase in the intensity of the world demand for the important Canadian products, the adoption of a sounder and more far-sighted commercial policy and of a more conservative policy of capital investment in questionable enterprises — these would substantially lessen for Canada the severity of the task of liquidation of its foreign indebtedness. Confidence in the economic prospects of Canada for the near future must rest on the expectation of the early attainment of some, if not all, of these objectives.

BIBLIOGRAPHY

BIBLIOGRAPHY

OFFICIAL

CANADA

Department of Customs: Annual Reports on Trade and Navigation. Unrevised Monthly Statements of Imports and Exports. Shipping Reports (annual).

Department of Finance: Public Accounts (annual). Monthly Statements of the Chartered Banks of Canada (also published as monthly supplement to Canada *Gazette*). List of Shareholders in Canadian Banks (annual). Annual Reports of Superintendent of Insurance. Abstract of Statements of Insurance Companies (annual).

Department of the Interior: Immigration Branch, Annual Reports. Immigration Facts and Figures, 1911 and 1920 editions.

Department of Labour: Wholesale Prices, Canada, 1890–1909; Special Report by R. H. Coats. Wholesale Prices, Canada (annual since 1910).

Department of Mines: Mines Branch, Annual Reports.

Department of Railways and Canals: Railway Statistics (annual).

Department of Trade and Commerce: Annual Reports, Part I: Imports into and Exports from Canada; Part IV: Miscellaneous Information. Canada Year Books.

Post Office Department: Annual Reports.

Board of Inquiry into Cost of Living: Report of the Board, 1915. Vol. I. Report of the Board. Vol. II. Supplementary Report: The Rise in Prices and the Cost of Living in Canada, 1900–1914; Exhibit by the Statistical Branch, Department of Labour, Prepared under Direction of R. H. Coats. Synopsis of Exhibit by the Statistical Branch, Department of Labour.

House of Commons: Budget Speeches.

King's Printer: The Canada *Gazette* (weekly). — Contains Monthly Statements of Chartered Banks and Monthly Reports of Receiver-General (on gold in government reserve and circulation of Dominion notes).

FRANCE

Bulletin de Statistique et de Législation Comparée du Ministère des Finances, 1902, tome II.

GREAT BRITAIN

Statistical Abstract for the United Kingdom (annual).

House of Commons Returns: Annual Statements of Emigration and Immigration, 1912, 1913, 1914. Annual Statements of Foreign and Colonial Trade.

Parliamentary Papers: Reports of British Trade Commissioners to Canada on Trade of Canada: Cd. 3868 (1908); Cd. 5591 (1911); Cd. 6870 (1913). Dominions Royal Commission, Final Report, Cd. 7971, (1917); Minutes of Evidence taken in the Central and Western Provinces of Canada in 1916: Cd. 8458 (1917).

United States

Commissioner of Immigration: Annual Reports.

Director of the Mint: Annual Reports.

Immigration Commission: The Immigration Situation in Canada (61 Cong., 2d Sess., Sen. Doc. 469).

Department of Commerce: Consular Reports, Annual Series, No. 4. Canada: Trade for the Year 1907. Monthly Consular and Trade Reports, Nos. 262 (July, 1902); 268 (January, 1903); 278 (November, 1903); 305 (February, 1906); 345 (June, 1909); 351 (December, 1909). Miscellaneous Series, No. 59, Methods of Computing Values in Foreign Trade Statistics. Miscellaneous Series, No. 92, Stowage of Cargoes. Statistical Abstract (annual).

Department of Labor, Bureau of Labor Statistics: Bulletin No. 181, Wholesale Prices 1890 to 1914.

UNOFFICIAL

Bacon, N. T. — American International Indebtedness. *Yale Review*, November, 1900.

Bastable, C. F. — On Some Applications of the Theory of International Trade. *Quarterly Journal of Economics*, October, 1899. Theory of International Trade. 4th edition. London, 1903.

Becqué, Émile. — L'Internationalisation des Capitaux. Montpellier, 1912.

Blake, William. — Observations on the Principles which Regulate the Course of Exchange; and on the Present Depreciated State of the Currency. London, 1810.

Boggs, T. H. — Capital Investments and Trade Balances within the British Empire. *Quarterly Journal of Economics*, August, 1915.

Bonar, James. — Canada's Balance of Trade. *Proceedings of the Canadian Political Science Association*. Toronto, 1913. Canadian Currency. *Economic Journal*, June, 1914.

Breckinridge, R. M. — The History of Banking in Canada. (U. S.) National Monetary Commission, 1910 (61 Cong., 2d Sess., Sen. Doc. 232).

Bullock, C. J.; Williams, J. H.; and Tucker, R. S. — The Balance of Trade of the United States. *Review of Economic Statistics*, Preliminary Volume No. 3 (July, 1919).

Burgess, C. H. — Review of the Municipal Bond Market, 1896–1913. *Monetary Times Annual*. Toronto, January, 1914.

Cairnes, J. E. — Some Leading Principles of Political Economy Newly Expounded. London, 1874.

Crammond, Edgar. — British Investments Abroad. *Quarterly Review*, July, 1907; July, 1911. The British Shipping Industry. London, 1917.

Eckardt, H. P. M. — Manual of Canadian Banking. Toronto, 1909. Articles in *Journal of the Canadian Bankers' Association*, January, 1903; October, 1908; July, 1911; July, 1913.

Field, F. W. — Capital Investments in Canada. Toronto, 1911 and 1914 editions.

Flux, A. W. — Measurement of Price Changes. *Journal of the Royal Statistical Society*, March, 1921.

Giffen, Sir Robert. — On the Use of Import and Export Statistics. *Journal of the Royal Statistical Society*, June, 1882.

Harpell, J. J. — Canadian National Economy. Toronto, 1911.

Hobson, C. K. — The Export of Capital. London, 1914. The Measurement of the Balance of Trade. *Economica*, May, 1921.

Hobson, J. A. — Canada To-Day. London, 1906.

Hollander, J. H. — International Trade under Depreciated Paper: a Criticism. *Quarterly Journal of Economics*, August, 1918.

Howard, B. E. — A Few Fundamentals — Credit Currency. *Monetary Times*, March 30, 1923.

Johnson, J. F. — The Canadian Banking System. (U. S.) National Monetary Commission, 1910 (61 Cong., 2d. Sess., Sen. Doc. 583).

Laughlin, J. L. — Principles of Money. New York, 1903.

Leacock, Stephen. — The Canadian Balance of Trade. *Journal of the Canadian Bankers' Association*, April, 1915.

Lehfeldt, R. A. — The Rate of Interest on British and Foreign Investments. *Journal of the Royal Statistical Society*, January, 1913; March, 1913; March, 1914.

Malthus, T. R. — Depreciation of Paper Currency. *Edinburgh Review*, February, 1811. (The article is unsigned, but is commonly attributed to Malthus. Cf. Bonar, J., Malthus and His Work. London, 1885, p. 162, note.)

McCulloch, J. R., editor. — A Select Collection of Tracts on Paper Currency and Banking. London, 1857.

Mead, F. S. — Bank Reserves in the United States, Canada, and England. *Quarterly Journal of Economics*, May, 1907.

Mill, J. S. — Essays on Some Unsettled Questions of Political Economy. London, 1844. Principles of Political Economy. London, 1848.

Nicholson, J. S. — Principles of Political Economy, vol. II. London, 1897.

Paish, Sir George. — Great Britain's Investments in Other Lands. *Journal of the Royal Statistical Society*, September, 1909; January, 1911. *Statist Supplement*, February 14, 1914. The Trade Balance of the United States. (U. S.) National Monetary Commission, 1910 (61 Cong., 2d. Sess., Sen. Doc. 579).

Patterson, E. L. Stewart, and Escher, Franklin. — Banking Practice and Foreign Exchange. Canadian edition. New York, 1914.

Ricardo, David. — The High Cost of Bullion. 1810. Appendix to 4th edition; in Works, pp. 291 seq. Letters of David Ricardo to Thomas Robert Malthus, 1810–1823, James Bonar, editor. Principles of Political Economy and Taxation. London, 1817. Works, J. R. McCulloch, editor. London, 1846.

Rutter, F. R. — Statistics of Imports and Exports. *Publications of the American Statistical Association*, XV, pp. 16–34. (March, 1916.)

Shortt, Adam, and Doughty, Arthur G., editors. — Canada and Its Provinces. Toronto, 1914. Vols. 9 and 10; Industrial Expansion.

Speare, C. F. — What America Pays Europe for Immigrant Labor. *North American Review*, January, 1908.

Taussig, F. W.—International Trade under Depreciated Paper. *Quarterly Journal of Economics*, May, 1917; and a Rejoinder (to Hollander). *Ibid.*, August, 1918. Germany's Reparation Payments. *American Economic Review Supplement*, March, 1920. Principles of Economics. New York, 1913. Wages and Prices in Relation to International Trade. *Quarterly Journal of Economics*, August, 1906. (Also Chapter IV in Free Trade, the Tariff, and Reciprocity. New York, 1920.)

Thornton, Henry. — An Enquiry into the Nature and Effects of the Paper Credit of Great Britain. London, 1802.

Tooke, Thomas. — The State of the Currency; 2d edition. London, 1826.

Victor, E., editor. — Canada's Future. Toronto, 1916.

Walker, Francis A. — Money. New York, 1883.

Whitaker, A. C. — The Ricardian Theory of Gold Movements. *Quarterly Journal of Economics*, February, 1904. Foreign Exchange. New York, 1920.

Wicksell, Knut. — International Freights and Prices. *Quarterly Journal of Economics*, February, 1918.

Williams, J. H. — Argentine Trade under Inconvertible Paper Money, 1880–1890. Cambridge, 1920. (Harvard Economic Studies, vol. XXII.)

Williams-Taylor, Sir Frederick. — Canadian Loans in London. *United Empire* (Journal of the Royal Colonial Institute), December, 1912.

Wood, E. R. — Annual Reviews of the Bond Market in Canada. (Published by the Dominion Securities Corporation, Limited, Toronto.)

Bank of Montreal, *Annual Reports*.

Canadian Annual Review, Toronto.

Canadian Bank of Commerce, *Annual Reports*.

Canadian Journal of Commerce, Montreal (weekly).

Canadian Pacific Railway, *Annual Reports*.

Economist, London (weekly).

Financial Post of Canada, Toronto (weekly).

Globe, The, Toronto. Annual Survey of Financial and Commercial Affairs.

Industrial Canada (Journal of the Canadian Manufacturers' Association), Toronto.

Journal of the Canadian Bankers' Association, Montreal (monthly).

Monetary Times of Canada, Toronto (weekly).

Monetary Times Annual, Toronto.

Statist, London (weekly).

INDEX

INDEX

THE CARLETON LIBRARY